A
MIND
FOR
MURDER

Book Belong To: Shanice Bernard

A MIND FOR MURDER

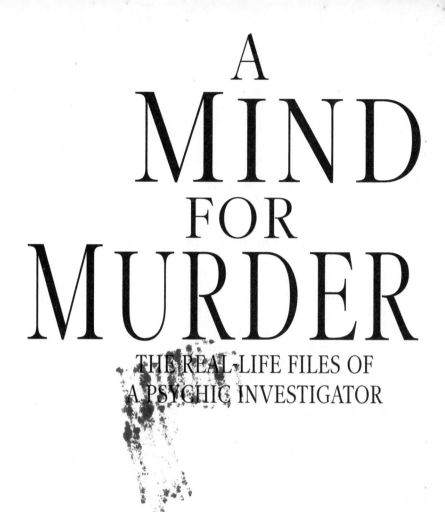

THE REAL-LIFE FILES OF A PSYCHIC INVESTIGATOR

NOREEN RENIER

HAMPTON ROADS
PUBLISHING COMPANY, INC.

Cover design by Frame25 Productions
Cover art by JordiDelgado c/o Istockphoto.com and
Shutterstock.com

Hampton Roads Publishing Company, Inc.
1125 Stoney Ridge Road
Charlottesville, VA 22902

434-296-2772
fax: 434-296-5096
e-mail: hrpc@hrpub.com
www.hrpub.com

If you are unable to order this book from your local
bookseller, you may order directly from the publisher.
Call 1-800-766-8009, toll-free.

Library of Congress Cataloging-in-Publication Data

Renier, Noreen.
  A mind for murder : the real-life files of a psychic investigator / Noreen
Renier.
      p. cm.
  Summary: "A psychic relates her dealings with police and FBI to solve
murders and missing persons cases"--Provided by publisher.
  Includes bibliographical references.
  ISBN 978-1-57174-573-6 (6 x 9 tp : alk. paper)
  1. Renier, Noreen. 2. Parapsychology in criminal investigation. 3.
Parapsychology and crime. 4. Extrasensory perception. 5.
Psychics--Biography. I. Title.
  BF1045.C7R45 2008
  133.8092--dc22
  [B]
                                                2008000812

ISBN 978-1-57174-573-6
10 9 8 7 6 5 4 3 2 1
Printed on acid-free paper in Canada

CASE NUMBER ___30945___

CASE NUMBER ___13701___

To all the detectives and law
enforcement agencies courageous
enough to use an unconventional
tool in their quest to
solve unsolved crimes.

CASE NUMBER ___13701___

CONTENTS

CASE NUMBER _____ 13701

ACKNOWLEDGMENTS

I would like to express my deepest gratitude to those who believed in me: my mother, Florida Uzdavinis, who loved even the first draft of my book and always encouraged me on my psychic path; both my beautiful daughters, Reené and Karla, for their priceless insights; Ellen Burns, who was there in the very beginning, offering invaluable enthusiasm and levelheaded logic as we searched together for the truth about psychic phenomena.

To David E. Jones, author of *Visions of Time;* I was so fortunate to meet him early in my psychic explorations. He is a wonderful man who is so knowledgeable about psychic phenomena and was kind enough to share his knowledge. He taught me so much, but above all to believe in my psychic abilities and in myself.

Several parapsychologists crossed my path and enriched my understanding. William Roll, who invited me to the Psychic Research Foundation to do research at the beginning of my search, was so important. He introduced me to the world of parapsychology, science, and intelligent skepticism. Joanne McMahon, PhD; her dedication, knowledge, and help were always inspiring.

I must also thank my attorney, Lee Werdell, who tried my libel case against the skeptic brilliantly and saved my reputation. He will always be my hero.

I would be remiss if I left out four "exes" who have always supported my work. I can't say enough wonderful things about former Colonie, New York, police lieutenant Ray Krolak, whose confidence in the truth of what I saw made it possible for him to solve an unsolved case. I must also thank former Williston, Florida, Chief of Police Olin Slaughter, an avowed skeptic who made an exception for me, and whose perseverance brought needed closure to the family of a missing man. Former Montana Agent Joe Uribe, who believed in me when many didn't, and got his murderer. And a very special thanks to former FBI Special Agent Robert Ressler, author of *Whoever Fights Monsters: My Twenty Years Tracking Serial Killers for the FBI,* for opening the doors that started my career as a "monster fighter." He is an extraordinarily insightful man and a good friend.

Finally, I wish to thank Robert Friedman, my editor at Hampton Roads Publishing, for being committed to republishing this book. The value of his help cannot be overstated.

PREFACE

Welcome to My World

Where do you turn when you've got a murder and you haven't got a clue? Enter Noreen Renier, psychic.
—48 Hours

I have had my throat slit. I have been shot, knifed, stabbed, raped, drowned, and strangled. I have been inside the last moments of many murder victims. I feel their pain, I speak their words, I live their deaths. I see the faces of their murderers, and sometimes I become them. I don't like to get killed more than two or three times a week—it's just too exhausting.

During my career as a psychic detective I have held the bloody earrings, watches, shirts, and shoes of murder victims. I have received the images and feelings that somehow reside in a piece of skull, a vial of blood, a few hairs, the murder weapon. Just as a dog picks up a scent trail that we humans can't detect, my mind taps into the turbulent energy left behind by a moment of explosive violence and I relive the brutal event.

Call it a hunch, a gut feeling, intuition. How do I do it? You tell me. You've been using your logical, rational mind for many years. Explain it to me: How do you use your mind? How did you learn math? How does your memory work? You can't explain it and neither can I. But you can use your mind, and I can use mine.

I've had quite a ride. Almost twenty-five years ago, on a sunny morning in the midst of an ordinary life as a working single mom, an unconventional career chose me. Since then, I've never looked back. Establishing my credibility in a field that fights for credibility has been daunting, but I have been rewarded in countless ways. In 1981, when I first lectured at the FBI Academy in Quantico, Virginia, my work with the police was considered controversial. Now, I'm a well-known psychic detective who has worked on more than four hundred unsolved homicides, missing persons, and rape cases with city, county, and state law enforcement agencies in thirty-eight states and six foreign countries. My work has been featured in the newspapers, on television, and even in a textbook for homicide detectives.

Like everyone else, I once thought that anyone who had psychic abilities was either a charlatan or a fraud. And just like you, I know that not everyone who calls themselves a psychic really is one. But even though there's no way I can prove to you I'm a psychic, I don't mind being challenged. In 1986, I even took a skeptic to court for calling me a fraud—and won.

I enjoy my work, but it's certainly not the life I would have consciously chosen. Most of all, I want you to understand that psychic abilities are another part of a normal life. They involve no fear, no evil. This ability—the opening of our own minds—is a gift that we can develop for good and use as a wonderful and amazing tool.

Over the years, I have encountered a great deal of fear and ignorance concerning my ability and psychics in general. However, I have discovered one very important thing: If you believe in yourself and in your own efforts, nothing can stand in your way.

CASE NUMBER _____ 13701 _____

INTRODUCTION

The Psychic Connection

I believe that educating people about psychic phenomena is the best way to help people spot charlatans, and the best way to help them open their own minds to new possibilities. It will probably not surprise you to learn that most law enforcement officials are skeptical of my psychic ability the first time we work together. Why shouldn't they be? After all, they are trained to work with facts they can see, touch, and prove. It follows, then, that most of them have not received any training about the best way to work with a psychic on a case. That's why I give the following information to every law enforcement officer I work with before we begin a case.

———————◆●◆———————

Let me state early that I do not solve crimes . . . the police do. I am merely an aid or an investigative tool for the police. By picking up images and feelings that the untrained mind cannot, I can provide clues, information, and perhaps a new angle to an unsolved crime.

The first time a law enforcement officer or agency uses my psychic ability as an investigative tool, it is important to understand a few simple techniques. The following information will help you enhance my psychic abilities during our session and, I hope, bring an unsolved crime to a successful conclusion.

1. A psychic should be called into an investigation as a last resort, when traditional methods for solving a crime have been exhausted.

2. I prefer not to know any details or personal background of the victim or the crime other than the first name of the victim and the type of crime. The less you tell me, the more I will be able to tell you.

3. I use psychometry, which involves touching an object that the victim wore or the suspect left behind.

4. It is important to start slowly. Initially, I try to see psychically what the victim looked like, or to re-create the scene of the crime. I do this for two reasons: to make sure I am "tuning" in to the case and to give the officer/agent confidence in me as a psychic. If this is successful we can continue with the case.

5. Questions. How you question me will determine the quality of information I receive psychically. *Be prepared*. Know in advance what your objectives are. Think of a profile you want me to fill in, information that will help you to identify and/or locate a suspect or body.

6. The way the questions are phrased is extremely important. An incorrect way to question is: "Where does he (suspect) live?" "Did he (suspect) do it?" A

productive way to question is: "Stand in front of the house (body) and walk toward it. What do you see? Look to the right, to the left. Fly above it, what do you see?"

7. Leading questions are not productive. Such questions include: "Is his hair black?" "Was he driving a blue Ford?" Instead, let me describe him/her to you, as well as any other pertinent information. Questions should have direction and not merely need a "yes" or "no" answer. It is very helpful to give me feedback when you know I have accurately described something or someone. The logical mind can analyze, but the psychic mind just receives information. The feedback keeps my confidence up and the images flowing. "Yes, we understand," is sufficient.

8. Try not to analyze the data that I give you immediately. Think of this part of the session as "fact gathering." Get as much information as you can. Later, you can analyze the information you have received and separate the wheat from the chaff.

9. During the session, I will use all five of my senses to some degree. Ask questions that will make use of these senses. Example: "Is there a special sound near his house (body), a different odor?"

10. My psychic memory is very short. Therefore, it is important that our session be taped. My answers can then be replayed repeatedly or transcribed in order to detect any information that didn't seem important or pertinent earlier.

I do not claim to be 100 percent accurate in my interpretations. Nor do I claim to be able to work on all cases with an equal degree of effectiveness.

I do not mind skepticism. However, continued skepticism and negativism hamper my work and concentration. Retired New York Detective Sergeant Vernon Gerberth, writing about my psychic abilities in his textbook *Practical Homicide Investigations,* states: "Practically speaking, if an officer feels that he or she cannot accept or work with the psychic, then this officer should not get involved in this segment of the investigation. Instead, someone who may be skeptical, but is able to put aside this personal prejudice, should be assigned to work with the psychics."[1]

CHAPTER I

Lightning Strikes:
My Psychic Abilities Speak

On that early Sunday afternoon Ellen, Joanna, and I sat at my round kitchen table. The hot Florida sun filled the room with bright light. We started off as usual, breathing slowly, growing calm, silently repeating our word. Suddenly, a surge of energy pulsated through my body. I felt as if I had been plugged into an electric circuit and all that electricity was racing through me. My stomach hurt terribly and I cried out from the pain. Then things really started happening.

As the phone rang for what seemed like the hundredth time that morning, I stifled an urge to throw it out the window. Instead, I thought of all the deadlines I had to meet in the next few hours. It was 1976. Disney World had opened four years earlier and millions of visitors were pouring into Orlando, Florida, looking for a vacation from their responsibilities. I envied them. As a young single mother of two girls, I rarely found time for myself before or after work. And as director of advertising and public relations for the Hyatt Hotel, my responsibilities didn't let up from the moment I walked in until the day was blessedly over: I had ad layouts to approve, out-of-town VIPs waiting to tour our convention facilities, advertising salespeople to talk to. Over the ringing, I could hear an irate hotel guest snapping at my secretary in the outer office.

With a sigh, I picked up the phone. It was my friend Mary. More aggravation! I liked Mary, but what was she thinking? She knew what my days were like, yet she continued to pester me at the office, asking for help in promoting a lecture by a well-known local psychic, Ann Gehman. She wanted me to book Ann into the Hyatt.

"Just meet Ann, that's all I'm asking," Mary pleaded.

I could think of any number of reasons to refuse: Psychics are all frauds and charlatans. Management will never go for this. And I just don't have the time! With two daughters to support and no husband to help me, I needed every minute I could get. But then I thought of the precious minutes that I had already wasted this week arguing with Mary. Maybe I should just bite the bullet, meet with her, and get her off my back. I lit a cigarette, leaned back, and gave in. With a sigh, I told Mary I would meet her at Ann's office at seven that evening—after work.

At least the meeting gave me something different to look forward to. Throughout my hectic day I found myself contemplating the evening's appointment. I smiled when I tried to picture how Ann would look. I figured she'd be dressed in gold jewelry and colorful skirts. Maybe she would look like a witch, dark and mysterious. Or Halloween-style—ugly, with a wart. What would my bosses say when they found out I was booking gypsies into their hotel?

By seven o'clock, when I met Mary at Ann's office, I was actually looking forward to meeting this exotic creature and was ready to be ushered into a dark, candlelit den. So I was a bit disappointed when the receptionist ushered us into a small but expensively furnished room—nicer than mine, in fact. And when Ann rose from behind her elegant French provincial desk to greet us, all of my preconceptions were shattered. Petite and charming, dressed in a tasteful pale blue business suit, she looked like a high-powered executive. No crystal balls in sight.

I must have looked as astounded as I felt because Ann smiled when she saw my reaction. Seeing me for the skeptic that I was, she asked if I would like a mini-reading. Sure, why not? I was already here.

She closed her eyes and began speaking in a gentle, soothing voice, telling me things about my two teenage girls, Karla and Reené, my recent divorce, the large surgical scar I had on my stomach—she even saw the new chair in my office. I felt a slight tingle run through my body. Oddly, what most impressed me was that she knew about the chair. Mary could have told her about my two girls and my divorce, and even about the scar. But how could she have known about my wonderful new chair? I had just gotten it and hadn't had time to tell anyone about it. She was still speaking, telling me more, and her accuracy amazed me. The tingling grew stronger.

I had to admit she was fascinating—and not at all what I had expected. Maybe my bosses wouldn't mind if she graced their hotel. Before the evening was over, I had agreed to promote her forthcoming lecture and rent her the Hyatt's small auditorium, at the hotel's lowest price. I didn't care if got in trouble—this could be interesting.

———————•◆•———————

As the next few days and weeks went by, my fascination did not leave me. I wanted to learn more about psychic phenomena. Maybe people like this really *did* exist. Ann was real enough. She gave me a few books about psychics and psychic phenomena, and I read them with great curiosity. But I was raised to be skeptical about outlandish claims, and I found it hard to believe the stories: dreams that came true, seeing into the future, visiting the past. . . . It was very difficult for me to accept that people could do those things. And none of the books told you how it worked. For my money, a good science-fiction thriller would have been more plausible.

The psychic world, however, wasn't going to let me off the hook that easily. One morning my friend Joanna called. Joanna was a great person, but I thought she had some odd ideas. She was a Winnebago Indian, and her spiritual connections grew out of that identity. She found spiritual activity in all things and felt everything had "vibrations" and "auras." Now Joanna was calling to ask me if I wanted to come over and meditate. I had never tried meditation before, but I was willing to give it a go. I had read a little about it, and I knew that it was supposed to relax you. I could certainly use some relaxation!

My best friend, Ellen, would also be there. Ellen reminded me of a redheaded pixie with a large bust—and she had once been a nun. After ten years in a convent, followed by another ten years of marriage, she had lost her faith and now proclaimed that she believed in "nothing." I wasn't surprised that she was reluctant to join us.

"Ellen, there's no hocus-pocus involved in meditation," I told her firmly. "It just relaxes you." I was projecting more ease than I felt about the project—I needed some company in this adventure. In the end she agreed to come, but only because it gave her an excuse to get away from her husband's visiting relatives.

Despite our reservations, we liked it. Joanna taught us how to breathe slowly and evenly and feel our muscles relax, and then to do a mantra meditation. As I focused on a single word, and repeated it over and over, I could feel all of the tension around my responsibilities grow softer and less pressing. It was very pleasant, and we held another meditation session the next week. But at our third meeting, something happened that would change my life forever.

On that early Sunday afternoon Ellen, Joanna, and I sat at my round kitchen table. The hot Florida sun filled the room with bright light. We started off as usual, breathing slowly, growing calm, silently repeating our word. Suddenly, a surge of energy pulsated through my body. I felt as if I had been plugged into an electric circuit and all that electricity was racing through me. My stomach hurt terribly and I cried out from the pain. Then things really started happening. A voice that sounded nothing like mine came from my mouth, saying things I had no control over. I could see passing images as the voice spoke, but my ordinary self wasn't listening or paying attention. Instead, while the voice spoke I was thinking, *What's happening to me?* It was an eerie sensation, it scared me, and I wanted it to stop.

I forced my eyes open and looked around the table. Joanna had tears flowing down her cheeks. She was saying, "That's Grandma. She called me Ginger Bear and we called my mother Memaw. That was my Grandma. My Grandma. Thank you, Noreen. God bless you. Thank you so much."

"Joanna, what are you talking about?" I was scared and mystified.

"The message. You gave me a message." Joanna looked from me to Ellen.

"I don't think she remembers," Ellen said. Ellen, the realist, reached across the table and took a sip of my cup of coffee. "What the hell is in your coffee, Noreen?"

Joanna murmured softly, her dark eyes still wet from the tears, "You're a medium, Noreen. You have just spoken to my grandmother, who died three years ago."

Uh-huh, I thought. *Sure.* I was too tired to care. Whatever had happened, I was completely exhausted. "My hands feel like they are on fire." I blurted out, ignoring them both.

Joanna placed her hands on mine and said to Ellen, "Feel this. Heat is just radiating off her hands. Noreen, you may be experiencing healing powers."

Ellen rolled her clear blue eyes in exasperation.

My hands were very hot, but I found that I could tolerate the sensation after my initial surprise wore off. I could handle what was happening to me physically, but Joanna was frightening me.

"Noreen," she was saying, "please come over here and take away my headache. I have a violent headache. Use your hands to heal me."

I didn't believe in touch-healing any more than I believed in talking to dead people, but I really wanted to put an end to this. So, to pacify her, I did what she asked.

Standing behind her, I placed my hands around her head without touching it, and took a deep breath. At once, that jolt of energy reentered my body, and again the voice came out of my mouth. I thought to myself, *I'm going crazy! I bet there's insanity in my family that my mother never told me about. What the hell's happening to me?* After a few minutes, my eyes opened and I went back to my chair rather sadly, figuring I had really lost it.

But Joanna was thanking me again. "Oh, thank you, my dear, and God bless you. You have made me so happy with your messages. And guess what?"

What?" I responded absently. My head was throbbing.

"My headache is gone."

"Break time! Break time!" Frantically, Ellen made the football "time-out" signal and put a protective arm around me. She really was a good friend, I thought, to stick by me when I had so clearly lost my marbles.

Finally, Joanna went home to tell her family about the message from Grandma. After she left, Ellen looked at me with concern. "Noreen, what the hell is going on? Did you make up that stuff?"

Damned if I knew. "I'm so confused, Ellen. I don't know what's going on, but I didn't make it up." I thought maybe Joanna's fervent belief in all things psychic had been working on my subconscious. "Look, Ellen," I said, "Let's get together tomorrow after work and see what happens when we do it without her around."

This marked the beginning of our practice sessions. Over the next few months, we met almost every night. After work, I would cook dinner for my girls and rush over to Ellen's apartment. Her husband, Len, was a reporter for the local newspaper. He worked evenings, so we had the place to ourselves.

After a long meditation, I would enter into what we called the "weird state of consciousness." Then the tolerant skeptic Ellen and I would approach the problem like research scientists, conducting tests and experiments on me. Unfortunately, we had no real under-standing of what we were doing.

But it wasn't for lack of trying. In my spare moments at work, I read every book on psychic phenomena I could get my hands on. I mined every resource—from Edgar Cayce to J. B. Rhine's classic experiments at Duke, from spiritualism to Tibetan Buddhism—for clues about new ways to explore the possibilities of my growing ability to enter deep trances at will. During my evenings with Ellen, I practiced what I had read about. With her cold logic and skepticism, she was the perfect counterbalance and kept me from feeling like I really was losing it.

One night Len came home early and caught us in the middle of a session. Throwing his suit jacket over an empty chair and loosen-ing his tie, he laughed. He was a good-looking Sicilian with dark eyes and a great body, but he also was a cynical reporter who didn't believe in psychics.

"When are you two going to start chanting, 'Bubble, bubble, toil and trouble'?" he teased us. "When do the eye of the newt and the liver of the toad come out?"

He was just leaving the room with a beer when I asked impul-sively, "Do you want to test me?"

Len stopped and smiled strangely at his wife's nutty friend. Ellen felt tense and rose to playfully shove her husband out of the kitchen.

"No, wait a minute now," he said, lightly moving her aside and stepping toward me. "Test you? How?"

"Just give me a name of a deceased relative. I don't care how far back in history you might want to go. I'll tell you about him—or her."

Len sat next me to, sipped his beer, and slowly set the can on the table in front of him. "Albert," he said. "His name was Albert." It was a challenge. Len crossed his arms and stared at me. I closed my eyes and wiggled in my seat to get comfortable as I pushed my long dark hair back from my face.

"I want to see Albert. I want to see Len's Uncle Al—" I opened my eyes and suddenly looked at Len. "*Was* he your uncle?"

"Could be. Go on."

I closed my eyes again. Suddenly, images came into my mind and I began to describe his Uncle Albert. "He has dark hair, a receding hairline. He's got an olive complexion and pockmarks on his face—he looks kind of sinister." Then a cold feeling ran through me when I saw that he had a rope around his neck. Then I saw his feet, in worn brown loafers, swinging a few inches above the floor. He had hung himself. I opened my eyes and looked straight at Len.

I was accurate—Uncle Albert really had hung himself. But Len still wasn't buying any of it. He pointed to an empty 7-Up can on the table and said, "If you can make that can move, you might convince me you're psychic."

"Let's do it, Ellen," I urged. Why not? We had never tried anything like that before, but I had read about Russian psychics who could move objects with their minds. It was called psychokinesis. Ellen and I sat on opposite sides of the table with the can between us. Taking deep breaths, we focused our concentration on the 7-Up can.

Naturally, it didn't move.

Maybe we should both be on the same side of the table. Again, we took deep breaths and focused our minds on the can. It didn't budge, but a thundering crash came from the bedroom—it sounded like a car had hit the wall. Len rushed into the bedroom to see what happened and came back into the room shaking his head and looking confused. Nothing was amiss in the bedroom. Ellen and I looked at each other smugly, but said nothing and continued our concentration. A few minutes later, a shattering noise made us all turn to look at the large plate glass window in the living room. But nothing had happened. Even I had to admit this was a little strange.

Len stood up abruptly and said, "That's enough of this foolishness. I need to get some sleep. We'll see you later, Noreen."

When I saw Ellen the next day, she told me that Len tossed and turned all night. Every time he closed his eyes, he said he felt something sitting on his face. He kept hearing loud noises in the apartment, and finally ended up sleeping on the couch with the lights and radio on. He told Ellen he didn't want her to do any more "psychic stuff" with me.

But Ellen was my best friend. Naturally, she ignored his request and we continued our development. Our sessions just ended earlier.

Slowly, this "psychic stuff" began to take root in my life. I didn't understand it, but I couldn't deny it either. I was completely captivated by the amazing new world that had opened in my mind. I started neglecting my job. All I wanted to do was practice what other people claimed they could do in the books I was reading.

Once the word got out, the hotel's maids, secretaries, and waiters became willing participants in my experiments. I would touch their rings or watches, and see pictures in my head that told me about them and their lives. They loved it and I loved it. My boss, however, did not love it. He was becoming suspicious of the heavy employee traffic in and out of my office. I didn't want to be caught—or stopped—so I devised a new way to practice during office hours.

On Mondays, I would make several phone calls to business-people in Orlando, inviting them to see our hotel facilities and join me for a magnificent complementary lunch. After the meal, I would casually mention psychic phenomena. If they didn't scream "evil" or hold up a cross, I'd pursue the subject further. Finally, I'd be pulling off their watch or ring and giving them my psychic impressions. I hoped to see things they could confirm—body scars, the place where they lived, what their loved ones looked like, and the kind of car they drove. Mostly, I could. My accuracy amazed my luncheon guests, and it still amazed me. When I look back on those days, I am astonished that I lasted as long as I did at my job. I think I was driven to do all these impromptu readings just to prove to myself that my strange talent was real.

The exciting new ability that had been switched on that morning in Joanna's kitchen didn't go away, and I didn't want it to. I loved being able to do this, and I couldn't get enough of it. I was hooked. To no one's surprise except my own, after three months of practicing my psychic abilities at home and at the office, and letting my work slip at the hotel, I was fired.

Some psychic I was turning out to be. I didn't even see it coming.

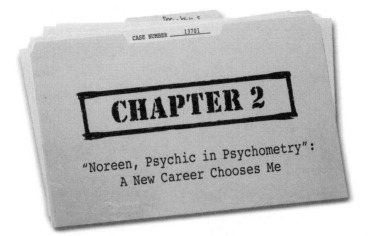

I didn't really know what a hotel's psychic-in-residence should wear, but I didn't think my Orlando businesswoman persona would work in this setting. I decided to go for the sexy, mysterious angle, and bought an expensive-looking gypsy outfit: a thin, off-the-shoulder blouse tucked into a tight waist-cinched Kelley green satin skirt, and voluminous purple petticoats that rustled when I walked. As the crowning touch, I added large gold hoop earrings. With my long dark hair, I just about pulled it off. Although I cringe to think of it now, I bravely dressed up and went to my new job each day, sitting in a booth in the hotel lounge and waiting for clients. All I needed was the crystal ball and bandanna to look like a tearoom gypsy from a movie.

The loss of my job left me devastated. How was I supposed to support my girls? Karla was in high school, and Reené had just gone off to college. The need for money wasn't going to suddenly stop, but neither was my fascination with this new ability. In my naiveté, I decided that if my psychic exploration was getting in the way of my work, maybe I should just work as a psychic.

But could I make a living at this? I was pretty sure the unemployment office had no job opening for a psychic, and I had never seen such a position offered in the help wanted ads. Later, Dr. William Roll of the Psychic Research Foundation told me that almost no one made a living out of being a psychic—there just wasn't any money in it. Good thing I didn't know that then, because I just went ahead and created a job for myself at another hotel as the "Resident Psychic." I was young, fired up, and full of energy. And I have never been at a loss for ideas and motivation!

The hotel was the Sheraton Jetport, a sprawling complex covering two acres near the Orlando Airport. The lounge seated more than a hundred people, and a bar ran the entire length of one side. Next to the bar was a raised platform for a band and a small dance floor, and padded booths lined the remaining walls. Tables and chairs filled the floor. I thought I would need a little quiet, so I chose a booth as far from the band as possible. The lounge's clientele was mostly airline personnel and passengers waiting for flights. Perfect! No one I knew would come in here. And if I wasn't any good, it didn't matter—my clientele would be flying away and I wouldn't see them again.

I didn't really know what a psychic-in-residence should wear, but—even though Ann Gehman was a great role model—I just didn't think my Orlando businesswoman persona would work in this setting. I decided to go for the sexy, mysterious angle, and bought an expensive-looking gypsy outfit: a thin, off-the-shoulder blouse tucked into a tight waist-cinched Kelley green satin skirt, and voluminous purple petticoats that rustled when I walked. As the crowning touch, I added large gold hoop earrings. With my long dark hair, I just about pulled it off. Although I cringe to think of it now, I bravely dressed up and went to my new job each day, sitting in a booth in the hotel lounge and waiting for clients. All I needed was the crystal ball and bandanna to look like a tearoom gypsy from a movie.

Whatever it was, it worked for me. The hotel gave me a free meal, a few glasses of wine, a booth to use, and wished me luck. I wasn't given any salary or commission. I had to provide my own advertisement, so I had table placards printed up with my portrait in soft but stark black and white: dark, piercing eyes staring out of a shadowy background, leaning slightly forward in a low-cut dress, arms clasped demurely. I played it up for all it was worth.

The fancy type at the top of the placard proclaimed that I was "Noreen—Psychic in Psychometry." Clients would pay me—five dollars, I hoped—to tell them about what I saw when I held something of theirs, usually a ring or watch or other jewelry. From my reading, I had learned that what I did had a name: psychometry. According to the books, the objects apparently held a field of energy that carried information, images, visions, and feelings about the owner that I could somehow "read." Sometimes I would see images in my mind when I psychometrized an object, sometimes I would just get an impression or a feeling. Anything a person had touched or worn seemed able to tell me something about them. They were astonished at my accuracy, and, frankly, so was I. Secretly, I thought I must be reading their minds—how else could I be doing it?

When my friends heard about my new job, they tried to discourage me—some gently, some not so gently. They gave all sorts of reasons: I was too new at all this. I wasn't ready. Real psychics don't do readings in bars. I wouldn't be able to concentrate. Only Ellen thought it was good idea, but even she was a little worried.

The first few nights, Ellen sat at a nearby table to watch over me and give me moral support. Maybe she thought I wouldn't get any clients, but I was surprisingly busy right away and continued to be during my stay at the Jetport. After a while, Ellen could see I was okay, wished me luck, and stopped coming. I was on my own.

* * *

After a while, true to my restless nature, I got bored with working at the Jetport. I wanted a new place, a larger establishment, and no more gypsy outfits. I didn't have to search very long before I found just the right place—the Twin Towers. By coincidence, it also was a part of the Sheraton chain.

I made an appointment with the nightclub manager for an interview. Confident that I was an experienced psychic, I went to the meeting feeling almost cocky. I was only slightly fazed by the size of the hotel when I arrived. It was huge, and I could see why it was one of the most expensive hotels in Orlando. Located near Disney World, the hotel consisted of two towers that shot up twenty stories. The sprawling ground level was its own world—a lobby, conference and convention rooms, and myriad eating and drinking establishments.

I don't know whether this manager had talked to the one at the Jetport, but I suspect he had. He hired me without hesitation.

My working conditions were the same: I received the exclusive use of a booth, a free dinner, and wine. I supplied my own publicity and brochures. The general configuration of the Twin Towers's lounge was similar to the one at the Jetport. But there the similarity ended. This new nightclub was larger—it seated three hundred people—and classier. It was decorated in a dramatic red and black, with thick drapes providing a lush background for the heavy, comfortable furniture in this windowless room. Even the band had more class—the musicians wore tuxedos. My method and rules for psychic readings remained the same, but I did make a couple of changes: I doubled my fee, and I spent a small fortune buying new working clothes. No more of that gypsy outfit! I bought seductive, sleek satin and silk outfits befitting a nightclub. My favorite one was a slinky black gown cut to the thigh. I was reading for the big time now. I had no idea, however, how big the big time could be.

The new hotel was working out wonderfully. The band and I established a good rapport. One of the advantages of having the same band for six months was getting to know the musicians and not having to explain to them what I did and the need for an introduction. They helped people know I was there and that helped my business. One evening, I had just finished a reading when John, the hotel manager, bent over my table. "Noreen, could you give a reading in the restaurant?"

"No," I answered. "The restaurant is too bright and noisy. Why can't they come to my table in the lounge?"

"These people aren't allowed in the nightclub. You're not that busy anyway. It won't hurt you."

"Okay," I nodded, wondering why they couldn't come to the nightclub. Still, he had a point: the evening was slow, and I could use the money.

I stood up, grabbed my cigarettes and lighter, and followed him as he led me to a table where two teenage girls giggled as I sat down. One was thin and one was plump, but both had deep brown eyes and long dark hair. They were dressed in clean but hardly fashionable blouses and skirts. Maybe they were maids at the hotel, too young to be allowed into the lounge. I smiled at them and sat down, nodding goodbye to John.

"Who's first?" I asked.

The thin girl deferred to her friend. She spoke with a strong accent that I couldn't place. I asked for her ring, told her my basic rules, and we began. She was particularly interested in a young man she had left in another country. Would she see him again? Yes, I told her that I could see her rejoining this man at a later time. For twenty minutes, I answered her questions and encouraged more.

At the end of the reading, they thanked me profusely and the girl asked how much she owed me. They were so sweet that I was momentarily tempted to say "No charge," but I overcame this desire to be Ms. Charity and asked for my regular fee. Then I went back into the dark, noisy nightclub and thought no more of the two girls with the strange accents.

Two nights later, the hotel manager again approached my table. He walked straighter and taller than usual. Beside him was a sophisticated Latin-looking woman. He introduced us, almost bowed to her, and left. Who the heck was this mysterious woman who had John on his best behavior?

I soon found out: She was a lady in waiting to a Saudi Arabian princess whose entourage had rented the entire top floor of the Twin Towers. Speaking very seriously, she explained that the princess had made a royal command: she requested a psychic reading. The woman explained that they were celebrating the religious month of Ramadan, and fasted from sundown to sunset. She would return at midnight to escort me to the princess. She also gave me some ground rules: I was to address the princess as "Your Highness," I could not speak unless I was spoken to, and my reading could see no negative aspects of her life.

I was stunned, to say the least. I had never met a princess before, and I couldn't imagine how she had heard of me. As the lady-in-waiting turned to leave, I said, "Wait, I have one question. How did the princess know about my psychic readings?"

She smiled for the first time and said, "You read her daughter in the restaurant a few days ago. She spoke of your amazing powers to her mother." I guess those girls weren't maids after all.

Feeling particularly unworldly, I ended my readings in the lounge at 11:00 p.m. I waited impatiently, smoking and drinking ginger ale, thrilled about this new adventure but a bit anxious about what I might encounter. A few minutes after midnight, the lady-in-waiting came for me. After she made sure I understood the rules for meeting the princess, we walked in silence to the private elevator and rode to the top floor. I was getting more nervous by the second.

The woman opened the door to one of the suites and I stood there in amazement. It seemed as if an entire town was in residence. The large room was filled with people of all ages. Children were running around, small groups of young people stood together talking loudly and gesturing wildly, and a woman in her forties was playing a board game on the floor with a young man. My escort led me to a chair in the middle of this chaos and abandoned me. For some time no one paid the slightest attention to me. Was I suddenly invisible? This was not doing much for my confidence. I couldn't even listen to the various conversations since I didn't understand Arabic.

I was getting more and more embarrassed just sitting there with all this commotion going on around me, but I didn't feel that I could leave. Failing to make eye contact with anyone, I said loudly to the room in general, "Does anyone mind if I smoke?" No one answered, but an ashtray soon appeared on the small table beside me. I lit up and inhaled gratefully. I was still being ignored, but at least I had something to do. Finally, the lady in waiting returned. I was so glad to see her I could have hugged her. She led me into a room that was as empty as the other one was crowded.

She left me alone there for thirty minutes. By this time it was around 1:00 a.m., and I was getting very tired. It was way past my bedtime. And a night's work combined with my anxiety in this strange situation left me completely exhausted.

I came alive, however, when the door suddenly opened and two women entered. One was an older woman, the other was the one who had been playing a game on the floor. She was the princess! She was beautifully and tastefully dressed in a tailored, embroidered silk dress, right out of a Paris couturier. She was covered with jewelry—gold bands on her wrists, diamond brooches, and simple red stones I took to be rubies in her earrings. Several lovely chains hung around her slender neck.

The older woman was the interpreter. I was angry after being ignored for so long, and forgot all about the rules the lady-in-waiting had been at such pains to tell me. Looking straight at the princess, I haughtily explained my own rules for a reading. The interpreter looked shocked. When she told the princess what I had said, she was also in shock. But she acquiesced and unclasped one of the pendants, a simple religious medallion.

The reading lasted for almost an hour because everything had to go through the interpreter. After a while I didn't even worry if she translated my answers correctly. The princess asked about various people, mostly relatives, but the one thing she asked most about surprised me: money. Finally, the session ended. I was now really exhausted and drained. But they wanted another reading!

Before I could respond, a young man entered the room. The interpreter explained that this was one of the princess's sons. He was in his late teens, still with some baby fat, but extremely good looking. I noticed two things in particular about him: his large, sparkling eyes and his white dress shirt. Maybe it was the late hour and the overall strangeness of the experience, but all I could think was that this shirt was the whitest thing I had ever seen, terrific for a laundry commercial. Fortunately, he spoke English. I told him my rules and he handed me his wafer-thin gold watch. It was exquisite.

He was more fun than his mother. He asked about girls, travel, and the usual teenage boy stuff. I did see, however, that there was a person he loved very deeply, someone he didn't get to see very often. When the reading was over, I asked him about this person. He hesitated, and then shyly told me that it was his father. The prince was so busy, and had so many children, that this boy was only allowed to see him for one hour a week.

When the teenager left, I was alone again. Again I waited, but not for long. The lady-in-waiting appeared, told me that the princess was very pleased, and gave me some folded money. I stuck it in my purse without looking at it. At this point, I couldn't care less. I just wanted to go home to bed.

I rode back down to the lobby alone. As I left the hotel to get my car, I was shocked to see the sun coming up. It had been a long, strange night, I thought, as I pulled out of the parking lot. At the first stoplight I came to, I opened my purse and unfolded the money to find three one-hundred-dollar bills. I began to laugh hysterically when I remembered that I almost hadn't wanted to charge the young princess in the restaurant.

———————◦•◦•◦———————

One evening, a cocktail waitress came over to chat. After a few brief moments of idle conversation she blurted out, "You know, most people who work here don't believe in you and that psychic stuff."

"That's okay," I replied with a smile, "because I believe in me and what I do." At that moment I realized that my enthusiasm for my new career was so strong that I was oblivious to the beliefs of others. For better or worse, this unshakable faith has stayed with me to this day.

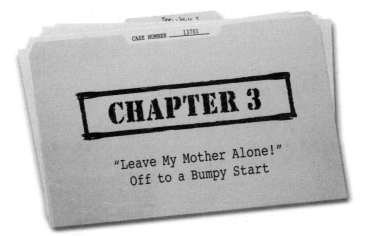

CHAPTER 3

"Leave My Mother Alone!"
Off to a Bumpy Start

"You're weird, Mother, really weird," Karla moaned. She flopped down on the living room couch. "It was so embarrassing coming home with my friends and finding you and Ellen sitting in the dark talking to ghosts. Mother, how could you!"

"But, Karla—"

"No! I don't want to hear about it! And quit telling all my friends what you're doing." She shook her long blonde hair in anger and stomped out of the room.

What had I done?

The more comfortable I became with my psychic abilities, the more I came to accept them and the more I enjoyed just being myself. It was a different kind of life than I had planned on, but I felt happy and curious and excited to learn more.

Unfortunately, my children didn't see it in the same way. My younger daughter, Karla, was especially upset. The more involved I became in the psychic world, the further she withdrew from me. She was a teenager, and just the fact that I was her mom was embarrassing enough. Now, having witnessed my transformation from straight mom with a respectable P.R. job to gypsy to resident psychic, she knew she didn't want me anywhere near her friends. I could not convince her to listen.

"You're weird, Mother, really weird," Karla moaned one afternoon, flopping down on the living room couch. "It was so embarrassing coming home with my friends and finding you and Ellen sitting in the dark talking to ghosts. Mother, how could you!"

"But, Karla—"

"No! I don't want to hear about it! And quit telling all my friends what you're doing." She shook her long blonde hair in anger and stomped out of the room.

What had I done? In all of her seventeen years she had never ever heard me even speak of psychics, and now I was professing to be one. This certainly was not the future I had planned for me or my family.

I guess I'd never had much of a plan at all. I grew up in Turners Falls, Massachusetts, a small town on the Connecticut River. We lived outside town on a few acres of land, and I spent most of my youth playing in the woods and the river. I was always a fearless, free-spirited child, and something of a tomboy.

In fact, I'd rather have been playing creative games in the woods by myself than studying for school. Needless to say, my grades suffered. I loved sports, especially the ones the boys played, like football, basketball, and baseball. I also loved posing for pictures and was always putting on plays for the neighborhood kids. I wanted to grow up to be a movie star.

But instead of running off to Hollywood, I married young, and I had my two daughters before I was twenty. My husband and I were like innocent babes ourselves, in some ways. Working to raise our kids, we pretty much missed the sixties youth revolution. Even after my divorce, I only allowed myself an evening out once a week. And now—well, I could understand why Karla thought her mother had flipped.

Unexpectedly, her door opened and she shouted down the hall, "And what's Reené going to think?" And the door banged shut in exclamation.

Karla had touched a nerve. Reené was coming home from college for Easter break soon, and I was worried about our relationship. I had written to her about what I had been doing in the nightclub for the past few months, but she never mentioned my psychic work in her letters. At 5'7", my beautiful Reené was the tallest in our family of women. She and her sister had the same blue-green eyes. The divorce had affected her greatly. She was six years old at the time and went through a lot of emotional turmoil, but by high school she seemed to have worked things out. She became a cheerleader in her sophomore year and was voted most popular in her senior year and was voted the sweetheart queen. Her grades were always good and her teachers had nothing but praise for her. We were very close. I hoped we would stay that way.

Reené arrived home looking even more blonde and beautiful than I remembered. She brought stories about college and the plans she had for a party the following evening. She was inviting all her high school friends. We had an intimate talk, and I tried to explain to her about my new career. I showed her the books about psychics and psychic phenomena that I was reading.

"You mean those psychics in the books work in a nightclub, too?" she asked.

"Well," I answered, "not in a nightclub, but the psychics in the books do the same thing."

Reené gazed deeply into my brown eyes as she asked, "Mother, do you really believe you can talk to dead people?"

"Sure I do. Just think, when I die I can come back and chat with you. Won't that be nice?"

"Mother! Don't talk like that! It scares me! You know I love you. But I don't believe in that stuff." And she rushed off to do some last-minute errands for her party.

At least Reené was more tactful in her disbelief, I consoled myself. Karla would just snicker and refuse to listen.

The night of the party they both made me promise: "No fortune telling, no talking to dead people, and no strange rapping on the walls." But I did not promise I would not try levitation! Up to a point, it had been successful in the nightclub. I was eager to try it again.

That evening the small house was filled with busy young bodies, loud music, and laughter. When I thought the girls weren't looking, I approached their friends and soon had a small group interested in levitation. I explained to them how it worked. One person sat in a chair, two stood by her knees, and two stood by her shoulders, facing each other. I stood behind the chair. After some deep breathing and practice synchronizing their arm movements, they simultaneously placed fingers under her head, thigh, and arms. Before long, we were levitating each other with our fingers, and soon everyone at the party wanted to be lifted into the air. It was great fun. My girls couldn't complain; everybody loved it, though Karla did scowl at me when she thought no one was watching. The party was a great success, and the next day the girls didn't mention the levitation.

A few days later, I was invited to entertain at a cocktail party. A friend of a friend had heard about my psychometry feats and thought it would be great amusement for her guests. On a whim, I asked Reené to come with me, and to my surprise she agreed. As we drove together to the house I tried to explain what I was going to do at the party.

"It's not difficult. I just touch a watch or ring and tell the person about the information I get from the object."

"You mean the watch tells you things, like talking to you?"

"In a way, Reené, yes. It doesn't talk the way we talk to each other. It skips my ears and sends my mind the information with pictures."

"Oh," she said, polite but clearly unconvinced.

The hostess greeted us at the door and led us into her living room. Magnificent paintings and sculptures decorated the large room, and her well-dressed guests were casually scattered around with drinks in their hands.

I chose a modern, no-nonsense-looking chair to sit in and they soon formed a semicircle around me. Their rings, watches, and gold chains had been collected earlier, before I arrived, and were on a small table nearby.

Reené sat a few chairs away and quietly watched as I chose an object and pressed it to my forehead. With my eyes closed, I began speaking. The readings were generally quick. This was a party, and everybody wanted a turn:

"This individual recently had an operation that left a scar on her lower stomach."

"Yes, I do have a scar on my lower stomach," the owner of a ring confirmed.

"I see construction around your home."

"Yes, I'm building an addition onto my house," responded the owner of a watch.

"You are expecting company from a distance, a female relative."

"How did you know my sister was coming to visit me?"

I continued reading the objects for about an hour. Everything was going smoothly until I picked up a delicate gold chain with a small cross. Immediately, the chain's owner said: "I think it's all tricks. I don't believe in what you're doing. If you're real, tell me who John is and how he died."

The chatty group went silent as I tried to switch my psychic attention to "John." But she just kept protesting loudly, "You're wrong!" I didn't know what to do.

But Reené did. She didn't like seeing her mother attacked, and without thinking she leaned over and grabbed the cross from my hands. Closing her eyes, she imitated my gestures and began giving the irate woman information about John.

"I see John as a young red-headed boy in his late teens," she stated. "I see a gold chain . . . There's water around him—a lake, I see waves. He was your son and he drowned in a lake," Reené said, opening her eyes and staring at the woman. The woman began to cry. "John, my baby," she said. "I gave him the gold chain two days before he drowned in a water-skiing accident in the lake behind our house."

Reené reached over and handed the woman her gold chain and cross, saying, "Now leave my mother alone."

I was flabbergasted. Reené had defended and protected me using her own psychic ability.

I collected my check, said my goodbyes, and left.

On the drive home I thanked Reené for her help and told her she was a wonderful psychic, her abilities seemed to be exceptionally strong.

"No, I'm not, don't say that anymore," she insisted. She was set on being "normal," and I guess I didn't blame her. We didn't mention what happened for a very long time.

Even though Karla and Reené weren't interested in learning more about psychic phenomena, I was. I couldn't get enough of it. I knew my readings were accurate, but I did not know how I did them. I didn't understand where the information was coming from. I suspected that, through the object I held, I was tapping into the other person's thoughts and feelings. Then one day, something happened that utterly changed this perception.

A woman who had been especially pleased with our session returned a few weeks later. Her nephew had been in an auto accident, she said. She thrust a ring into my hand and demanded I see what was wrong with her nephew. The images came quickly and vividly. "I see a young man . . . curly brown hair . . . a scar on the left side of his head. Fourteen . . . fourteen." Twice the number came into my mind. The impressions vanished abruptly, the same way they had arrived. The woman was terribly upset. She snatched the ring back from me and started screaming at me.

"No, no! My nephew has long, bleached blond hair. He doesn't have any scars on his forehead or anywhere else, and I don't know what the hell number fourteen means." She grabbed her drink, downed it, and left—without paying me.

I was confused. I had seen it so clearly, and yet her denials were sincere. I began to wonder about this strange ability I had spent so much time developing. How could I be so wrong? I had misinterpreted visions before, but never when the vision was so clear.

To my surprise, she returned a few days later, much calmer and quite contrite. She apologized as she paid me and told me she had not seen her nephew for a while. He had cut his hair four months before the accident, and had let it grow out into its natural light brown curl. The accident had left him with a scar on the left side of his head. He had been in a coma from which he emerged exactly fourteen days and fourteen hours later.

It was then that I truly understood that I wasn't reading my clients' minds: But how was I doing it? I had some serious questions about my ability, and I was determined to find the answers.

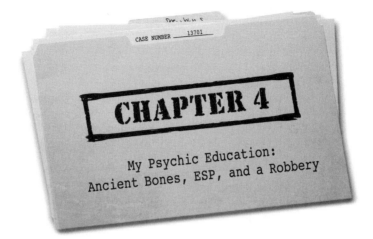

CHAPTER 4

My Psychic Education:
Ancient Bones, ESP, and a Robbery

Nervous but excited, I stood at the woman's front door—holding my new tape recorder. If I was going to be a psychic investigator, it was important to document my cases. Armed with Dr. Jones's instructions, I thought there was a chance I could actually help find out who had robbed this woman's house.

She greeted me warmly, and then introduced me to her friend, Detective Grady, who looked at me suspiciously. He turned out to be a very nice guy and a good cop. Naturally, he was skeptical. "Are you kidding?"

I started to defend myself, but instead I looked him right in the eye and said, "Look, you don't have any leads, you don't have any suspects. What have you got to lose? Let's give it a try." I sounded much more confident than I felt, but it worked.

Grady shrugged. "Okay," he said, "Let's give it a go."

"Hello, is this the Duke University Parapsychology Laboratory? I'm a psychic in a nightclub. Can you please test my ESP and tell me what it's all about?"

The answer was polite but direct: Thanks, but no thanks. Looking back, I'm not surprised that the academic world was skeptical about me. I guess they'd heard that story before. But I wouldn't take no for an answer. I wanted to learn as much as I could, and I wanted to learn from the best.

I was skeptical myself. It's the way I was brought up. My mother was and is a very creative woman. She's a gifted painter and a world traveler, curious about everything. Like me, she was on her own from an early age. But she also had a very strong French Catholic upbringing, and she was pretty skeptical about what I was doing. My father never said a word about psychic phenomena. It was not until I had become a psychic that he told me his Lithuanian mother would sometimes have neighborhood women over to "read the cards" for them.

I'm not particularly religious, and I'm not one for blind belief. If I was going to "read the cards" for someone, I needed someone to help me understand *how I was doing it.* I wouldn't take no for an answer, so I dug deeper and found out that a man named William Roll was the head of the Psychic Research Foundation near Duke University in Durham, North Carolina. I wrote him a letter telling him the things I could do and expressing my bewilderment about how it worked. I may have made my living in a nightclub, but Dr. Roll could see that I was sincere—and sincerely confused. Almost immediately, he invited me into the program.

———— ·•· ————

I felt like I had struck gold. William Roll had done research for seven years with J. B. Rhine at Duke's Parapsychology Laboratory. Rhine is generally acknowledged as the founder of modern parapsychology. Dr. Roll is the president of the independent Psychical Research Foundation (known as PRF), which began at Duke University back in 1961. I was thrilled that Dr. Roll, a man who knew all about the meaning of the words I could barely pronounce, was so willing to share his knowledge and patient enough to answer my many questions.

My first visit was a real surprise. I had expected to find a big laboratory building on the grounds of Duke University, but the PRF turned out to have its headquarters in a small house down the road. This little house was like a home, filled with an extended family of assorted researchers and assistants. Dr. Roll's secretary was a beautiful blonde who seemed to know a lot about psychic research. One of the researchers was a handsome, charming guy whom all the women were clearly in love with. I think my favorite person was Joan, a young college student who was interning there. With her dark hair and large dark eyes, she was a wonderful young woman who wasn't afraid to ask questions or say what she felt. I found her honesty and truthfulness exciting.

Dr. Roll himself had a lovely British accent, and was always very professorial and nicely dressed. Everyone else who worked there was much more low key—sandals seemed to be the footwear of choice. I probably stood out in my suburban suits, but the staff always made me feel at ease. Over the next five years, I drove to Durham as often as I could. I would spend a week, sometimes two, involved in research. They tested my psychometry and mediumship ability, and my telepathy. I would try anything they wanted me to do with my mind.

For some reason, I tend to remember the times I felt I *didn't* do well. In one early experiment, they asked me to hold big padded envelopes and tell them what I saw inside. But no matter which envelope I held, I saw the same thing: a dark building, with people rushing in and out of it. I was crushed. How could I keep seeing the same thing? I must be wrong. Later, I found out that each envelope contained a different object from a different person, but all of the people who owned the objects worked in—you guessed it—the same dark office building.

I remember one experiment vividly. Before we started, they asked me a very good question. Instead of locking me up in a brightly lit lab cubicle, they asked me how I worked best. I had to be honest. I said, "Well, I like to have the energy from an audience." So they got me a little audience of secretaries and researchers, and I did some of what I call "showing-off psychometry." They handed me an object and said simply, "This belonged to Jay, and he's dead. Tell us how he died." An image poured into my mind. I saw a man step into traffic, get hit by a car, and shoot way up into the air. "And that was just how he died," I finished. I heard a lot of "wows" all through that presentation. Sadly, it turned out that I was right on target: Jay was a friend of theirs who had recently been killed crossing the street.

Of course, not all of the experiments were so dramatic. Some really were just as scientific and rigorous as I had imagined, and we would go to Duke to use their psychology lab facilities. I remember one research project I did with a parapsychologist named Ed Kelley. He hooked me up to an EEG machine to monitor my brain waves and placed me in a glass booth. I felt like I was in a science fiction movie. First, he and his colleagues monitored my brain pattern when I was just talking normally. Then they would give me rings and watches to psychometrize, and they would monitor my brain patterns again. Later, they told me that the EEG readings indicated that I was using a different part of my brain when I was psychic.

I was really excited about the information these tests were providing. I knew how I felt, but now they were giving me real, verifiable feedback about what I was experiencing. Kelly and his colleagues at the PRF didn't have any cut-and-dried explanations for the things I did, but they did make me aware of two issues that were very important to me: First, they assured me, I was *not crazy*. And second, I was *not special*. They helped me understand that everyone has this intuitive part of the mind, but it's usually a lot quieter than mine turned out to be. The reason is pretty simple: Our society encourages us to use the logical, rational, thinking mind—the left hemisphere of the brain. Although right-brain thinking is getting a lot of well-deserved attention today, back then this perceptive, creative, and emotional part of the mind was the part we were conditioned to ignore. As I learned from the researchers, we need to use, develop, and respect all parts of our mind.

Above all, I learned that my newly awakened abilities were something that could be seen in the light of day and verified. Some people—even some of my friends, and certainly some of my clients—seem to want the illusion of secret rites and magic potions. They wanted to see me hovering mysteriously over a Ouija board, reaching across the border of consciousness to the "dark side." But I was learning that it's not a gift a few lucky individuals have acquired through magic: We *all* possess psychic ability, no matter how rudimentary. Your sudden hunches, flashes of insight or intuition, and moments of inspiration are all coming from the same place: the right hemisphere of your eight-pound universe, your brain.

Part of what I love about my work is that I get to meet so many interesting people. During this period of intense research, I was also fortunate enough to meet Dr. David E. Jones, a man who was to become my friend and mentor. Dr. Jones is a cultural anthropologist, author, and parapsychology investigator. At that time, he had already carried out research among Comanche and Kiowa Indians in Oklahoma, was extremely spiritual, and seemed to know a great deal about everything. When I first met him, he was a professor of anthropology at the University of Central Florida. Very tall and thin, he reminded me of a figure in an El Greco painting. I thought he was great.

Dr. Jones was different from the psychic researchers I had met at the PRF. He was not trying to understand what psychic phenomena are all about, or whether psychic ability was valid or invalid. Instead, he was interested in exploring the practical applications of extrasensory perception—ESP. He was trying to answer a very specific question: Could people who profess to have psychic ability touch archeological artifacts and the physical remains of ancient people and convey information about the objects that cannot be obtained in ordinary ways?[1] When he offered me the opportunity to get in touch with the past by touching artifacts, I leaped at the chance.

I loved his office at the university. It was covered with bones and books and all kinds of things you might see in a museum. At our first meeting, he gently unwrapped an ancient human jawbone he had carefully packed. I picked it up and stroked it, concerned. "David," I asked, "why is he in a hole with a bunch of other people?" This image upset me, and I didn't know why.

I guess Dr. Jones was used to working with psychics, because he didn't bat an eye. He just told me that this was the fossilized mandible of an adult Native American man who had been buried in a mass grave east of the Great Lakes more than two thousand years go. Then he asked me, "What kind of weather do you feel he experienced?"

I closed my eyes, shifted in my chair, and pursed my lips. "He didn't like the cold," I said. "There was snow. Cold winters and short summers."

Dr. Jones was testing me in his own way. He later told me that he was trying to decide if I was capable of touching a nondescript human bone and conveying specific information that would locate its historical, geographical, and cultural origins. "Noreen," he continued, "where does this bone come from? Who is it?"

I opened my eyes and searched through my purse for cigarettes, saying casually, "Oh, he's an old Indian man from up north somewhere."

He took the bone from me and placed it back in its packing box. "How do you think he died?"

I leaned back in my chair, exhaled a cloud of smoke, and told him what I saw. "He didn't die from old age or sickness. He was hit in the head and killed. He didn't have a chance."

Dr. Jones later told me that the man's cranium, which was being packed in a separate container in the archeology laboratory, indicated that death had been caused by a crushing blow to the left side of the head. Intrigued by my accuracy, he asked if I would participate in more experiments. "Hell yes," I said. This was exciting work for me, and about as far away from nightclubs as I could get. I had found a new way to use my abilities. Not only was it helping Dr. Jones, it was also helping me learn more about what I could do.

Working with Dr. Jones was an extraordinary experience. He gave me a great deal of respect, and I appreciated that. He also taught me an important lesson: that I could do more with my psychic ability than work parties and hotel lounges.

———————◆———————

My friends all knew about my new career, and most of them were intrigued. At least they were still loyal friends. During this time, Karla also left for college. Both of my daughters were now over eighteen and had left home to start their own lives—still more or less aghast at my new profession but resigned to it. I was on my own for the first time in decades, and it was time to get to know myself. Anyway, I was having too much fun learning about psychic phenomena to have time left over to worry.

About this time, Dr. Jones unwittingly started me on my way to being a psychic detective. A woman he knew had been burglarized, and she was frantic to get her things back. No one had seen a thing, and the police couldn't find any clues. It looked like she was just going to have to write her possessions off to a bad experience, but she wasn't ready to give up. Desperate for help, she called two old friends: a seasoned police detective and David Jones. Dr. Jones, bless his heart, thought I could be of some assistance

I was surprised. Why me? I was just beginning to learn about ESP and other psychic phenomena, and I knew even less—in fact, nothing—about police work. But if Dr. Jones wanted me there, I couldn't say no. Still, I told him all my doubts. "How will I know what to do? How can I help her? I can't use psychometry. They didn't leave anything behind, so I don't have anything to touch." I felt completely out of my element.

Dr. Jones listened without interrupting and then gently replied. "Of course, they left something behind, Noreen. Energy."

"What?" Now I was even more confused.

"Relax, Noreen." Dr. Jones was so patient—that's what I really liked about him. "Listen to me. The individuals who robbed that house left something we can't see but which you—as a psychic—can pick up and interpret."

I still wasn't getting it.

"Look," he continued, "you know those search and rescue dogs? You and I can't smell the scent the way the dog does, but that doesn't mean the scent's not there. The scent *you* are going to pick up is called energy. It's left behind just like the scent the dog follows," he continued patiently.

"She needs your help, and you can help her." I listened attentively as he calmly explained what I needed to do. By the time he was done, I thought, *Okay, if he thinks I can do this, maybe I can.*

The next day, nervous but excited, I stood at the woman's front door—holding my new tape recorder. If I was going to be a psychic investigator, it was important to document my cases. Armed with Dr. Jones's instructions, I thought there was a chance I could actually help. The woman greeted me warmly, and then introduced me to her friend, Detective Grady,[2] who looked at me suspiciously. He turned out to be a very nice guy and a good cop. Naturally, he was skeptical. "Are you kidding?"

I started to defend myself, but instead I looked him right in the eye and said, "Look, you don't have any leads, you don't have any suspects. What have you got to lose? Let's give it a try." I sounded much more confident than I felt, but it worked.

Grady shrugged. "Okay," he said, "Let's give it a go."

Following Dr. Jones's instructions, we moved through her new house room by room. I sat in each room, turned on my tape recorder, and let any images flow into my mind. I didn't receive too much information, but I was able to say that I saw two men, and I also described their gray van.

A few weeks later, the police made an arrest and Detective Grady confirmed that my visualizations were accurate. In fact, he told me that he thought my accuracy was damn good—way beyond chance. He even gave me a few back-handed complements. I lapped it all up like a happy puppy.

I had just had my first taste of a direction that would take me out of the smoky world of hotel lounges and into a much darker world of violent death. But I didn't know it then. Then, as now, my own future unfolds from one mystery to the next.

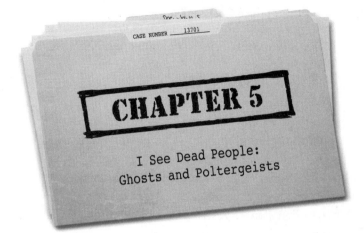

CHAPTER 5

I See Dead People:
Ghosts and Poltergeists

"Noreen," said Detective Grady without preamble, "I have a case that seems like hocus-pocus stuff, not police work."

"What do you mean?" I asked.

"It's weird as hell, and I don't know what to make of it." For Grady, who was a pretty quiet guy, this was really saying something. I listened closely.

"A family in our town called us a few weeks ago, scared to death. They claim things are flying around rooms, chairs are shaking, sinister voices are on the telephone—strange stuff. We don't know what the hell is going on in that house. But I can tell you that people outside the family have seen some of this going on."

"Tell me more!" I said. I didn't know what it could be either, but it sounded pretty exciting.

———•◦•———

I didn't think I'd ever see Detective Grady again, but a few months later I picked up the phone and heard his gruff voice. "Noreen," he said without preamble, "I have a case that seems like hocus-pocus stuff, not police work."

"What do you mean?" I asked.

"It's weird as hell, and I don't know what to make of it." For Grady, who was a pretty quiet guy, this was really saying something. I listened closely.

"A family in our town called us a few weeks ago, scared to death. They claim things are flying around rooms, chairs are shaking, sinister voices are on the telephone—strange stuff. We don't know what the hell is going on in that house. But I can tell you that people outside the family have seen some of this going on."

"Tell me more!" I said. I didn't know what it could be either, but it sounded pretty exciting.

"Well, when I interviewed the family, they claimed it started with unexplained voices over the telephone. Later, these voices seemed to come through the walls. Books and small vases and other objects are flying across the room without anyone touching them. The family's terrified."

"How many people live in the house?" I asked.

"Four," he replied. "All females—an older woman, her daughter, and two granddaughters, six and ten years old. The young girls are from two different marriages. The grandfather died a few months ago."

"What about the phone calls?" I prompted.

"When the mother or grandmother picks up the phone to make a call, they claim a strange voice is there and identifies them. The voice tells the caller what she is wearing and what the caller just finished doing . . . and what the caller planned on doing." That seemed really disturbing, and I felt a chill.

"At times the voice sounds like a child's voice; sometimes the voice sounds like a white woman, at other times a black woman. The voice uses foul language and makes threats laced with sexual overtones, often threatening the life on the other end of the phone."

"What about the phone company?" I began. "What do they think is happening?"

"The telephone company has been investigating, and our department has phone taps on the telephone, but we can't figure out the source of the calls.

"Noreen, this family is scared to death. They're a very religious black family, and they suspect voodoo and witchcraft, and they just don't know what to do."

Okay, now I was hooked. No way I was going to miss this opportunity. I had recently seen the movie *The Exorcist,* and the temptation to see what might be an example of this in my own backyard was too much to resist.

"Wait," Grady said, "there's more. Whenever the family sits down to eat, one of the little girls' chairs starts shaking like crazy. The kid's feet can't even touch the floor. Many people, including their Baptist minister and some local reporters, have seen this stuff happening. So we can't ignore it, but we can't seem to find a suspect behind these events. I figured this was your territory. Is there anything you can do?"

It may have been psychic phenomena, but this was new territory for me. Still, why not? "I can't promise anything, but I would sure like to give it a try." I agreed to meet with Detective Grady the following evening at his office, which was an hour's drive from my home in Orlando, Florida.

I only knew what I'd read, but this sounded a lot like what I'd dug up about ghosts and poltergeists. So right away, I called Dr. Roll, who was an expert on such matters. After I told him everything Detective Grady had told me, I asked, "Do you think this is a haunting?"

"No," he said. "It sounds like a poltergeist, Noreen. If it is a real poltergeist, if we feel the case is valid, I'll send a researcher down to investigate it further."

The next evening it was raining as it can only in Florida. My windshield wipers were losing their battle against the downpour, and I felt like I was driving my laboring old Ford under water. To make it even more melodramatic, the rain was accompanied by thunder and lightning. It was a great night for a ghost story! If I hadn't been so nervous about driving safely and finding the police station, I would have found the situation humorous. I was on my way to a haunted house.

Like many Florida towns, this one has grown in recent years and has a population of thousands. But in those days, only a few hundred people lived there and the roads were pretty dark. After several wrong turns on obscure county roads, I found the police station. I parked as close as possible and ran quickly through the rain to the front door, giving my name to an expressionless woman behind a wire cage. A large man sitting nearby leaped up immediately. He glared at me with hard eyes, and grunted as he opened the locked door for me and walked stoically down a long corridor. I interpreted all this to mean "follow me," so I did. He pushed through a door to an inner office marked "Chief." Without introducing himself, he told me Detective Grady was no longer on the case and he had taken over the investigation.

The Chief clearly did not want me there, and he interrogated me relentlessly and angrily for a solid hour. Why was I there? What was I planning to do? Who was I? I answered as honestly as I could. Having only recently started to develop my psychic abilities, I didn't really know a heck of a lot, and the Chief apparently interpreted my uncertainty as caginess. Dissatisfied with my answers, he pushed a dirty green mimeographed paper at me. "Read this!" he demanded, his face going from red to purple with rage. The faded print said that all fortunetellers, palmists, astrologers, and psychics were followers of Satan. It cited certain passages of the Bible.

I was shaking inside, but I tried to reply calmly. "None of those descriptions fit me," I said with as much dignity as I could muster. "I'm a *psychometrist*." And I pushed the dirty paper back over his desk. That must have unsettled him because he blurted out, "What church do you go to every Sunday?"

Maybe he thought I would say "The First Church of Psychometry," but instead I replied honestly. "I don't go to any particular church. I find truth in all religions."

Ignoring my answer, he repeated the question. "What church do you attend every Sunday?"

I sat a little straighter in my chair and slowly and clearly repeated my previous answer, "I do not attend a specific church every Sunday."

He loomed over me and pointed his thick finger toward the door. "Out of my office!" he bellowed. "You're evil!"

I had never been treated like this in my life. I was furious, but helpless. I walked slowly toward the door, wishing with all my heart that I really was an evil witch so I could put a curse on him. With my hand on the doorknob, I turned to stare at him and said, "You're wrong." He glowered at me and I got out of there as quickly as possible. It was still pouring. As I drove back home in the driving rain, I really wondered if I was in the right business.

The next day, to my great surprise, Detective Grady called and told me that I was back on the case. We met for coffee, and he kindly filled me in on what had happened.

After I left the Chief's office, he had gone on to the house alone. Although he'd been there a number of times before, he'd never witnessed anything out of the ordinary. This time, however, things would be different. I like to think that perhaps a transfer of energy occurred from me to him. Maybe it shook him up so much that it flipped a switch and opened up his mind to some new things. All I know is that when he got there all hell broke loose.

Thunder and lightning from the storm made a dramatic setting for his arrival. The family—a mother, grandmother, and two young daughters—was sitting down to eat when he arrived, and they invited him to join them. He refused their invitation, but took off his wet jacket and sat in a comfortable chair to observe. Everything was orderly and quiet in the small house as the thunderstorm continued to rage outside.

The grandmother and mother were both sitting at opposite ends of the table in the tiny dining room, and the two girls sat across from each other, between them. As the Chief watched, not expecting much to happen, the oldest girl's chair suddenly started to shake so violently it knocked the fork from her hand. The other members of the family sat fearfully still. The Chief, big and strong, confidently walked over and placed his hands on the back of the chair. But it kept shaking, and his body involuntarily began to quiver.

He let go of the chair and started across the room toward the phone to call the police station for backup. The family all sat silently at the dining table, watching as small objects left their place on shelves and tables and flew at him. Bobbing and weaving to avoid the flying ashtrays and books and knickknacks, the Chief finally managed to reach the phone. But when he picked up the receiver to dial, a strange woman's voice was already on the line. She said, "You're going to call your office, Chief," then added (appropriately, I thought), "You're not smart enough to solve this case. Get your white ass out of this black house." He did.

I told Grady that this case really sounded interesting, and I couldn't wait to meet with the family.

So, on a nice sunny day, I headed over there. I stood in front of the one-story, one-family house for a moment, wondering what I'd find. I don't know what I was expecting, but I walked into a scene right out of a movie. I stood in their small living room surrounded by more crosses, cheap reproductions of Jesus, holy scenes, and religious inscriptions than I had ever seen in one place in my life. Having religious pictures and icons in a home is not uncommon, especially in Florida; many of my relatives are very religious and have reverent pictures hung about the house. But this family had pictures and crucifixes not only on the walls, but propped up on tables and even on the floor, leaning against the worn furniture. Clearly, this family was determined to ward off something they perceived as evil.

I noticed that the mother, grandmother, and younger daughter were all terrified, but the older girl, whom I'll call Sarah, seemed to be shyly enjoying all the attention. I asked the family questions and drew diagrams of the house where the phenomena had occurred. I noticed that if I ignored Sarah and centered my attention on her younger sister, small objects would leap off the tables and bookcase and head in my direction. I had never experienced anything remotely like this. It was absolutely amazing, and it seemed very clear who was creating all this excitement.

At one point, Sarah walked angrily into the bathroom. As I watched, I was astounded to see the toilet paper quickly unraveling—all by itself. Almost simultaneously, the water in the toilet overflowed and water poured from the sink faucets. Sarah had not touched anything. I could feel Sarah growing stronger, her unconscious powers magnifying. Naturally, especially given all the religious symbolism in the house, I couldn't help but think of *The Exorcist* and I shuddered.

The family, all devout churchgoers, had been holding daily prayer meetings ever since the occurrences started. But even with the pastor of the local Baptist church praying with them, the events continued. Loud thumps on the walls and flying crucifixes would sometimes disrupt the pastor during the prayers.

So, what was going on here? I'd been told that the girls were intelligent and they did well at school, but they had to obey their grandmother's excessively demanding house rules: No friends could play in the house with them and they could not play outside; no television, no phone calls, no snacks in between meals. Harsh discipline was imposed for the slightest violation. Their mother argued constantly with the grandmother about the rigid rules.

Apparently, the sudden death of the grandfather had left a feeling of emptiness in all their lives, especially the girls'. He was the only male they loved, and they both missed his hugs and loving attention.

As I had seen, the incidents at the house always happened when Sarah was home, and they were centered on her. Eventually, she began to have emotional attacks combined with muscle spasms. Although she was observed for a week in a hospital, the doctors could find nothing physically wrong. Yet the attacks recurred. The family refused to let Sarah see a psychiatrist.

After I had visited the house several times, I knew I was in over my head. I contacted Dr. Roll and explained what I had seen. He sent Joan as an observer. She stayed with the family for a week studying the strange phenomena. She later wrote a report about the case, which was published in a parapsychology journal.[1]

Was this family haunted? Was the girl possessed, like the girl in *The Exorcist*? I later learned that I had observed classic poltergeist phenomena. The word *poltergeist* is German for "noisy ghost," but no ghost is actually involved. In cases that have been studied and have not been found to be frauds—and yes, there are frauds in the psychic world!—the source is generally thought to be the unconscious or subconscious result of an adolescent or young person in the house who has learned or been forced to suppress strong emotions such as anger, fear, or hate. The "too good" little boy or girl who has not been able to vent strong emotions has a volcano of frustration inside, which can erupt in psychic energy.

Sometimes this energy is triggered by a chemical change in the person's body. That's why in many cases a child approaching puberty is the culprit. Reaction to the stress causes the outburst, like a subconscious temper tantrum. The poltergeist always fades as the child matures or the emotional trauma subsides, and that's what happened to Sarah. Although she hadn't hit puberty, her energies were severely repressed. She missed her grandfather and had no way to express her anger and grief and confusion. Fortunately for this troubled family, as the weeks turned into months the phenomena subsided. Maybe all the attention the girl was getting as a result of the case actually helped to calm her down. I wasn't able to help this family, but I felt privileged to have been invited as a witness. And anything I could do to further my own psychic education was welcome.

In my work with the Psychical Research Foundation, I became involved in a number of interesting and quirky cases. Although I ended up using my abilities in the real world of crime and criminals, this early work led me into investigations of hauntings. Are there ghosts? I don't know. My own conclusion is that ghosts are a form of energy, similar to the energy Sarah generated in the poltergeist case. Where that energy comes from—whether from a dead person or from somewhere else—is open to debate. I can tell you this: although the usual setting for a ghost story is a rambling and dilapidated Victorian house, a drafty castle, or a musty, magnolia-draped Southern mansion, people actually report ghosts in more mundane places.

One day, while I was involved in psychic research experiments for the PRF, Joan pulled me aside. "Will you have time this evening to investigate a haunted business?" she asked. "If you think you'll be too tired, just say so."

At the beginning of my career, I was always willing to try anything that might improve my developing ability. "No, problem," I replied. "I'll go. But what type of business would be haunted?" I figured a ghost who haunted a business would have to be sophisticated and nonviolent—no typewriters flying around the room.

"Sorry," Joan said, "but I can't tell you anything. In fact, just to make sure you don't use telepathy, the boss is only sending those of us who don't know anything about the haunting."

Late that night, Joan, her two assistants, and I piled into Joan's small imported car. Crammed in there with all of our recording and monitoring devices, we were severely overcrowded. Fortunately, the business was only a few miles away.

When we turned into a modern shopping center, I thought, *Oh, no! Not a haunted Safeway!* But we drove past the supermarket and pulled into a parking space in front of a health spa. A haunted spa?

We unloaded the car, pushed open the glass doors, and entered a reception room where two worried-looking young women in leotards awaited us. The young women gave us a quick tour of the facility, and settled us in the middle of an exercise room. In the mirrored walls, our small group looked huge.

It was distracting to see our group's reflection in every direction my eyes looked. I couldn't concentrate and asked that the lights be dimmed. The two young women were clearly excited, but also anxious about what might happen. What we wanted to happen was to contact the spirit and learn why it was haunting the spa.

We had plenty of recording equipment set up, but I felt like I needed some paper and a pen. I rarely used automatic writing—becoming a channel for a spirit that communicates a message through writing—but I felt compelled to make this request. I was learning to trust my instincts. One of the employees quickly left the room and returned with a notepad and pen, and we began.

The six of us sat in a circle on the highly polished hardwood floor. I relaxed myself and the rest of the group with some deep-breathing exercises, and I soon entered an altered state of consciousness. I found myself suddenly watching a woman who seemed to be in her late fifties. She was sitting in swirling, bubbling water, her flaming hair floating wildly on the surface. Suddenly, she grabbed her chest and cried out. I opened my eyes and said: "This older woman with dyed red hair died in your whirlpool bath."

The two spa employees looked at each other blankly. They had only worked there for a short time and couldn't verify anything I had witnessed.

Joan took charge. "Noreen, go back in and tell us more."

I closed my eyes again and immediately more images poured into my mind.

"She's upset," I said. "I'm having a hard time with her. She's very demanding. I keep seeing water overflowing. She's telling me she's been trying to communicate with people at the spa. She keeps phoning, but they don't hear her when they answer the phone. Sometimes you hear her on the back steps leading to the women's locker room."

Impulsively, I picked up the pad and pen and began writing. My eyes were still closed so I had no idea what I was writing. The information was completely bypassing my conscious mind—it was going straight through my hand to the paper. Almost as suddenly as it started, the writing stopped. Once again I was listening to this angry woman and repeating her words: "You tell my attorney to get going. He's had too many delays, too many interruptions. Tell him to finish my case." I could feel her agitated emotions in my own body as she added, "I'd like to tell him a thing or two."

Suddenly, I was jarred back to reality as all four phone lines started ringing simultaneously in the offices. The sound came through to the exercise room loud and clear, but no one was on the phone. By this time I had been working about forty minutes, and I was getting tired. We decided to stop. Joan said she would type up the information from the tape recorder and try to find out who the people were whose names I had unknowingly written down.

Later, I learned the whole story from Dr. Roll. The names on the pad were the dead woman's and her husband and lawyer. The woman had been a member of the health spa—and apparently, she had been just as acerbic in life as she was in death. She had indeed had a fatal heart attack in the whirlpool bath. Soon after, the haunting started. Every Wednesday, the whirlpool would overflow at a specific time—the day and hour she had died. The water stopped as mysteriously as it started, and plumbers couldn't find a problem to fix.

At the same time, the phone would ring, but no one was ever on the line. The telephone company checked and rechecked the phones, but could find no answers.

Almost all of the spa instructors had heard the footsteps on the back stairs. They usually began just before the spa closed, and members who were there late also heard the sounds. Understandably, none of the employees wanted to work late by themselves.

The husband had filed suit against the spa, but the attorney who was handling that case and the woman's will had delayed settling to attend to other pressing matters. Now, with this new information, the husband urged the lawyer to finish. The case was finally completed and quickly settled, and the haunting stopped.

I've never encountered another haunted spa, but over the years I have encountered a great deal of fear and ignorance concerning my ability and psychics in general. I have also been fortunate to have the continued support of my friends, my mentors, including Bill Roll and David Jones, and some wonderful people in law enforcement and the FBI. And I have to credit the angry red-haired woman with teaching me this valuable lesson: If you believe in yourself and in your efforts, nothing can stand in your way!

I felt a heaviness fall over me, leading me, and I walked away from the group. It was drawing me toward the kitchen, and I went where I was led. On my left, I saw a small storage room with a door that opened on the outside stairs. I looked in and "saw" the rapist standing in a dark corner of that small room. The unexpected vision was shocking. "He was waiting for you there!" I screamed. I must have looked wild, pointing my finger repeatedly to the spot where I saw him.

By 1979, I had left central Florida and moved to the town of Ruckersville, Virginia, near Charlottesville, to be closer to my mother and sister. I packed my belongings into a twenty-four-foot U-Haul rental truck and dragged my old blue Ford Taurus behind. At the last minute, my daughter Karla came by and said, "Mother, take this dog with you!" She threw in a big, friendly—and thoroughly untrained—mutt and waved goodbye. (This poor dog was frightened of stairs. I'll never forget having to carry all eighty pounds of him up the stairs to a motel room on that trip. But that's another story.)

The drive up was glorious, and I felt like I was starting over. As the scenery changed from sultry Orlando to Virginia's smoky Blue Ridge Mountains and the changing foliage of the Shenandoah Valley, I could feel my excitement rise.

After looking for a while, I found the perfect house: a one-hundred-year-old wood frame farmhouse on a few acres in the country. Looking back, I can see that it was way too big for me— I really don't know what I thought I'd do with four bedrooms— but I had a great time painting it and fixing it up. My mother lived with me for a time and put in a garden. I'm not a gardener myself, but I loved breathing in the energy of growing things and the pungent scent of dirt. Mostly, I loved being out in the garden because I could go for days without thinking a psychic thought. It was healing and grounding, in more ways than one.

I was driving to Durham on a regular basis to visit the PRF, and I was gaining more confidence in my abilities. They were still testing me in laboratory settings and sending me out on all sorts of wild cases. I loved never knowing what to expect, and I loved the people I was working with.

My career, too, was moving ahead. People were beginning to take me more seriously. More and more clients came to my house for private readings. And, to my great surprise, I found myself lecturing on ESP at the beautiful and historic campus of the University of Virginia, with its genteel dorms designed by Thomas Jefferson, and at Blue Ridge Community College near the small town of Staunton.

I couldn't believe I was lecturing at colleges—my formal education had stopped sometime short of that. But I have always loved to read—psychology, philosophy, religion—and I am always eager to learn new things. My work with David Jones had been particularly exciting, in part because I got to learn so much about things that had happened long ago.

My college teaching happened by accident, as so many things seem to do in my life when I'm on the right path. I was trying to make a living and get my name out there in Virginia, doing small talks and readings around town at all sorts of venues—bookstores, people's homes, even singles' clubs—and I guess I was getting known. One day, a friend of mine who taught at the University of Virginia suggested that I could teach a continuing education class in ESP and that people would be interested.

I did, and they were. By now, of course, I had completely abandoned my gypsy look. I dressed in plum-colored skirts and matching jackets, my dark straight hair cut to my shoulders. No crystal balls, no smoke and mirrors: just Noreen. And the audiences seemed to like me. I would always tell them a bit about myself, the public relations work I used to do, my two kids, and my basically skeptical nature. Almost always, I knew that people wanted me to "prove" I was psychic. I didn't mind the proving part—no problem, just listen to me!—but I didn't want people to become dependent on me, to come back every week and ask me what they should do with their lives. I told jokes to put them at ease. I told them the story of how I became psychic, the story of my involvement in psychic activity, of encountering spirits and poltergeists. I told them about the power of the mind and how they could use it too. I held their rings and watches and keys, and told them about their scars and their dreams and their lives.

I have to admit, I loved what I was doing. In fact, I couldn't imagine doing anything else. But it was during one of these talks that my first serious police case came into my life and I changed course once again.

All through the hot summer and into the fall of 1979, a rapist had been terrorizing the citizens of Staunton, a quiet town in Virginia's beautiful Shenandoah Valley near where I lived. In this small town, where nothing much ever happened, a man with a stocking mask pulled over his face had already raped five women and attempted to assault several others over a period of eight months. The police, under pressure to find the man, kept hitting dead ends. The story was a big one, and the end of the rapes didn't even seem close. By this time, the women and girls who lived in Staunton were terrified. It wasn't a matter of locking their doors and staying inside: The man came right into their homes to attack them.

In early December, I was lecturing on ESP in a nearby town that snuggled into the Blue Ridge Mountains. I always showed people a little of what I could do and tried to encourage them to use the untapped ability in their own minds. Some people were eager to learn more, some were skeptical, some even fell asleep. Although I didn't know it at the time, a reporter was in the audience, tape-recording my words. On this evening I had just finished my psychic demonstrations with the audience when a dark-haired young woman in her twenties abruptly stood up. Her voice trembled as she blurted out, "Can you use your psychic ability to help my sister?" This young woman was clearly troubled.

I could feel the tension in the room rise as she explained that her sister had been brutally attacked by the stocking-masked rapist. The police had no clues or suspects in her case, and she and her family were desperate. "Would you please help?" she pleaded.

I responded "Yes" without thinking twice. Of course I would try to help. Then she gave me a ring to hold and asked me if I could tell her about her sister. I was able to say enough about her sister that she was convinced. She tape-recorded my response and so did the reporter, who was sitting in the back of the room.

The next day, the young woman took her tape to the Staunton Police Department and begged them to work with me on her sister's case. I guess they really were at the end of their resources because they contacted me immediately and invited me to meet them at the victim's apartment. In those days, the police were not trained in profiling and parapsychology, and working with a psychic was a new thing for them—this was a case of "We'll try anything once." I have to say it was new to me too, and I was also curious to see if my psychic ability could help them with their case.

On a cold winter's day, I drove up to the address they had given me and met two plainclothes detectives outside a small apartment. They greeted me cordially and introduced themselves. Detective Lacy King was the lead detective,[1] and Detective

Whisman was his partner. As I would find with police through the years, they didn't give me any information about the crime ahead of time. They wanted to test me, to see if I could really reveal the truth of what happened. I couldn't blame them for having their doubts. Why should they believe something they'd never witnessed themselves?

As I climbed the stairs to the apartment with the two men, a fleeting image entered my mind. Abruptly, I turned to Detective King and said, "He was waiting for her inside the apartment, wasn't he?" The men exchanged a glance, but said nothing.

A young woman opened the door and politely invited us into her one-bedroom apartment. As we introduced ourselves, I felt a heaviness fall over me. It was like a pressure, leading me, and I walked away from the group. I was in the room with the two detectives and the woman, but my mind was being filled with other, more disturbing images. The pressure was drawing me toward the kitchen, and I went where I was led. On my left, I saw a small storage room with a door that opened on the outside stairs. I looked in and just "saw" the rapist standing in a dark corner of that small room. The unexpected vision was shocking, and I screamed, "He was waiting for you there!" I must have looked wild, pointing my finger repeatedly to the spot where I saw him.

The young woman nodded and the detectives quickly exchanged startled glances. They later told me that only the victim and a few police officers knew that fact. King and Whisman immediately became more attentive and offered me a seat.

Gratefully, I settled myself in a large, comfortable chair. I took a few deep breaths to try to relax, while the others sat nearby, waiting to see what would happen next. I had told the police about my psychometry work, and the woman who had been raped handed me a ring that she was wearing when she was attacked. Holding the ring in my hand, I closed my eyes and silently directed my mind to see through the eyes of the rapist. I knew from experience that in a few moments images would begin to form in my mind.

People think it's strange—*I* think it's strange—but when I investigate crimes, I just seem to somehow "become" the perpetrator or the victim—sometimes both. I see through their eyes, and I feel what they feel. Sometimes the words pour out in a rush, some-times I manage to stammer out a few fragments. This time, the rapist started speaking, telling us where he lived. "I live in a brick building . . . it's old . . . across the street is a theater . . . I've been in jail."

Then I came back to myself, and my mind searched the rapist's body for imperfections. "I see a scar on his right leg, near the knee . . . the sprained ankle." Maybe it wasn't grammatically correct, but it was information. And as the information flowed, the two men wrote furiously in their notebooks.

I was getting all kinds of images and impressions, not only of these mundane details about the rapist, but of what had happened that horrific night—from the point of view of the rapist. As I struggled to see, the chaotic emotions of the rape victim kept intruding. Her fear was overwhelmingly strong, and I was feeling embarrassed. I didn't feel I had any right to see these horrible, pri-vate moments.

I opened my eyes, and saw the young woman was sitting on the edge of her chair, staring at me with fear-filled eyes. I could see that this experience was hard on her. Thinking I could save us both some embarrassment, I asked her if she would mind waiting in the next room for a short time. She shot straight up out of her chair and left the room, clearly grateful for the chance to escape.

That was my cue to reenter the mind of the rapist. I closed my eyes and we worked a little longer, and a little more information came through. Then the detectives got up from the sturdy sofa on which they were sitting and conferred in a corner of the living room. I assumed we were through, so I was surprised when they asked me if I had time to visit another rape victim that day. I read-ily agreed. I really felt like I might be able to help these women, and I didn't want to stop. So they called the second rape victim on the phone and explained that we were going to stop by her apart-ment.

We drove a few short blocks to a small modern building that had recently been painted. We knocked on the door of an apart-ment on the first floor and were greeted by a young dark-haired girl in tight-fitting jeans and a freshly pressed shirt. She was petite with friendly eyes and welcomed us in. She too gave me a ring she had been wearing during the rape. I sat on her bed and focused on the rapist. I guess I was primed because the words and images came quickly, floating effortlessly into my mind. I was only dimly aware of the three faces that watched me as I worked.

I told the young woman that the rapist had been very apologetic, and when I spoke about the attack, I began to stutter. Wide-eyed, she backed away from me and whispered something to the detective sitting next to her. I know it sounds like a strange thing to say about a rapist, but this man seemed really torn. He felt bad about what he did and wanted to apologize. Unfortunately, he was too out of control to stop.

I just kept going. I was inside the rapist now and describing what I was seeing. "The rapist is driving a truck with something on it that goes round and round . . . he is mechanically inclined. He can fix machines. I feel heavy material on my body. The shirt and pants match . . . he has a uniform on. He delivers something in his truck." I also said that I thought the man had been in prison, and that the detectives would find a lot of evidence in his home that would make his guilt clear. I told them he was very polite, and that he always apologized to his victims. And oddly, I kept seeing the rapist's mother standing in a kitchen.

Suddenly, I felt exhausted, drained. When I opened my eyes, the light was fading outside the windows, and the small room felt very cold. It was time to stop. It had been a very long day.

As they walked me to my car, both detectives shook my hand and thanked me warmly. Whisman laughingly asked, "When will we get our man?"

"Before Christmas," I said without any hesitation. I drove home, dragged myself into the house, and slept like the dead.

━━━━━◆━◆━━━━━

On a bright winter morning in early February, Detectives King and Whisman met with me in a family restaurant near my house for coffee. Belatedly, they laughingly thanked me for their Christmas present—the arrest of the Staunton rapist on December 22.

Of course, I knew all about it by this time, and so did everyone else in town. The newspaper reporter who had been at my lecture also attended my class, and the woman's sister told the class and the reporter what had been happening. This reporter and others wrote feature stories for the local papers about my involvement in the case before the arrest. "Ruckersville Psychic on Trail of Rapist,"[2] read Charlottesville's *Daily Progress.* And the *Richmond Times-Dispatch* proclaimed, "Psychic's Sensitivity Is Pitted against Rapist."[3] Some reporters misreported the information I had given the police. They wanted a quote from me, but I certainly wasn't going to comment publicly on the case—the police had enough on their plate without me getting in the way. As I told one reporter, "The rapist is not that stupid. He can read the papers too."[4]

So now I was the "Ruckersville Psychic," and the name stuck for a while. In the end, when the police arrested the rapist, even the *National Enquirer* picked up the story, framing it much more spectacularly than any of our local reporters: "Psychic's Clues Help Police Catch a Brutal, Knife-Wielding Rapist."[5]

It turned out that I'd gotten most of the details right—or, as one paper put it, "Psychic's Details Mostly Accurate." In fact, the article reported that "Lt. Jack Benton said . . . that, with one exception, the information given police by University of Virginia ESP teacher Noreen Renier was both accurate and unknown to authorities when she described the rapist after visiting two houses in Staunton where the rapes had occurred."[6]

I was pleased, but I wasn't surprised. I knew what I'd seen. The rapist turned out to be an ex-convict, James Bruce Robinson, who had a distinguishing scar on his leg. He lived in a brick building in downtown Staunton, across the street from the Dixie Theater, and his house was filled with things he had stolen over the years. The truck he was driving turned out to be a cement mixer—definitely something that goes "round and round"!—and he used it to deliver cement to construction sites. His parents used to own a restaurant, and I guess that's why I kept seeing his mother in the kitchen. In fact, the only thing they could catch me out on was my insistence that he had something wrong with his teeth. In the end, Robinson was convicted of five rapes and sixteen felonies and went to prison to serve twenty-one consecutive twenty-year sentences.[7]

I didn't catch this rapist; the police did that. And I want to make it clear that they didn't use my information to go out and track this man down. They got him because they were routinely staking out and arresting peeping toms and questioning them about the rapes. Once he was arrested, Robinson confessed to being the stocking-masked rapist. Then, as Lt. Benton said, "We looked back and saw [the clues] were true."[8]

It took me some time to come to grips with this experience because it was so different from what I was used to. First, I was usually sitting sedately at home, receiving people and doing private readings. Some of the readings were unusual, but mostly people had questions about love and health and work. Now I had traveled to crime scenes, met crime victims, and actually experienced the mind of a rapist.

It was a disturbing and exhausting experience—and the first of many to come. Fortunately, working on cases like this does not give me bad dreams. As my mentors explained to me, when I'm being psychic—in a trance or doing psychometry—I use a different part of my brain than the part I use in daily life. When I'm in a deep trance, I have no real consciousness of what I'm saying while I'm saying it—which is why I always insist on tape-recording these readings—and afterward I have very little memory of what happened. One time, however, trying to be helpful, the police showed me a crime scene photo of a dead woman, half-naked with one eye staring directly at me. That horrible image burned itself into my conscious mind and I had nightmares about it for days.

This experience encouraged me to follow a path I had never imagined. If these two cops had been mean and derisive, I never would have done work like this again. But they were encouraging and gentlemanly, kind and courteous, and treated me with respect.

Although I never worked with Detectives King and Whisman again, I ended up helping law enforcement agencies around the world, lecturing at the FBI Academy, appearing on national television shows, and getting a lot of attention—some good, some I could have done without. In becoming a "psychic detective," I had entered into uncharted waters, and I had no idea where my explorations would take me next.

CHAPTER 7

Murder, She Saw:
Again and Again

I wasn't Sally anymore. I could no longer feel her pain. Now I was watching Sally and it was terrifying; I could see a man lean over and cut Sally's throat. There was blood everywhere, a shocking, repulsive amount of blood. Then I saw her killer bend towards her lifeless body. My eyes snapped open. I was gasping. That was it; I had had enough. I could not go on with this scene another moment.

The pretty dress I held in my hands was covered with dried blood. The stench of the blood mingled with the scent of eleven different colognes from the eleven police detectives huddled around me in the small interrogation room. I was a nervous wreck with all these stoic gun-wearing people watching me. I looked around the room for support—it was filled by a large oblong table and nothing else. The faded yellow walls were bare except for a large round clock. It was 10:00 a.m. *I am going to be sick*, I thought to myself. *What in the world am I doing here?*

I was there because I'd gotten a call I couldn't refuse from Chief Pat Minetti of the Hampton Police Department. He had read one of the articles about my work, and the detective in charge of the homicide squad had recently attended a lecture at the FBI Academy in nearby Quantico on the use of psychics in solving crimes. They were desperate and pretty much ready to try anything—and that meant me.

My work on the Staunton rapist case a few months back had gotten me a great deal of attention from other police departments. Since then, I had worked on other police cases and had even been flown across the United States to work on cases in Texas and Arizona. Over the last twenty-five years, of course, I've been called in to help police with hundreds of cases—more than I have room to write about in this book. But on that morning, sitting at the table in the Hampton, Virginia, interrogation room holding a bloody dress in my hands, I was about to become involved in my very first murder case. And I was also about to throw up.

I was determined not to throw up with everyone observing me, and I was desperate to relax, so I asked for a glass of wine. Relaxation enhances my psychic abilities, but deep meditation in this environment was out of the question. They wanted me to start work immediately. The young detective sitting closest to me said, "We don't have any wine at the station, but I think I can get you some Scotch."

"Great," I said, forcing a smile. "With water."

He returned with a white paper cup. As I put it to my lips, I could tell he hadn't heard my request for water—the undiluted Scotch was overpowering. *What the heck,* I thought, and took a large sip, which almost choked me. Regardless of how I got there, I did feel more relaxed, and I got to work.

I picked up the bloody dress again and closed my eyes, trying to shut out the presence of all those people in the room. They had told me the victim's name was Sally. I knew nothing else about the case, except that she had been killed two days earlier. Soon, images began to appear. Unfocused at first, they gradually cleared and I saw a young woman, not overly pretty but attractive, with clear blue eyes and light brown hair that curled. Tall and slender, she looked to be in her middle thirties.

The image expanded, and I could see where the murder had occurred. "It's a trailer," I said. In my mind, I walked into the trailer's small kitchen and began picking up even stronger signals. Suddenly, I was Sally, and I felt a knife tearing repeatedly through the flesh of my back. It hurt! I moaned softly, then more urgently, as I felt the stabbing pains over and over again.

Then I wasn't Sally anymore. I could no longer feel her pain. Now I was outside Sally, watching, and it was terrifying: I saw a man lean over Sally and cut her throat, blood gushing out. There was blood everywhere, a shocking, repulsive amount of blood. As I watched her killer bend toward her lifeless body, my eyes snapped open. I was gasping. That was it; I had had enough. I could not go on with this scene another moment. My heart was beating wildly. Now I really did need that Scotch.

But the detectives did not want me to stop, and they implored me to keep on going. What was wrong with these people? Couldn't they see I was in pain? "She is dead and he is raping her!" I screamed. "Why do you want me to experience that?" I later found out that a hundred stab wounds had been inflicted on Sally's body. The police had gone over the room with everything they could think of, including laser beams, but they'd come up with nothing. So they really did need any help I could give them. But I didn't know that at the time.

They tried to explain that they needed to know more. I tried to explain that I definitely could not go on; in fact, I would not! Then I had an idea. "Please," I pleaded, "let's go to the scene of the crime and I'll describe the murderer for your artist."

Thankfully, they agreed, and we headed out toward the police cars. Before we filed out, I glanced at the clock. It was 10:55. I was stunned. Only fifty-five minutes had passed—to me, it felt like five hours. Exhausted and shaken, I took another sip of the undiluted scotch and lit a cigarette. I'd been warned by the people at the Psychic Research Foundation that drinking and smoking generally impeded psychic abilities, but that didn't seem to be the case with me. Anyway, at that moment I really didn't care. I knew more horrors awaited me.

The City of Hampton, founded in 1610, is America's first continuously occupied English-speaking settlement. It sits on the Chesapeake Bay, right between two popular tourist destinations, Williamsburg and Virginia Beach. But on this day we weren't going to visit historical sites or play on the beach. We were traveling down the highway to the scene of a violent murder.

I was right—it was a trailer. When we arrived there, the signs of brutality overwhelmed me. It looked like a battleground. There was blood everywhere, along with the black powder that crime scene investigators use to dust for fingerprints. The scene was dark and eerie, and I will never forget it.

I forced myself to look down at the chalk outline that marked the spot where Sally had last lain. The violent vibrations were overpowering. I was grateful to be able to sit down with the police artist on a cream-colored couch—coated, like everything else, with black dust and dried blood. I closed my eyes and concentrated, and details of a face began to materialize. First an eye, then an eyebrow, then a mouth appeared. As I described the features, the artist began to draw a face on his clean white pad.

When I finished, I opened my eyes and looked at the artist's sketch of the face. There he was, just as I had seen him: a slender, boyish-looking man in his early thirties. He had a high forehead with deep creases, neatly trimmed light brown hair, a long slender nose, thin lips, and an oval chin. I wondered who he was.

The artist held his sketch up for the detectives to see, and I watched the expressions on their faces. I saw recognition—they knew who this individual was. Then, rather abruptly, we all got up, piled in the police car, and rode in stony silence back to the station.

Back at the station, my energies depleted, I told them that I had to leave. They thanked me, paid me (not a great deal), and I drove home, weary but deeply grateful to get away from the emotional experience.

But I couldn't seem to get away from Sally's murder. Maybe because I had actually visited the crime scene, replays of the violence bombarded me day and night. I was exhausted; all I did was sleep. I had recently acquired a cat, and she curled up next to me for comfort.

Days later, when the memories were finally fading, I got a call from one of the detectives. He told me what I already suspected: The face the artist had drawn was someone they knew—the victim's neighbor, who lived two trailers away. He had found the body with another neighbor, an older woman. Unfortunately, the detective said, the drawing wasn't enough. Could I come back and answer more questions about the suspect?

My mind reeled. I truly did not want to go back into that nightmarish experience. "I don't see how I can be of any further help," I protested. "I've told you all I can."

But the detective wouldn't take no for an answer. "Noreen," he explained patiently, "we can't make an arrest until we find the murder weapon or his bloody clothes," he explained. "We know he did it, but without evidence, we can't arrest him."

Again, if he had been rude or bullying, I would have stuck to my guns and stayed home. But he was asking so politely, and he sounded so desperate, that I reluctantly agreed. "Just for a few hours," I emphasized.

"That's fine," he replied, and then he hesitated. "The captain doesn't have any more money in the budget," he finally blurted out. "Could you donate these hours?" he asked sheepishly.

"Sure," I said. Why not? It was the least this woman deserved.

Later that afternoon, at the police station, I was again overwhelmed by the number of police waiting for me. I sensed a different mood in the station—a negative tone leaning to downright hostility—and I felt it leveled directly at me. I couldn't figure out why: Was it because I was an outsider, or a woman? Did they object to a psychic intruding into their investigation?

I could understand why they might feel that way. First of all, a psychic's findings are not admissible as evidence in a court of law. I just give them clues to follow and directions to go, insights into the criminal's character that they may not have had before. I don't go out and solve the crime for them: that's their job. Second, a psychic is not a police officer—a psychic is an outsider. And a weird outsider, at that. I know that when police detectives first meet me, they are almost always surprised to find that I don't have a crystal ball, and I don't miraculously pull the name of the criminal out of thin air. Not only that, they think I'm down to earth, someone they might meet and even like in the course of their off-work lives. Sometimes, I suspect, they're disappointed.

The detective who had asked me to return filled me in on the problems with the case. The suspect had failed a lie detector test, but they did not have enough evidence to arrest him. He had agreed to be interrogated (or "interviewed," as the police called it), but he knew it was within his rights to leave the interview when the questioning got dangerously close to things he didn't want to talk about. And that's exactly what he would do. As soon as the interview got hot, he'd take off. He wasn't officially under arrest, so they couldn't stop him. To make an arrest, they needed something that would tie him to the crime, like his bloody clothes or the knife.

They knew I needed something to hold, so they gave me the wires that had been attached to him during the lie detector test. I sat in the wooden chair they used for polygraph tests, held on to the wires, and concentrated. Soon, images began flooding into my mind. "I see a small dog, the dog is barking a lot . . . it's the knife! The knife is in his trailer."

I began to describe the weapon I saw. It was a fancy hunting knife. The point of the long blade was slightly curved and the handle was carved. Then, as seems to happen, my mind went somewhere else: under the bed, where I saw a long box-like object that pulled out like a drawer. I felt this box contained his bloody clothes. The detectives gathered around me, along with two new members of their ever-expanding team: a consulting psychologist and a vice cop. This was getting to be quite a crowd.

They questioned me for a long time. I was beginning to feel like my mind was a new toy that everyone wanted to play with but no one knew how to use.

Suddenly, one of the detectives had an idea. The suspect was due to come in for another "interview" in about fifteen minutes. Maybe I could psychically read him to obtain more details that would help them solve their case. They suggested that I go out and pose as a new receptionist.

"Hmmm," I said with some trepidation, "That's an interesting idea." I wasn't sure I could do it, but—being game for just about anything—I agreed to try.

I sat nervously at the front desk. One of the detectives taped a recording device under it so they would be able to hear what we said. Then he went into the back room to wait and listen with the rest of the group. I was alone, waiting for a murderer.

Minutes later, he came in. I looked up from my pretend typing and smiled at a slim, boyish-looking young man—who was wearing the crisp blue uniform of a police officer. He gave me his name and asked for one of the detectives. This was the suspect? A police officer? I couldn't believe it! I was shocked. Even though I had seen it happen in my own mind, and felt it in my own body, the reality was completely jarring. How could anyone who looked so harmless commit such a vicious crime?

In my best receptionist manner, I told him Detective Smith was busy but would see him in a few minutes. But my nerves got the best of me, and I started babbling. "Hi," I said, "I'm the new receptionist, Noreen." I couldn't believe I'd given him my real name. I really fretted about it later, but then I just kept chattering away. "Do you want a cup of coffee?" I asked brightly, like I thought a good receptionist would. As soon as the words were out of my mouth I realized I had no idea where the coffee pot was! I hoped that he would refuse, and he did.

To occupy myself during those tense moments, I kept pretending I was typing a letter. When I started to run out of paper, I opened a dictionary to pretend to look up a word. The only word

I could think of was "murder." He sat and watched me, which started to unnerve me more.

So, of course, I began to talk. "Everyone's so excited that you're coming," I gushed. That got his adrenaline going, so I added, "I bet you're going to help them solve Sally's murder."

He looked closely at me, and his answer was not what I expected. "Hey," he said suddenly, "I think I will have that coffee. One cream, one sugar."

I stood up and smiled at him while I willed my legs to move. I opened the door leading to the offices in the back and wandered into the first hallway. I had only walked a few steps when a hand reached out and yanked me into the room where all the detectives were sitting, listening to me babble. They didn't look too happy.

"Can you do it?" the chief detective asked gruffly. "Are you getting anything?" they all asked at once.

"No," I said, sadly shaking my head. "I'm too nervous. It's not working." A hulking detective thrust a Styrofoam cup of coffee with one sugar, one cream into my hand.

"Go back and stall," said one of them. "We'll buzz you and tell you Detective Smith is ready to see him."

As I walked back into the reception area, the suspect's blue eyes examined me, making me even more uncomfortable. I handed him his coffee and tried not to look at him too closely or to give anything away. I was tense. I could hardly take my eyes off the gun at his waist. Finally, the buzzer sounded and I told him Detective Smith was ready to see him. As soon as he was gone, I left the reception area and joined the group to listen to the interview—a hidden microphone in the interrogation room relayed the sound to a speaker. The detectives were battering away at him, trying to get his permission to search his trailer. I guess they didn't have enough evidence to get a search warrant. Finally, and reluctantly, he agreed. As if on cue everyone in our cramped room got to their feet. The chief detective pointed his finger this way and that like a gun, assigning the detectives and other personnel to various cars.

"You," he said, aiming his finger at me, "come with me."

We got into an unmarked car and headed toward the trailer park. With lights flashing and siren screaming, we got there faster than I thought physically possible.

Once there, the police cars emptied quickly, but we were stopped in our tracks by a small, elderly white-haired woman, a neighbor who had positioned herself in front of his trailer door and refused to let us in.

I thought the chief detective would explain to her we had a warrant, or permission to search the trailer, but he didn't. Instead he turned to another officer and said, "Arrest that woman, she's obstructing justice!" Horrified, I couldn't imagine this poor old lady was really being hauled off to jail.

But before I could spend any more time thinking about it, I was immediately distracted by the sound of barking—it was the dog I'd seen. I was impressed by this plucky little dog's attempt to guard his master's space, but the detectives weren't. I'd never been involved with a homicide case, and I was dazed and amazed by police procedure.

Seconds later, however, the suspect arrived and took the dog to the back bedroom. When he emerged, he'd changed out of his police uniform and into a freshly ironed shirt and faded jeans. He looked incongruously like a preppy college boy, so young and innocent. He noticed my gaze and returned it with a smile. I felt embarrassed being part of this scene.

I looked around his trailer. It was immaculate, perfectly organized. But the detectives destroyed that pretty quickly as they began to tear the place apart. They couldn't find the knife, so they asked him about it, describing it as I'd described it to them. He produced it immediately.

Next they asked about the box that pulled out from under his bed. He explained, without any hesitation, that it was outside and led us to it. It was under the trailer—a long box-like object that he pulled out. Although it was under the trailer, it was directly below the bed, as I had described. But it was clean—too clean. Where there should have been dirt, there was none. Like his trailer, it was spotless.

The police didn't bother with goodbyes. We all piled back into the cars and screamed back to the station, where they gave the knife to the forensics lab. Earlier, one of the police officers had taken the white-haired neighbor to the police station. They tried their best to get information from the old woman, but the interview proved frustrating—she really didn't know a thing about the murder—and the mood was getting very pessimistic. We had no clues, no bloody clothes. Even the knife proved worthless as evidence. It had been meticulously cleaned and soaked in bleach, something a cop would think to do.

The detectives were stymied. They wanted another crack at the suspect, but they had no real reason to ask him back to the station. I suggested they call him and ask him to come pick up his neighbor. They agreed, but they wanted something more.

"Noreen, we want you to let him know that you're psychic," the chief detective said. "Tell him what you saw when you held Sally's dress. If he believes you, maybe we can scare him. It's our last chance. You'll be waiting for him in the lobby and Detective Smith will be sitting near you. We'll wire the area, and we'll hear everything that's exchanged between you. Don't worry, armed officers will be watching you constantly."

I agreed, and forced myself to relax while I was waiting. I sat there and breathed deeply and slowly. As I mellowed, I could feel my psychic powers increasing. This time, it was easy to pick up what was going through the suspect's mind when he came into the station. He was asking himself, "Her again? What the hell is she doing here at this hour of night? Who the hell is she anyway?"

When he sat down, I told him the truth. "I'm not a secretary, I'm a psychic." He looked at me suspiciously, so I kept going. Talking quickly, I began laying it all out. I told him the details of the murder, but I didn't feel the right reaction; he didn't believe I had received these facts psychically. I could read his thoughts, but he thought I'd read the police reports.

This was pretty ironic—making a murder suspect believe that I was psychic so that he would confess! But I had to prove my psychic abilities to him, so I began a psychic reading. I told him facts about his life, things no one could possibly have known. As I did, his skepticism began to crack.

Before I could finish, the detectives came back. They told him that they wanted him in the interrogation room, and he agreed. As we walked along the long corridor together, shoulders almost touching, he asked what I'd thought of him when we first met. "I thought you were good-looking," I replied, "but I knew you killed Sally." He shrugged with a small smile, and nodded.

Unfortunately, this was as close as he ever got to a confession. The police were sure he had killed Sally, but were unable to produce any evidence. He was a professional—he knew that without evidence, there would be no case. Our suspect is a free man today.

So that was my first murder case. Never before had I experienced, psychically, another person's death. It was tough, exhausting, horrifying. I didn't know if the police would ever call me in on such a case again, and I didn't know if I wanted to go back to such a dark place again. But, as it turned out, I did: again and again and again.

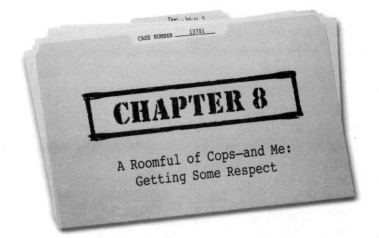

CHAPTER 8

A Roomful of Cops—and Me: Getting Some Respect

The small auditorium was set up for lectures, with tiered seating that looked down on a small stage. I sat nervously, way up in the back, several seats into the row, feeling rather alone amid the audience of about two hundred police officers—almost all men. I listened intently to the first lecturer, a parapsychologist, as he stood behind the wooden lectern and expounded on the paranormal to the stoic audience. The skepticism was so thick you could see it.

"Noreen, this is the Peninsula Tidewater Academy of Criminal Justice in Hampton, Virginia. We heard about your work with the Staunton rape case, and we'd like you to come lecture."

He explained that they were planning a program to introduce police to the use of psychics as an investigative tool—far from a recognized practice in any law enforcement agency. The fact is, when the police call me in on a case, it's often because they are pressed to the wall and have nowhere else to turn. Even though the police are asking for my help, I know they have their doubts. Still,

I had a little success under my belt now, so anything I could do to ease their apprehensions was all for the good. I was flattered and scared, all at the same time. "Count me in," I said.

They explained that the academy program would give all sides of the issue. The panel would consist of a parapsychologist for the scientific angle, me (the practicing psychic), and a behavioral scientist from the FBI Academy in Quantico, Virginia. I had no idea how they would react to me, but I was prepared to lecture on how I worked with the police—that's what I did in my classes at UVA. But a roomful of cops? I got up my nerve and went.

The small auditorium was set up for lectures, with tiered seating that looked down on a small stage. I sat nervously, way up in the back, several seats into the row, feeling rather alone amid the audience of about two hundred police officers—almost all men. I listened intently to the first lecturer, the parapsychologist, as he stood behind the wooden lectern and expounded on the paranormal to the stoic audience. The skepticism was so thick you could see it.

Their attitude didn't surprise me. Cops are not predisposed to believe in psychics, or to believe that psychics can help them do their job. But with the case of the Staunton rapist, apparently, I had changed a few minds. Staunton Police Lieutenant Jack Benton told the news media, "The information the psychics gave us proved to be the break we had been looking for." In Staunton, it seems, they had consulted not one but two of us! Apparently, based on the information I had given them, an anonymous male psychic came forward to offer his assistance—and they took him up on it. We were making progress. "The clues they gave us definitely helped us to get to the rapist. It was really amazing what one psychic (Renier) could come up with. It's weird, almost unbelievable, how accurate her 'feelings' were."[1]

Police are predisposed not to trust. I usually say, "Look, just try to believe for a couple of hours. You can be as skeptical as you want later, when you put the pieces together, but believe for right now." Sometimes, after they hear what I come up with, they think that someone must have told me about the case, or that I must have somehow gotten my hands on the files. That's why I prefer not to know any of the details of the crime, or anything about the victim. I just want to know the first name of the victim and the type of case we're working on, and I take it from there.

This was the kind of thing I wanted to talk about. I sat there tapping my foot and wishing for a cigarette to calm my nerves as I went over my lecture in my mind. Earlier, I had asked the parapsychologist to pass out envelopes to police officers at random, ask them to place a metal object like a ring or a watch inside, seal it, and write their initials on the outside. I planned to do a psychometry demonstration during my lecture, and I didn't want the police to think I had tampered with the envelopes in any way.

As I sat there trying to concentrate, a tall, good-looking man came in and sat down at the end of the aisle. He had tremendous presence. Who was this guy? I could feel his intense energy from two seats away.

The polite applause from the audience broke into my thoughts, and I joined in. The lecture was over and I was on next. Thank God we had a fifteen-minute break. I really needed to get my thoughts together. When I turned to get up and walk outside, the tall man had already disappeared. He must have gone out the other end of the aisle. Meanwhile, my nose followed the scent of smoke outside. Alone in a sea of smoking police officers, I tried to calm down and think about my lecture.

After the break, I walked onto the stage. This was not the kind of audience I was used to. My students were usually ready to open their minds and learn something new. Looking out at these stony faces, I was struck by how quiet they were. Polite, staring, unmoving. Still, even with this tough group, my nerves were steady. It's funny—I think of myself as something of a loner. Traveling exhausts me and being with people takes a lot of energy. But I must have been an actress in my last life, because I'm good at telling stories and I know what to do when I'm on a stage to hold an audience.

I began with a little drama, telling them about my electrifying experience in my kitchen, and how I dressed as a gypsy to work in the hotel lounge. That story got a small laugh out of them, at least. I told them about my work at the PRF with Dr. Jones and explained what little I knew about psychic phenomena—"The last speaker knows a lot more than I do," I said, and got another laugh.

I have always believed that all talk and no show is a bit of a bore, so next I offered to demonstrate my psychic abilities. The parapsychologist had given me the envelopes he had gathered earlier. After I briefly explained how psychometry worked, I announced, "By touching an envelope—and without opening it—I'll describe the individual to whom it belongs." No oohs or aahs from this group.

Bravely, I picked up the first envelope, read out the initials, R. T. I stroked the envelope with my fingers, and placed the envelope to my forehead. An image of a man with reddish brown hair and large blue eyes behind thick glasses floated into my mind's eye. I felt a small, wiry body with an old scar on his upper arm. The images and feelings were very vivid, and I felt quite confident. I opened my eyes and asked the person with the initials R. T. to stand up.

A huge man stood up, rubbing his bald head with both hands. In a loud voice, he announced, "I don't need glasses, I don't have a scar on either shoulder, and I don't have *any* hair!"

I wanted to burst into tears. I couldn't feel any sympathy in the room. Two hundred police officers had watched me bungle this. I figured I'd never get any work from these guys again, let alone any respect. I wanted to run off the stage. Instead, I smiled and said, "Well, I guess that didn't work. Let's try it again." As I reached for another envelope, looking far more calm than I felt, I prayed, *God, please let it work this time!*

Holding the second envelope, I began, "This is S. P. You have thick brown hair. Your eyes are brown too, and you have a scar high on your right cheek. You have a long, thin face, and there's something about your stomach." Automatically, my hands rubbed my own belly. "You had an injury there recently." This felt right. I started to breathe a little easier. The details were pouring in. "When you're at target practice, you tend to shoot a little to the lower left. I feel you're happy about a recent raise. You have two daughters." I looked up. "Okay, S. P., where are you?" As a thin-faced, brown-haired man rose, my smile grew wider. I thanked

God silently. "How'd I do?" I asked. He nodded his confirmation of my impressions, clearly bewildered and grudgingly impressed. The audience actually applauded their approval.

Now my cocky attitude returned full force. I leaned forward, lowered my husky voice even lower, and said, "You guys must remember this is not a full reading. Think of it as a quickie—nice, but not totally satisfying." They groaned. I had them.

I finished up by successfully psychometrizing a few more envelopes, thanked them for their attention, and walked off to some applause. Thank God that was over.

Out in the courtyard again, I joined the other smokers for another break before the final speaker. This time, they smiled at me. I was deep in conversation with the parapsychologist, thanking him for his help, when the good-looking man from my aisle walked up with the bald giant in tow. He smiled and introduced himself as FBI Special Agent Robert Ressler. "This is Detective Toller,"[2] he said, turning to the bald man. "He has something to tell you."

Detective Toller grinned at me sheepishly and began, "It was just a joke. We didn't mean any harm. I put my initials on the envelope that my friend Mike put his watch in. You nailed Mike." He stared at me as I stared at him. "It was just a joke," he repeated, and stuck out his hand to shake mine. "No hard feelings, I hope."

"No hard feelings," I agreed, but inside I was still fuming. *Not funny,* I thought to myself. Still, I was grateful to Agent Ressler for making Toller confess.

We all trooped back into the auditorium for the final speaker. Again, I sat in the back and looked down at the stage. As the speaker was introduced and walked onstage, I was taken by surprise to see that the behavioral scientist from the FBI was my new best friend, Agent Ressler.

I was even more surprised when the first words out of his mouth were about me. "It took a lot of guts for Noreen Renier to stand up in front of all of you skeptical cops," he began. Then he asked Detective Toller to confess to the whole group.

Toller rose, grabbing his friend Mike and bringing him up with him. There stood Mike in all his glory—wiry body, thick glasses, blue eyes, and reddish-blond hair. "She was right," Toller admitted. "He even has the scar she mentioned on his shoulder." He explained how he had put his buddy's watch in the envelope and signed his initials—"as a joke." There were some catcalls for Toller and some applause for me. I even saw a few smiles.

Then, in the biggest surprise of all, Agent Ressler invited me—in front of all these skeptical cops—to lecture to his criminology students at the FBI Academy at Quantico. I was stunned—and I leaped at the chance. But I'd have a few more cases under my belt before I finally got there.

As it turned out, this wasn't the last time I would lecture to a roomful of cops. After my rocky but ultimately triumphant beginnings, I went on to develop a police workshop designed to train members of the force in the most effective techniques for working with psychics and to help them understand why (and when) working with a psychic can aid an investigation. But I have to admit, I had an ulterior motive: I wanted to help them understand that they had intuition too. Call it a hunch, call it a gut feeling—it's all the same to me. I knew that if I could help them work with these feelings instead of discount them, they would become more effective police officers. And maybe I would get a little more respect!

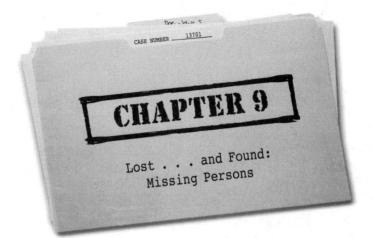

"I feel a lot of brush. . . . I would be stuck in branches. I don't think I drowned immediately . . . I went quite a ways. . . . There's rocks!" I felt panicky, unable to stop. *"I'm getting hit. I'm getting hurt . . ."* Then I was floating, the river was wider.

"I'm more quiet. I can see that damn gas station . . . I can see it up there!" Someone should be able to save me. I could see them, why couldn't they see me? *Up above, I saw steep, wooded bank.*

———————◆———————

In Waynesboro, Virginia, in the early 1980s, Richard Wayne Painter was swept away by a terrible storm—almost four inches of rain had pelted the area for two days, sending the river swirling through town at around thirty miles per hour and causing flooding, whirlpools, and mudflows. When the storm subsided, mud and debris were everywhere, but there was no sign of Mr. Painter. What had happened to him? Where was he?

"I'm under a bridge or an overpass. There's cement. I'm flowing. It's not just straight, there's a curve . . . it's curved. There's a gas station up there. I hurt."

I winced in pain, soaked and chilled, feeling the sharp pain of rock on bone. My body was in my office, warm and dry, one of the lost man's possessions in my hand. But my mind was in Richard Painter's body, being swept along in the raging storm. Images flooded across my vision like scenes in a movie, and words came pouring out of my mouth, almost as fast as the swollen river had overflowed its banks.[1]

I was fearful, in pain, helpless, and unable to stop.

"My body is going downstream," I continued. "I do pass a bridge, and the water starts going wider. I feel suction; I'm on the right. Let me stop!"

Suddenly, I came out of the trance, breathing hard. I was confused for a moment—Painter's fear had become mine. The police investigators who were questioning me comforted me, but I told them I needed a break. Sitting there in my warm office, sipping my wine and inhaling deeply, I could feel my muscles start to relax. Time to go back in.

When I started again, the detectives kept interrupting me, trying to figure out where I was—Virginia is filled with trees and rivers and hills, and I hadn't been to this town before, so I really had no way to help them.

"I feel a lot of brush. . . . I would be stuck in branches. I don't think I drowned immediately . . . I went quite a ways. . . . There's rocks!" I felt panicky, unable to stop. "I'm getting hit. I'm getting hurt . . ." Then I was floating, the river was wider.

"I'm more quiet. I can see that damn gas station . . . I can see it up there!" *Someone should be able to save me. I could see them, why couldn't they see me?* Up above, I saw steep, wooded bank.

"I'm walking on land. My head hurts. You will find an injury to the head. I've been hit very strongly by a rock.

"Oh, this is interesting. . . . I see a tree joined up with another tree. There is a space—the tree grew two ways. . . ."

Then, suddenly, I was flying in the air, looking down on Painter's body from above. "There is a shack or building, possibly under construction, near the point. The roof is black, maybe shingled. It's dark, large."

And that was all the information I could give them. In this case, however, it wasn't enough, because back then I had no way to help them figure out *exactly* where to look. I simply hadn't been in the psychic detective business long enough to work out a reliable system.

In the end, the body was found by accident—at the bottom of a steep, wooded slope on the river—by a man who thought he was just going off for a nice day of fishing. Downstream from the site was a forked tree, much as I had described. Looking across the river, you could see a flat-roofed old building, and Hicks Service Station was visible up at the top of that seventy-five-foot slope, just a little further down but too far to help Richard Wayne Painter survive the storm.

In the cases that come my way, women are usually the ones who are murdered and men are the ones who are missing. For me, it has been relatively simple to access these men's energies psychically and see images of their location; but it has been much more difficult to learn the best way to communicate these clues to help police and searchers find them.

When you're trying to find a missing person, pinpointing the general search area is crucial. But think about it: How can I tell police which direction to go and where to look in a place I have never been? I gave up slogging through rivers and mud holes and dense wooded areas—the kinds of places most of my missing persons seem to be found—years ago. I'm usually sitting in my house, hundreds or thousands of miles away from the crime scene, seeing the scene of their disappearance like disconnected frames of movie film.

These images belong to these men: They are never connected to anything I know about personally. Not only that, they often don't tell a straight story. It's easy for me to follow a tangent and get lost in the information. If I'm not getting good directions from investigators when I'm in a trance, my mind is liable to go anywhere at any time. Disconnected impressions—that's all they are unless they can be fixed to a place and become a real map investigators can follow. That's why I was so excited when I stumbled on the idea of the "clock"— a simple map that gives me a way to fix real directions and points of the compass on vague descriptions of towers and bushes and bridges and pools of deep water.

Here's what I do: Right before I go into trance, I take a pencil and paper and draw a circle. Then I put an X in the middle of the circle—that's the person's body. Around the outside of the clock, I draw a square. I mark 12, 3, 6, and 9 on my circle, as if it were the face of clock. Now I have my focus.

Of course, I have no idea going in which way north, south, east, and west will be (and even if I did, my sense of direction in daily life is so bad I have literally gotten lost in Wal-Mart more than once!). So I identify the relative positions of landmarks I see with the hours marked on my clock. For example, if I'm on the ground, I might say, "There's a horse pasture at six o'clock." If I'm seeing the same general area from a height of twenty feet, I might say, "There's a radio tower at three o'clock," and so on. Sometimes we have two or three circles, all at different heights—from ground level to two hundred feet in the air—because I can see different types of landmarks from these different vantage points. Detectives can then use these landmarks to orient themselves and follow the clues to the missing person.

The way I am questioned also makes a big difference. How would you like to have a conversation with someone who only asks you yes or no questions, never gives you a verbal pat on the back, and is unable to respond spontaneously to an unexpected conversational turn? Right. You'd feel like you were being interrogated by the police, and your mind would clamp shut.

I was lucky that the police on the first few cases I worked on treated me with respect and dignity. In fact, most of the law enforcement people I have worked with have been great. Sometimes, however, the police just go on automatic—especially if they don't want to work with a psychic. Then they automatically suspect me and try to trip me up. Believe me, this does not help me to relax and establish an atmosphere of trust!

Over the years, I've learned what kind of questioning works and what doesn't, and I've written up some suggestions to help investigators who are working with me for the first time. Sometimes, I work with an assistant who handles the questioning. But when the police do it themselves, it's essentially a matter of getting them off a memorized script and into an engaged social conversation. I give them these basic rules:

1. I will touch an object from the missing person. I will need the first name of the missing person and the date she disappeared. For a warm-up, I will describe the individual. Please give me feedback to help confirm my accuracy. *Encourage me to describe everything that comes into my mind. I should not edit anything out of my response, even if I think it is trivial, out of place, or inconsistent.*

2. Ask open-ended questions. Use short sentences and a simple vocabulary.

3. Listen actively, conveying appropriate feedback.

4. Induce detailed descriptions by providing as much structure as you can. (In a normal line of questioning, you might ask a witness to describe the clothes of the "bad guy." But with me it is best to ask separate questions about the shirt, the shoes, the pants, etc.)

5. Stay on a specific topic, then move to another area of questioning. Don't jump back and forth.

6. To some extent, I can become the murderer or the victim, and I can also view things as Noreen. However, the key to using my intuitive ability is in

the way you elicit information. Individual styles may vary, but understanding from what perspective or person's eye I am seeing and obtaining information may help.

7. Use concrete reference points to guide my response. Through your questions, you can induce focused concentration. (For example, "Noreen, you are the victim. Start from your house and guide us to where you are now.")

Here's an example of how it works. Let's say that I am the lost person, and when I look up I see the sky. That's not going to help anyone locate me. So the detective might say, "Okay, Noreen, now float twenty feet above the body, face twelve o'clock, and tell me what you see straight ahead."

"I see a river that splits in two directions."

"That's great, perfect. Now turn left. What do you see at three o'clock?"

"I see a big red house, some large animals of some sort."

"Can you get any closer?"

"No, there's something in the way, a hill."

"That's fine, don't worry about it. Now turn left again. What do you see at six o'clock?"

"The river is disappearing into some trees, no leaves on the branches."

And so on. Usually, the detectives can pinpoint the area. Oh yeah, they'll say, that sounds like where the Brown River splits off near the Andrews farm. Then they take what they know about the landmarks and assign directions to my clock. This gives them a pretty good idea of where to look.

First, of course, they have to call me in on the case.

Most of the time, families tell me that they wish I'd been called in sooner. Since I normally work with the police, however, my input generally comes when all else has failed. During this same period in the early 1980s, I worked on a couple of missing persons cases in Maryland. On both, police had basically given up on finding the person before they called me. When Detective John Fasick of the Prince George's County Police Department in Hyattsville, Maryland, was asked when he thought it was time to call a psychic in, he replied, "If you've done everything you can possibly do, you have nothing to lose by using her help." I'd say they could have saved a lot of time if they'd called a bit earlier. In this case, he asked for my help in finding an eighty-year-old man who had wandered away from a shopping center. His family had looked everywhere and so had the police.

Fasick had a bit of an adversarial attitude at first, which was what I was used to from many of the police I worked with at that time. He gave me a toothbrush, a razor, a hat, and a shoe that had belonged to the man. I didn't want any other information, and he didn't give me any. It's important for me just to be able to tune in on the energy and information I get from the personal items—I don't want what I see or feel to be influenced by things I've already heard about.

I held the objects in one hand, brushing my fingers over them lightly, letting their energy pour into me and guide my mind. I became the confused old man, correctly describing what he had been wearing. I felt he was already dead. When Fasick asked where the man could be found, I saw "a river, a bridge, and a church steeple" visible from the site. Five days later, they found the man dead—exactly where I had described. Or, as Detective Fasick put it, "A lot of information correlated between what she predicted and what happened. . . . I wouldn't hesitate to use her again."[2] I guess he felt a little better about me after that.

Soon after, another Prince George's County detective, Mike McGraw, asked for my help. His wife had actually suggested he call in a psychic to help solve the case of another elderly man who had been missing for two weeks, and when he asked other cops, my name came up. It was a tough case, and the police were running out of ideas. As McGraw said, "We'd tried our best. Searched from the air, searched on the ground. We had horses, a helicopter. We had twenty men at a time in the woods out looking. I got stuck in quicksand, had to get pulled out and throw my shoes away. We were in every nook and cranny. . . . We had tried everything else. Made up a photo flyer, canvassed twenty-five hospitals, no luck. I dropped all my other cases and we worked all day searching and doing follow-ups. We were really frustrated."

And just like Fasick, he added, "I figured, what have we got to lose?"[3]

McGraw came to see me with a highly skeptical polygraph operator in tow—he wasn't taking any chances with me! I began by correctly telling them the day of the week he disappeared and that he was wearing a bathrobe. When they confirmed this information as true, I continued. "I see him shuffling along," I said, and McGraw said yes, the man had a problem with his leg. When they asked where he would be found, I saw a hole of some sort, with a radio tower or some sort of tower nearby, and an old bridge.

In fact, the man was found in a drainage ditch, near a tower, and they had to go over an old bridge to get his body back. Sadly, he was already dead.

------------◆------------

In 1996, seventy-four-year-old Philip Lester, who suffered from Parkinson's disease and had short-term memory problems, apparently wandered away from a seniors' tour at a funeral museum in Texas and walked through an open door, disappearing into the cold and rainy November night. Six months later, completely frustrated in their attempts to find him, the police had to stop looking.

I was pulled into the case by a police sketch artist I knew. Years ago, when I still traveled to crime scenes, she and I had met on another Texas case. We had developed an easy friendship then, and she thought maybe I could help this family. Mr. Lester's daughter had called her and asked her to try to get me in on the case.

"Noreen, please," she begged, "you *have* to do this." She told me the family couldn't really afford to pay my fee, but they were desperate. Then she added, "It will make you famous." *That's just what I don't need,* I thought, reflecting on the skeptics who had been trying to discredit me for years. I had been purposely keeping a low profile, working only with law enforcement, for just this reason. Still, my heart went out to the family, and against my better judgment, I said I'd do it. I even reduced my fee. I figured it would only take a few hours. I was wrong.

The main problem was that I wasn't working directly with the police. Nice as this family was, communicating with them was turning out to be a stumbling block. As usual, I told them I needed some things that had belonged to the lost man. The daughter sent me a shirt, a comb, and a hairbrush. I explained to the daughter and her husband how to question me, and we got to work—me in Orlando and them in Texas. Brushing my fingers over the items, I felt a strong reaction right away. I just knew he was dead, and his body would be found in a dense, wooded area near a main highway. For some reason, I knew exactly where he was—I could have walked right up the trail myself and pointed him out, the vision was that clear. So I told them just where to look, and they passed the information on to the searchers—the police had refused to work with me. But somewhere between my lips and their ears the information got distorted, and the searchers couldn't find him.

When the daughter called me back the following week and told me, I was really frustrated. What was the problem? I don't think I had ever been more certain of anything in my life. I tried to explain to them again exactly where to look, but they just didn't seem to understand what I was describing. So I asked them to send me a map. More time wasted waiting for mail.

Once the map came, we tried working from that—we each had a copy, and we talked through it over the phone. But it was an aerial map and it covered too much territory. I asked them to send me *another* map of the area, thinking it might be more specific. This was three Sundays gone already. Meanwhile, I knew this man's body was still out there.

Finally, they sent me a detailed map. By this time, I was really mad. They could have found him already! Frustrated, I took a big black pen and circled the area where they should look on the map, gave them some verbal directions again, and sent back the map.

That seemed to do the trick. The daughter gave the directions to one of the searchers who had befriended the family, and she went out searching with her boyfriend. Before long, the boyfriend stumbled across some business cards that had been in Phillip Lester's wallet. This was the first break in the case in six months. He immediately gave the cards to law enforcement officers, who sent out a search party right away. They soon found the scattered remains of the body pretty much where I said they would: Two miles from the museum and about forty yards from where the cards had been found.

My police artist friend was right: the case did make me famous, for a few days at least. My information was apparently spectacular enough to land me once more on the front page of the *National Enquirer:* "Psychic Finds Missing Man After Cops Give Up." The quote from the missing man's daughter made me feel particularly good. I even felt better about giving up four consecutive Sundays to work on this case. "Thank God for Noreen Renier," she said. "Without her, we never would have found Dad. . . . I believe God sent us Noreen Renier to help us find Dad's body."[4]

I don't know if God had a hand in it, but I was glad to have the validation—and, I must admit, the publicity *was* good for business. In the end, everyone was pleased with the outcome of the case. The family got their father's body back, the sheriff was able to close the case, and I had the satisfaction of knowing they had found Mr. Lester's remains almost exactly where I had told them to look. And the skeptics? They're still on my case. As one paper reported at the time, "Despite the satisfaction of both families in those cases [Lewis and Lester], the founder of a skeptics chapter in Florida said those cases prove nothing because no one can prove that psychic power is real."[5]

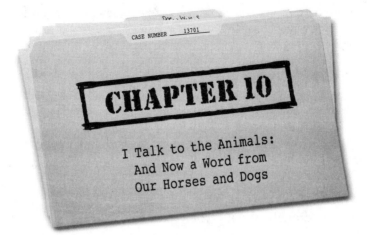

CHAPTER 10

I Talk to the Animals: And Now a Word from Our Horses and Dogs

As we stood in front of the two horses, I suddenly got a message: "I'll be dead in a month." One of the horses had sent it, but which one? I don't like to see death, even for animals. Sadly, I relayed this information to my client.

Carrie thought about it for a minute. "You must be picking up the old mare," she said. "She's been around a long time, and hasn't been feeling well lately." Carrie seemed pretty philosophical about this, so I began to relax and enjoy my animal "chat."

———◆———

One spring day, a client asked if I would come out to her farm and "chat" with a few of her animals. Carrie said she would pay me my regular fee. I had never read an animal before, but I thought it would be fun at the very least. So a few days later, off I went on a lovely drive through the Virginia countryside to her farm.

As the two of us walked up to the pasture, two horses stood by the fence. The older, wiser-looking white horse calmly assessed us, but the younger, brown horse kept gnawing on the wood fence as if his life depended on it.

I know about cats and dogs, but farm animals are a mystery to me. "Why is that dark horse chewing on the fence?" I asked.

"I wish I knew," Carrie replied, shaking her head. "That's called cribbing. If you can tune in and find out why, it would really help us."

As we stood in front of the two horses, I suddenly got a message: "I'll be dead in a month." One of the horses had sent it, but which one? I don't like to see death, even for animals. Sadly, I relayed this information to my client.

Carrie thought about it for a minute. "You must be picking up the old mare," she said. "She's been around a long time, and hasn't been feeling well lately." Carrie seemed pretty philosophical about this, so I began to relax and enjoy my animal "chat."

"Tune in to the younger horse and find out about his cribbing," she urged.

So I stood and concentrated my attention specifically on the brown horse and got a much more specific answer than I expected. Apparently, because of the way the horse had been bred, his system lacked a specific vitamin, and that lack made him nervous. He'd started cribbing to relieve the nervousness. Like a smoker with cigarettes, the more he did it the more he needed it, and he just couldn't stop. The message I got said that Carrie should give him and his offspring massive doses of vitamin B.

"Thanks," said Carrie when I told her all this. I guess it made perfect sense to her, because she just said, "Now let's move on to the dogs."

"Okay," I said, and trotted along after her. Dogs are nice, and I was eager to see what a dog or two might have to say. This was turning out to be a pretty interesting afternoon.

———— ◆ ————

The frenzy of barking as we got near the kennel told me immediately that it was more than a couple of dogs. I was overwhelmed when we entered the kennel and were greeted by at least ten large Irish Setters eager to be released from their wire pens. *Oh no*, I thought, *I have to talk to all these dogs.* Until that moment, I had no idea she was a dog breeder.

My dogs had always been lovable mutts, but these dogs were clearly royalty. They were beautiful, with long, silky red hair. To my eyes, they all looked exactly alike, but as I started my telepathy I soon found vast differences in their personalities.

She opened one wire cage at a time, and I bent to touch each animal, asking Carrie what questions she had for that specific dog. I have to say I felt foolish, but that's what the client wanted and I was intrigued to see if I could pick up impressions.

"Ask him if he is satisfied with the food we feed him," she said of the first dog. He had no complaints, and neither did the second one. But the third dog sent me a different message. I looked at Carrie. "He says he doesn't like the dog two slots down." I felt a strong wave of jealousy from this dog, and asked Carrie what the dog might be referring to. She knew right away. "The dog he's talking about is the only one in the kennel we allow in the house at night. I guess that could make him jealous."

Another dog was more picky about the food. He didn't like the fish meal they received weekly—he'd much prefer chicken or some other kind of meat. Still another dog was disappointed that he wasn't getting his special dog treats. I guessed dogs thought a lot about food.

After a few more dogs, I was starting to wind down. As I tuned in to the next dog, I felt a sharp pain in my hip and told Carrie what I felt. She confirmed that this dog had an injury in his hip, but she thought it had healed. She said she would look into it and take extra precautions with him.

Even though the dogs didn't discuss politics or world events, I enjoyed experiencing their lives a little bit and felt enthusiastic about my success with animals. But I was saddened when, one month later, Carrie called to tell me that the mare was fine, but the younger horse had died unexpectedly—just as he had told me he would.

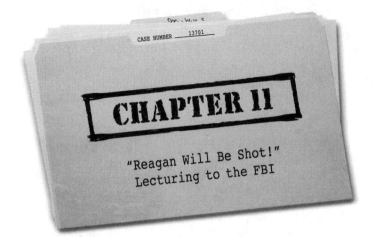

CASE NUMBER ___13701___

CHAPTER 11

"Reagan Will Be Shot!"
Lecturing to the FBI

When President Reagan was shot—in the upper left chest, as I had predicted—all hell broke loose. I didn't play up my prediction, but others tried to jump on the bandwagon. Lucky for me it was on tape and in print this time.

As usual around any tragedy, charlatans got into the act. The television show PM Magazine *in Charlottesville reported, "On March 30, President Reagan was shot in an assassination attempt. The next day, a psychic named Tamara Rand gained national notoriety by claiming to predict the event. It turned out to be hoax. And in all the excitement, another psychic who did predict the shooting was unnoticed." That other psychic was me.*

And not only was my prediction in the tabloids, I had actually managed to make a pretty detailed prediction in front of a classroom of law enforcement officers at the FBI Academy.

———————◆———————

"And now, WXAM Charlottesville invites you to join us for a very special hour with renowned psychic Noreen Renier. We will be taking your phone calls and putting you . . . *In Touch* with Noreen."

From public relations to gypsy fortuneteller to psychic detective . . . and now, a psychic Dear Abby! My life was moving along at quite an interesting pace.

> *Caller*: My initial is "C" and I received a diamond from a man I've been dating with the initial "R," and I just received a call from a guy that's been away in the service named "C." He's coming home in three weeks.
>
> *Noreen*: . . . and you're in trouble. You haven't been that honest with either man. You wanted a diamond and you wanted a boyfriend. But you don't love either man. You're going to hate to do this, but I think you should give back the diamond and start dating both of them. And be honest . . . for your sake as well as theirs.

In 1980, I talked myself into a local radio show. Frankly, I needed more business, and my public relations smarts told me that I could reach out and touch a lot of people on the radio. I had a mortgage to support now, and the $35 an hour I was charging—up from the $5 I was charging back in my hotel days—kept my bank account pretty slim. I was starting to pick up more private clients, and lectures and classes helped a bit, but I thought I needed a bit more local exposure.

I am nothing if not direct, and once I get an idea into my head, I don't rest until I have acted on it. So one morning I got dressed in my nicest business outfit, walked into the station, and asked—well, begged would be a more accurate term—the manager to give me a chance. I said, "Just give me your worst time slot, and I'll show you what I can do." Much to my surprise, he gave me Wednesday morning from ten to eleven, and announcer Josh Cohen to make sure everything was running smoothly. Almost immediately, we were off and running.

We had two phone lines that never stopped ringing. I regularly took calls for over an hour after the show was over—people would just call and want to be put on hold. Mostly, they asked questions about love: "I just met a man. Do you see a relationship developing?" Next was money: "I have an opportunity to be transferred to a new department." And finally, health: "My father-in-law is in intensive care. Will he get better?"

When they couldn't call me on the phone, they'd send personal items and ask me to read them. I didn't really want them to send their jewelry in the mail, so quite often they would send locks of hair—sometimes lots of hair. We had to be careful opening the mail.

The show was popular and soon word got out. *PM Magazine* did a feature on the radio show, and plenty of people were writing magazine articles about me. I was the local psychic of the hour for a while. By this time, I was being called by police in a number of cities in Virginia, as well as in other states. I was hopping on planes, tromping through mud, walking through rivers, and visiting crime scenes. I liked being able to help the police when I could, but it was tiring work and I can't say I enjoyed it.

I did have fun on this show, though, and I learned a valuable lesson: I could do this work over the phone. I did not have to travel to every crime scene.

Even when I'm not tuning in to a specific person or item, images and feelings pass through me. Most are fleeting and incomplete, and I let them go. Who knows where they come from or what they mean? But some seem serious, and they get my attention. In early 1980, one strong feeling kept coming back: Something bad would happen to Ronald Reagan. Before Reagan was elected, I would just see his chest. Then I would feel pain in the chest area. I kept pushing the image away because, frankly, I don't like to see negative things about people. It's upsetting. But I couldn't ignore it. The image kept coming back, and it got stronger and more detailed. Finally, I couldn't help blurting it out.

On November 5—the day after Ronald Reagan was elected president—I told my radio listeners at WXAM, "I'm feeling problems in his [Reagan's] chest. If it's not a natural problem, perhaps it will come from outside." Then, in December 1980, I prepared my predictions for the coming year for a Canadian publication. I simply wrote, "Reagan will be shot in the upper left chest." That prediction was published thirteen days before the assassination attempt.

When Reagan *was* shot—in the upper left chest—by would-be assassin John Hinckley, all hell broke loose. I didn't play up my prediction, but others tried to jump on the bandwagon. Lucky for me it was on tape *and* in print this time. As usual around any tragedy, charlatans got into the act. The television show *PM Magazine* in Richmond reported, "On March 30, President Reagan was shot in an assassination attempt. The next day, a psychic named Tamara Rand gained national notoriety by claiming to predict the event. It turned out to be a hoax. And in all the excitement, another psychic who *did* predict the shooting was unnoticed." That other psychic was me.

And not only was my prediction in the tabloids. I had actually managed to make a pretty detailed prediction in front of a classroom full of law enforcement officers at the FBI Academy.

It was January 1981, a cold winter day in Virginia. As I drove my increasingly more ancient Ford down the long, tree-lined roadway to the FBI Academy's headquarters at Quantico, I was intimidated as hell. Most U.S. citizens never get to see this bastion of American policing. What was I doing here? The bare winter trees formed a chilling backdrop to the large, granite building looming in front of me, which looked very imposing, as I guess it's meant to be. The FBI compound—a number of classrooms, offices, and lab buildings surrounded by an enormous wooded tract next to military facilities—feels like its own country. The perimeter is tightly secured with a barbed wire fence and monitoring devices. I wasn't going to sneak in or out of this place!

When Robert Ressler had asked me to give a lecture to his criminology class at Quantico, I was flattered that this impressive FBI agent was taking me seriously. But Special Agent Robert K. Ressler was no ordinary agent. It was Ressler, in his groundbreaking interviews with murderers, who coined the term "serial killer." The first investigator to interview multiple murderers—including Charles Manson, Ted Bundy, John Wayne Gacy, Richard Speck, Jeffrey Dahmer, and David Berkowitz—he formulated a theory. Other investigators had written off these people off as "monsters," but Ressler wanted to learn more about the criminal mind. Eventually, he developed a theory about the behavior of multiple murderers: He described them as "serial killers," people so demented that they were compelled to kill again and again until they were caught.[1]

When I met him, he was at the beginning of a career that has made him a legend as a criminologist and expert on violent crime. Ressler was the real-life inspiration for the investigator in *Red Dragon* and *Silence of the Lambs,* and his work as Supervisory Special Agent and criminologist at the FBI's Behavioral Science Unit inspired the television series *The X-Files.* He was also the first important law enforcement officer to understand the use of psychics in criminal investigations.

In 1980, using a psychic as an investigative tool was far from a recognized practice in any law enforcement agency, let alone the conservative FBI. The police are trained to look at the physical facts of a crime—the facts, ma'am, just the facts—and make their interpretations based on what they can see. They couldn't understand why they should consider what they can't see and can't get their hands on. Well, I decided, it would be my job to help them understand the importance of a mind open to many possibilities.

I drove past the simple marker that said "FBI Academy" and parked in a space marked VISITORS. As I walked into the spacious reception area, the young person behind the desk greeted me cordially. I signed in, and he gave me a preprinted name tag, saying with great importance, "Never take this name tag off." I was in a different world.

Agent Ressler had told me I was welcome to stay overnight, and I took him up on it. How could I turn down an offer like that? Now I was being shown to my room. It was small and sparsely furnished, like a dorm room: a desk for studying, with drawers for clothes. On a twin bed were sheets, towels, and a folded blanket. It wasn't the Four Seasons.

As I hung my clothes up in the closet and looked around, I noticed that the door to my room did not have a lock. That alarmed me for about thirty seconds, until I realized that I was in perhaps the safest location in the entire world.

As I prepared for the first class, I couldn't help but feel a bit nervous. I'm right at home speaking to a crowd of hundreds or a classroom of eager students. But this was going to be a small class of about fifty law enforcement agents and officials, there to listen to me—*and probably against their better judgment,* I thought.

I dressed conservatively for the occasion in a simple, dark, knee-length dress with a high neck. As I walked into the small classroom—the most uninteresting classroom you can imagine, with a white pull-down screen behind me for contrast—I looked at my students. The room was rife with male pattern baldness. Today, police officers look almost like everyone else in America: they are men and women, all sizes and colors. But back then, I was facing the most homogenous group imaginable: virtually all white men, all serious, hunched over, and staring at me quietly and politely. I took a deep breath and began.

As I talked, I started to calm down a bit, going off on tangents, telling my stories, waving my hands around, and asking them to remind me to talk to them about frauds and charlatans after the break. After about forty minutes, totally relaxed and feeling right at home, I blurted out, "Oh, I wish I could smoke! I'm desperate. Would you mind if I smoked?" Much to my surprise, they laughed and accommodated my addiction immediately—in fact, I think they may have realized at that moment that I was human, just like that. From that moment, I thought, *I've got them.*

The lecture went really well, I thought. I'd been able to explain my technique and how I worked with the police. I also got to tell them the best way to work with a psychic. "One thing that is vitally important is how you phrase your questions to me," I told them. "You should question me in a casual, gentle manner. Please don't interrogate me like a criminal, even when I am playing the criminal's part. And please don't ask me a series of yes and no questions—that tends to cause me to lose my train of thought." Instead, I told them, they should encourage me to describe the details of what I envision psychically, through questions that affirm my visions rather than call them into doubt. Some of them even took notes on what I was saying—I thought I was really mak-ing progress.

Just as I was finishing my talk and thanking them for being there, one officer who hadn't smiled at my jokes jumped to his feet and announced, "I don't believe one word you've said. Here's my watch. Prove it to me."

Normally, if an audience member had approached me in this way after a lecture, I would have said, "tough noodles, it's over." But I was intimidated and felt compelled to accommodate this irate officer. Snatching the watch from his hand, I thought to myself, *Please let me get this right!* and I sent my mind into his body to search for scars that he could confirm. I found several, but he kept interrupting me, yelling, "No! No! You're wrong!" But I didn't *feel* like I was wrong. Finally, I clearly saw a scar on his back in the shape of a cross—not an X, not a T, but a *cross.*

Again he yelled, "No! You're wrong!" I was exasperated.

Fortunately, the other students didn't believe his loud protests any more than I did. In their best police technique, they grabbed him, pulled him kicking and screaming to the back of the room, and stripped his shirt off his body. There it was: a scar in the shape of a cross. With his back literally up against the wall, he reluctantly confessed that everything else I had told him was accurate.

And that was my initiation into the world of the FBI Academy. It was to be the first of several lectures I would give there, and it wouldn't be the last time I was challenged.[2]

Some months later, I was lecturing to about two hundred and fifty officers in the academy's new auditorium. During my psychic demonstrations, an enormous man way back in the auditorium stood up and shouted belligerently, "If you can do all you claim you can, tell me about Jim!"

I asked him to repeat the name. "*Jim!*" he said again, his voice thundering through the room. He was gesturing emphatically, an unlit cigar in one hand. The choked emotion in his voice helped me to focus on Jim. I closed my eyes and prayed hard: *Please let me pick up on Jim, whoever he is.*

Suddenly, into my mind rushed blurred images and strong feelings that poured out of me in a rush of words. "Jim is a young person, but he is not related to you. He lives close to your family. He played with your son, you knew him." My face twisted in pain. "He is dead," I said. "He died a painful death, a lot of torture, a lot of pain."

The man crushed the cigar in his hand, threw it down, and fled the auditorium, clearly upset. What had I said? Often, when the words come through me like that, the feelings stay with me but I have little cognizance of what I have said. Agent Ressler rushed onto the stage to save me and enlighten the audience. He explained that Jim had been a victim of John Wayne Gacy, the Chicago serial killer who had tortured and killed thirty-three young boys over a period of years and buried them in his cellar. Chillingly, Gacy had been a well-liked and respected family man—often, he had dressed up as a clown and performed at children's parties. Jim was a boy who lived in the officer's neighborhood and had often played with his son.

Robert Ressler was very serious about the possibilities of the Behavioral Science Unit. He felt it was important for agents and officers to learn to keep an open mind about all sorts of possibilities, so he invited me back to lecture at Quantico a number of times. Over the years, he's gotten some flack for that stand, but he has always defended my integrity as a psychic and his decision to bring me into his program.

Agents and detectives from all over the United States and the world came to Quantico to study law enforcement theory and techniques. For me, one of the highlights of lecturing at the academy was the opportunity to socialize with all of these interesting people. The most interesting part was *where* we socialized: After hours, we all gathered in the "Board Room," a lounge located right in the FBI Academy.

A bar? In the FBI Academy? Most of these officers were the elite or most promising of their respective agencies. They came for a three- or four-month program, working hard under intensely stressful conditions for several weeks at a time. Without some release, the tension might become overwhelming. So when the officers—about 90 percent men—needed a safety valve in the form of alcohol and socializing, it was safer in every respect to keep on them on academy grounds. (They also had a casino room, where they taught agents how to cheat so they could catch crooked gamblers—but that's another story.)

Over a drink and casual conversation, the officers who had heard my lecture earlier in the day could see that I was—in the words of one police investigator—"a down-to-earth gal."[3] One by one, they would come over to me at my table in the evening and ask, "C'mon, tell me something about myself—here's my watch." What had happened to those tough, skeptical guys? It turned out that doing readings for the agents in the Board Room was not very different from my first job as a professional psychic in a nightclub.

I lectured at Quantico several times over the years, but it was that first lecture in early 1981 that eventually landed me in the news big time.

I end all of my lectures by asking for questions from the audience. On this day, soon after the inauguration of President Ronald Reagan, an FBI officer asked what lay ahead for the new president. As usual, I closed my eyes and answered without thinking. "The president is going to be popular," I began. Then I started patting my left side, saying, "some kind of pains, chest pains." Then I clarified a bit and said no, he is going to be shot in the upper left chest, in about three months. The room fell silent. I continued, saying that he would not die but would become a stronger president because of all the sympathy. The room began to buzz.

The lecture was over. It never occurred to me that talking about assassination in the FBI Academy was going to land me in hot water.

Later, Ressler said that he didn't really think too much about my prediction. In fact, he didn't actually report it until *after* President Reagan was shot by John Hinckley. Although it didn't occur to me either, sometimes I wonder if the White House might not have welcomed my prediction. It's well known that Nancy Reagan was fond of her astrologer's predictions, and the president was also known to have consulted astrologers over the years. Scott Jones, a staffer of Claiborne Pell, later quoted a White House source as saying, "This is a very psychic White House."[4]

Once the prediction *was* reported, the Secret Service launched an investigation of me. One brilliantly bright day in April, I returned home from my radio show and found a strange message on my answering machine. The man identified himself as Terry, and said he worked at the Department of Treasury. He wanted me to call him. The Department of Treasury—didn't they trace counterfeit money? I was confused, but I called him back. I really didn't know what he wanted and he wouldn't say too much on the telephone, but I agreed to meet with him the following week after my radio show. He asked me to bring him a tape of my radio show where I predicted the assassination attempt on President Reagan.

Terry turned out to be from the Secret Service. He was a nice-looking man of average height who could easily get lost in a crowd—a good quality for the job, I thought. He asked me a lot of questions, mostly about my psychic ability. He was agreeable to be with and we had a few drinks after lunch. We talked the whole afternoon.

The following week he came to my house. My sister was there, and I tape-recorded our time together. He wanted to know if I saw any danger to the president in the future. I closed my eyes, concentrated, and my mind raced to the future and danger. I saw a man in a foreign military uniform, a military parade, a reviewing stand, lots of people, machine-gun fire. This man would be killed by several of these people in foreign uniforms. A successful assassination. I think we both assumed it was Reagan because that's who we were talking about.

But then he asked me what branch of the service I saw, so I zoomed in for a closer look. I didn't recognize the uniform—it must be foreign, I said. Then again I heard the loud noises, guns shooting. I saw a palace, and someone getting shot in the stomach. He asked me when, and I said within a few weeks.

A few weeks later, Egyptian President Anwar Sadat—not Reagan—was shot to death by extremists in Cairo—just as I had seen in my vision. (Ressler later said that the "circumstances were uncanny in their accuracy.") Terry called me right away and asked me not to mention my prediction to anyone. And I didn't—until one evening, at a cocktail party, I overheard a wealthy socialite from Richmond relating my story to a rapt audience. Of course, she didn't know *I* was the psychic she was talking about! That really made me mad.

I decided right then and there that if she could tell my story, then I could tell it, too.

In 1997, after two years of trying, I got the FBI's forty-three-page report on me through the Freedom of Information Act. I didn't know what an extensive investigation they had done on me way back then. Impressive! I found out things even *I* didn't know: cases I had helped resolve, agencies they had interviewed, and their comments. They also checked to see if I had a criminal record and/or mental health problems—and found neither, of course.

The report also mentioned another of my predictions. Between 1979 and 1981, a series of horrible child murders had plagued the city of Atlanta. I had correctly predicted—again, on my radio show, and fortunately, on tape—that the body of the next victim would be found on Easter Sunday. (I remember that one because when I made that prediction, as sometimes happens with my psychic energy, all the power in the studio went off!) The report said, "to date she has provided information which was previously unknown outside the FBI and that she has been highly accurate."

Thanks, FBI. The discovery that they had all this information about me—almost more than I had about myself—was disconcerting. But I have to say I appreciated the recognition and the validation. Later, a police textbook in which I am mentioned would actually be used as a teaching tool at the academy.[5] But most of all, I was grateful when I read Robert Ressler's assessment in the *National Enquirer:* "She's an absolutely amazing woman."[6]

Robert and I stayed in touch over the years. One time, he called to say he was going to Europe on a business trip, and he asked me if I could tell him anything about what might happen. "I don't see you leaving when you think you're going to leave," I said. "And I see pain coming to your back and a dark-haired woman chasing you."

"Tell me more," he asked. But I didn't see any more.

A couple of days later he called me again. "You told me I wouldn't be leaving when I thought I would. You were right. The airline made a mistake. Instead of canceling just one person's ticket, they accidentally canceled everyone's ticket, so we're all going on different dates."

About a month later, he called again. "Noreen," he said, "I got to Germany and had the worst pain and headache. My wife"—a lovely woman with dark hair—"had been in a car accident and broke her back." He returned home immediately to find her "chasing him," in a way: in her hospital room, they had her going around and round on a circular apparatus designed to help people in her condition.

Robert was really worried. He got a piece of her hair for me, and said, "I must see the truth." I closed my eyes and focused in—and, to my great relief, I saw her working in her garden. I said, "I think she's going to recover about 90 percent."

And she did.

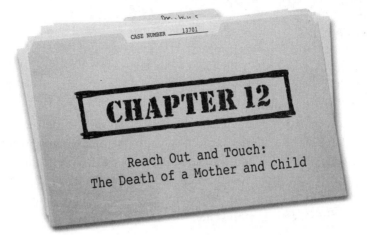

CHAPTER 12

Reach Out and Touch:
The Death of a Mother and Child

The pain was like ice and the blood flowing out of my body was hot. I was crying for my life as I was being stabbed to death, and the cry grew into a horrible, wrenching wail. Every cell of my body was experiencing the agony and horror of being stabbed to death. Suddenly, my eyes snapped open. I was Noreen, breathing hard, crying, and squeezing a bloody earring in my sweaty palm. I just stared at the phone, clutched tightly in my other hand.

⁕

The first time I worked on a murder case over the phone was a far cry from my radio show—it was a horrible experience. But when a distraught woman called and asked me for help in solving the murders of her daughter, Barbara, and her five-year-old granddaughter, Danielle, I couldn't turn her down. The last time Mrs. Jones had seen Danielle, the little girl had asked if she could spend the night.

After a three-month investigation, the sheriff's office in Cassopolis County, Michigan, had turned up nothing. Detective

Atkinson had never had any contact with psychics before and was naturally pretty skeptical, but Mrs. Jones had read about my work in a magazine and was impressed. She was determined to see these murders solved. She told Detective Atkinson about me, told him what I charged, and begged him to call me.

When he called, I explained how I worked, and he agreed to send me an earring the mother had been wearing at the time of the murder. At the arranged time, I sat in front of the phone with my black cat on my lap and the bloodstained earring in my hand, waiting a bit nervously for the call. As I waited I stroked Fat Cat, which calmed me down and seemed to make her happy, too. My cowardly Doberman pinscher was snoozing in front of the office door.

The phone rang, and we were off. I closed my eyes, targeted my mind on the earring, and all of a sudden, it was like I was looking in a mirror. I could see the murderer washing his hands and combing his hair. I could see him perfectly. I saw the tattoos on his arm, I saw his whole face, and I described him over the phone.

I figured that would surely be enough, but the police wanted more. Detective Atkinson asked me if I could see what was happening to the victim whose earring I was holding. I was hesitant because I knew what was probably coming would not be pleasant. Reluctantly, I agreed. Today I might not agree quite so quickly. But in those days, I was still learning what I could do, and I was pretty innocent about the whole thing.

So, all of a sudden, I was back inside the murder scene, and this time I was being murdered by the tattooed man. He was holding me tight by the wrists. I twisted and turned, struggling to escape with every muscle in my body, but his grip just tightened more. I was flailing my arms wildly as the razor-sharp knife tore into my body over and over and over. The pain was like ice and the blood flowing out of my body was hot. I was crying for my life as I was being stabbed to death, and the cry grew into a horrible, wrenching wail. Every cell of my body was experiencing the agony and horror of being stabbed to death. Suddenly, my eyes snapped open. I was Noreen, breathing hard, crying, and squeezing a bloody earring in my sweaty palm. I just stared at the phone, clutched tightly in my other hand.

From far away, a voice was saying, "Noreen? Noreen? Are you all right?" The voice on the phone was Lt. Atkinson.

"Yes, I'm okay," I answered, "but could you hold for a few minutes? I want to get something. I'm a bit stunned."

Shaking, I placed the receiver and the earring on my desk and went into the kitchen to pour myself a glass of red wine. I took a big sip and paused at the window and looked out over the fields, where cows grazed in the distance. The sight never failed to relax me.

When I got back, Atkinson was waiting dutifully on the phone. He'd been skeptical at first—this hadn't been his idea, he was a man who was far more comfortable dealing with facts, and he was good at his job. But after he heard my graphic account, the skepticism was gone from his voice. He asked me to continue.

"Yes," I said, picking up the earring. "I see a wooden house. Behind the house is an old car. It has a flat tire. The house is isolated on a few acres of land. Other houses are around me, but not that close. The lights are on in the house. I hear a television. I see a small child. I'm in the bedroom putting some clothes away, and he just walks in."

Then the detective prompted me gently, "Noreen, you said there was a child. Can you be the child? Tell us what happened to her."

"No! No!" I shouted. I did not want to do this. "You already know how she was killed. I don't want to do it. I don't want to be killed again."

"Noreen, please try," he said quietly. "We need to know what happened. You do not have to experience the pain." He was trying to be reasonable, but he really didn't know what he was asking me to do. I did it anyway. To this day, I don't really know why.

When I touched the earring, I was back in the violent vibrations of the crime. I could feel that awful energy coursing through my body as I shuddered and held the dead woman's earring tighter. I tried to relax and let the images flow. Finally I spoke. "I'm back in the house."

My mind found the child. She was a pretty little girl with short, curly blonde hair, and she was in the messy bedroom of a child. She was playing with her dolls on her bed. Now I was the girl. I heard my mother screaming from the other room, and felt afraid in my bones. I ran to hide in the closet, crouching at the back among forgotten toys and discarded clothes. I whimpered softly as footsteps came toward the room. I knew they were not my mother's and I tried to make my tiny body even smaller. I tried to control my sobs as the footsteps came closer.

Then a tall figure appeared. I started screaming and screaming as he yanked me out of the closet. He stabbed me over and over and over again. *I was only five years old.* I died in pain and terror.

As Noreen, I came out of the vision for a moment, crying uncontrollably and still experiencing the girl's primal pain and terror. Then I was back in, and my vision shifted. I was in the bathroom, and I was the murderer. I watched as I washed the blood from my hands. I became mesmerized watching the bright red blood merge with the flowing water from the faucet as they swirled together down the drain. I looked up into the mirror over the sink saw myself, as him. I watched as my hand reached up to comb back my receding hair, and I saw a tattoo with snakes on my right wrist. Noreen, somewhere in back of all this, felt frightened and fascinated at the same time. The scenes ended as quickly as they had materialized, and I dropped the victim's earring on the floor.

On the other end of the telephone, Detective Atkinson was repeating his question, "Noreen? Noreen? Are you okay?"

I wasn't okay. I was shattered. I took a long drink of the wine and gave him more details about the murderer, including the tattoo, and then I stopped speaking. I just sat there, breathing raggedly, hearing the detective's faraway voice saying, "Noreen? Noreen? Are you there? Talk to me."

I simply could not talk. I reached for a cigarette, lit it, took a drag, and finally said, "Yes, yes, I'm here. A bit shook up, but I'm here. Was I any help?"

"You were very accurate with your descriptions of the specifics of the crime," he told me. "Very. That's all I want to say for now.

Thank you for your time, and thanks on behalf of the family."
Then he hung up and I sat there listening to the dial tone.

Fat Cat had long ago jumped off my lap, probably when I
started screaming. The dog was looking at me with some concern,
as dogs do. I was depleted and wrung out. I literally crawled up the
stairs to my bedroom, lay down, and went to sleep. I had a private
appointment coming later in the afternoon, and I would need my
strength.

I heard from the detective again in a few weeks. Now that I was
done with the case, he could fill me in on the details. The mother,
he said, had been stabbed viciously, twenty-seven times. Her
young daughter had been found face down in her bedroom closet,
stabbed seventeen times. I felt sick when I heard that, even though
I knew the horror from my own experience. I was gratified to hear
that the police artist in Michigan had made a sketch of the murderer from my description, which they distributed nationally. A
few days later, the Cassopolis County Sheriff's Department
received a flyer from out of state that had a picture and the description of an individual who had been arrested as a suspect in a bank
robbery in Goshen, Indiana. He looked quite a bit as I had
described the murderer—and he had the same tattoo. In the end,
he was extradited to Michigan, where he was arraigned and convicted of double homicide.

In 1989, the case was featured on the ABC television show
Incredible Sunday, including a reenactment of the crime. When
Detective Atkinson was interviewed on camera regarding my work
in the investigation, he recalled our phone call. "I continued my
conversation with Noreen for approximately forty-five minutes to
an hour, with her describing the type of places the individual suspect might frequent. At this point I was somewhat confused. My
first impression was she must have called someone or somehow
got hold of some information. Then I realized that the information
she had, no one knew."

And my description of the murderer? Atkinson concluded, "His physical appearance was as she described. His social background was as she described. The tattoos she described were accurate. I believe that overall, the use of a psychic, and Noreen in particular, was a benefit to us. I believe that psychics are a good investigative tool."

Today, more than twenty years later, I do 90 percent of my casework over the phone. But even today I recall this case with chilling clarity. It was upsetting to experience such brutality, and confusing to have been both murderer and victim. It was especially horrible to be the child. I didn't need to have that experience in order to get information. The terror that I felt and had to pick up was overwhelming. She was just a little girl, playing with her dolls.

Afterward, Mrs. Jones came to Virginia and tried to give me a reward. I told her I just wanted to be paid for doing my job; I didn't need a reward. But she insisted, and I accepted.

Most of the time, I just wanted to forget my experiences of cases like the one in Cassopolis County, and the radio show was the perfect place to do it. For five years, I talked to whoever called. Sometimes, I even got to tell my own stories. The one I call my "tree story" is especially healing.

> *Announcer:* Okay, Noreen, we have time for a few more calls.
> *Noreen:* No, I don't want to take any more calls. I want to tell my tree story:
> Early in my psychic life, I worked with Dr. David Jones of the University of Central Florida in archeology research. In his book, *Visions of Time,* Dr. Jones wrote of the work he had done with psychics in uncovering the past. When he offered me the opportunity to get in touch with the past in this way, I leaped at the chance.

A group of archeologists were planning a dig, but wanted background information from a different source . . . a psychic source.

Of course I volunteered. Driving to the site, I asked Dr. Jones how he'd like me to establish contact. He mumbled, "Oh, go talk to a tree." I focused in on this bizarre suggestion and realized there was truth in his humor. Trees have energy. I have energy.

I chose my tree carefully. It was a huge, sprawling oak that had been around for a long, long time. I figured if trees could talk, this one would have a great deal to say.

I closed my eyes and placed both hands on its trunk, a forgotten cigarette dangling from my right hand. Instantly, vivid impressions flooded my mind. My oak chatted long and interestingly about the past. I saw a double burial site and many artifacts. I was told where the river used to flow, how fighting had taken place nearby, and other historical facts.

Dr. Jones and the archeologists had their tape recorders whirring and were taking fast and furious notes, when suddenly I was told by the ancient oak, "We have one fear and that is of fire. Would you mind not smoking while you're touching me?" Stunned, I quickly pulled my hands and the cigarette away from the tree.

The archeologists were pleased with the information I had been able to give them: I thoroughly enjoyed the adventure, even though I felt as if I'd had a close encounter with Smokey the Bear!

To this day, when I hear the song "I Talk to the Animals," I smile and think, *Good for you. I talk to the trees!*

NOREEN
Psychic in
Psychometry

Let Noreen speak to you
of yourself as you were,
as you will be....
as you could be,
revealing personal
insights.
Five dollar gratuity customary

My first job as a psychic

Noreen Renier—a young psychic

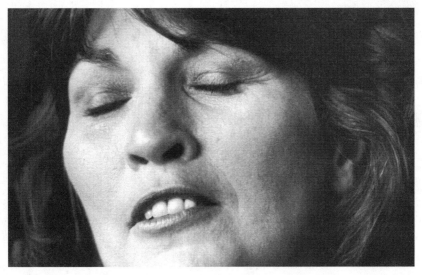

Psychic detective Noreen Renier enters a trance

During filming for Court TV's Psychic Detectives, *Noreen arrives in Shelby, Montanna. (Courtesy of Storyhouse)*

Undersherriff Dave Robbins (left) and Agent joe Uribe in Shelby, Montanna (Courtesty of Storyhouse)

*Original sketch drawn by
Barbara Tiffany
(12/1/1995)*

*Sketch of Eugene Moore
with beard added*

Bloody underwear and belt from a homicide case

Jackie Peterson's check to me

The handwritten envelope from Scott Peterson to me

Laci Peterson's shoe

Close-up of Laci Peterson's sweatshirt

My description of the New York Zodiac killer fit Heriberto "Eddie" Seda (shown here in his mug shot), who was eventually arrested and convicted.

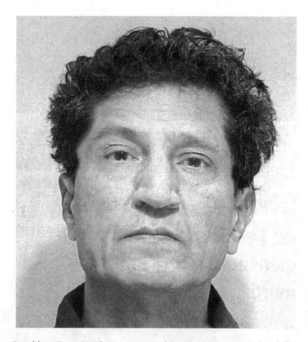

Jasubhai Desai as he appears today. Desai, sentenced to life in prison for the murder of Anna Turetzky, is serving out his sentence at Thumb Correctional Facility in Lapeer, Michigan.

FBI GOES INTO ACTION AS PSYCHIC PREDICTS NEW ASSASSINATION

Psychic sees death try, FBI listens

Psychic solves brutal 3-year-old murder for stumped lawmen

Psychic leads police to body

Some of the many headlines reporting my successes.

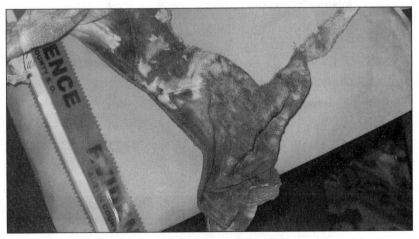

Evidence from a homicide case—a bloody bra

DEPARTMENT OF THE TREASURY
UNITED STATES SECRET SERVICE

131(8

ORIGIN ID	OFFICE Richmond, Virginia	CASE NO. CO-2-84,980

TYPE OF CASE	STATUS	TITLE OR CAPTION
Intelligence	Continued	Name of Subject:

INVESTIGATION MADE AT	PERIOD COVERED
Richmond, Virginia	4/22/81 - 5/8/81

NOREEN JEAN RENIER

Present Location:

INVESTIGATION MADE BY
SA

Route 2, Box 113
Barboursville, VA 22923

DETAILS

No

SYNOPSIS

Subject Noreen Renier was interviewed in
Charlottesville, VA. Law enforcement
officials in Charlottesville, Fredericks-
burg, VA, Montgomery County, MD; and,
FBI Academy, Quantico, VA were interviewed
and feel that the subject is a legitimate
psychic.

Renier provided cassette recordings from
her radio show at WXAM-Charlottesville,
as well as a cassette in which she predicts
that President Reagan will suffer a fatal
wound in November of 1981.

(A)   INTRODUCTION:

Reference is made to previous reports, the last being the Headquarters
teletype #371, dated 4/20/81, requesting Richmond to interview subject.

Reference is also made to telecon with IR: , ID, Region I.

DISTRIBUTION	COPIES	REPORT MADE-		DATE
Intell. Div.	Orig.			5/13/81
Buffalo (IO)	1 cc			
Rochester RA (IO)	1 cc	SPECIAL AGENT		
Richmond	2 cc	APPROVED		DATE
				5/14/81
		SPECIAL AGENT IN CHARGE		

MEMORANDUM REPORT   (CONTINUED ON PLAIN PAPER)   SS-1366 (66-72R)

☆ U.S. GOVERNMENT PRINTING OFFICE: 1976-633-864

*It took years, but I finally got my FBI file through the
Freedom of Information Act—all 43 pages.*

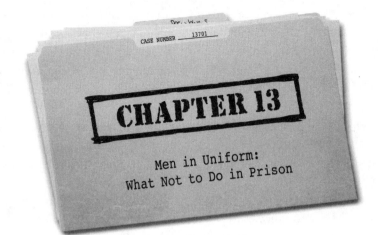

CASE NUMBER _____ 13701

CHAPTER 13

Men in Uniform:
What Not to Do in Prison

As we entered one inspection area after another, enormous steel doors clanged shut behind us. Finally, we were led into a small holding cell. It was stripped to the bone. Exposed toilet, barracks-type beds, and a long table filled the room. Around the table sat twelve strong young men in their twenties and thirties, neatly dressed in identical prison uniforms. There I was, locked in a cell with twelve criminals, one guard, and George.

I have visited men behind bars at two different times in my life. Once when I was just starting out in my career, and again after I'd helped to put a few of them there. Both of these journeys into the dead end of crime were harsh and depressing, infuriating and astounding, occasionally amusing, always eye-opening. The first, I have to admit, was an unmitigated disaster.

It happened way back when I was just getting started as a psychic and was eager to test the limits of this strange new skill. My old friend George, a dream interpreter, had been spending two hours a week at the local jail in Orlando helping some of the prisoners analyze their dreams. He thought it would be interesting for the men to learn something about psychic phenomena and watch me demonstrate psychometry. I was game for just about anything, and I figured that psychometry for prisoners would certainly be a new experience.

I didn't have a clue about men in prison. I'd never given them much thought, except to be glad they were behind bars and I was out of harm's way. For now, all I was concerned about was the logistics of my presentation.

"Will I be lecturing to the inmates from a raised platform or a stage?" I asked George as we left the freeway and headed for the downtown jail. He gave me a sideways glance and said, "Well, I guess you can always stand on the top of the toilet seat." *Ha ha*, I thought to myself. As he opened the door to let me out, I went from the air-conditioned car into the hot Florida sun. I hoped it was cool in that jail.

His toilet seat joke turned out not to be much of a joke. As we entered one inspection area after another, enormous steel doors clanged shut behind us. Finally, we were led into a small holding cell. It was stripped to the bone. Exposed toilet, barracks-type beds, and a long table filled the room. It was horrible. Around the table sat twelve strong young men in their twenties and thirties, neatly dressed in identical prison uniforms.

If you called me naïve, you'd be right. I was astonished that anyone in their right minds would do something that would land them in this hole. Most of these men were younger than me—they had their whole lives ahead of them. What did they do to be here? And why? What desperate needs propelled them to ignore honesty and trust and land here?

There I was—and let's face it, underneath the mysterious psychic trappings I was basically a nice, suburban mom—locked in a cell with twelve criminals, one guard, and George. I wasn't sure the odds were in my favor here. But after the initial shock wore off, I began feeling a bit more comfortable. It didn't look like I was in any imminent danger, and I was eager to share what little knowledge I had of ESP. Still, although I smiled and kidded and acted as calmly as possible, I was dumbfound that these young men were in jail. This was a different world.

Of course, what they really wanted was to see me demonstrate my psychic abilities. These men were all being held pending sentencing—they didn't know how long they'd be here, or where they were going next. There wasn't much for them to do except worry, and I was a nice diversion from the usual monotony and noise. So George collected rings and watches while I turned my back and promised not to peek. Finally, I turned around and selected one ring at random. Yikes. I hadn't begun working with the police yet, so the images I was receiving came as something of a shock. I blurted out, "Whoever this ring belongs to is a *terrible* thief. I can see that you're in and out of prison a lot. You've been caught every time! I don't want to hurt your feelings," I said politely, "but I would definitely suggest another occupation." The ring's owner laughed ruefully as he nodded his head in agreement with my assessment of his career.

Now I was enjoying myself. We were laughing together and relaxing, and I had some fun with the next few readings. But suddenly, as I held the last piece of jewelry in my hand and concentrated, I felt a sharp pain in my lower abdomen. It wasn't my own pain—I definitely felt like it was coming from the ring's owner. When the reading was over, I asked him if he was in pain right now. "Yes, ma'am," he replied quietly. He was a very young man. I couldn't imagine why he was in such pain.

At that time I had also been experimenting with healing. I had heard that people could heal with their hands and their energy, and I wanted to give it a try. My friend Ellen's cut finger had seemed like the natural place to start. When she reluctantly agreed, I placed my hands above and below her finger. Closing my eyes, I took several deep breaths, hoping the magic would work. I could feel the tingling heat as the energy flowed from me. After several seconds I slowly removed my hands and opened my eyes.

Ellen let out a piercing scream. "Noreen! My finger's on fire! What the hell have you done to me? If this is healing, it's hell! Don't help me anymore, okay?" But the pain was soon replaced by tingling. By the time I left, her finger was fine. We were both a bit stunned by my success.

Well, I thought, *if it worked on Ellen, maybe it will work on this young man.* Impulsively, I asked, "Do you want me to try to get rid of your pain?" I explained to him that the energy that emanated from me and my hands could affect him and his body. "I don't have to touch *you,*" I said. "I touch the energy that emanates from you. Your aura." I don't know if he really understood what I was talking about, but I certainly had his attention. In fact, all twelve men were giving me their undivided attention now.

I quickly went over to the suffering prisoner, took several deep breaths, and placed my hands above his head until I felt a connection with his energy. Then I let my hands hover a few inches away from his lower abdomen, where I had felt the pain in myself. As I felt the energy flowing between us, I assured him he would be just fine. When I looked up, he thanked me—with a strange, faraway look in his eyes. It left me puzzled, but then the whole experience had been unusual. *Job well done,* I congratulated myself.

George said the men had really liked me, and he invited me back the following week. They certainly greeted me very enthusiastically. But after my lecture and a few psychometry demonstrations, most of the men began complaining of pain. Some had it in their stomachs, others had it way up on their thighs. What was wrong with these guys? I figured that the food they were eating in prison must be pretty bad. Or maybe they were getting in a lot of fights. Jail was a dangerous place full of violent criminals. Of course they'd be hurting each other from time to time.

So, dutifully, I went on with my healing, my hands hovering over the nether regions of one man after another. After our session, I felt exhausted. I had never done so much healing at one time! Maybe this healing wasn't really for me. Still, I was delighted at their acceptance of me, and I left happy.

But I didn't stay happy. Two days later, a prison administrator called me at home and asked me not to return. I thought he sounded embarrassed.

"Why not?" I asked.

He cleared his throat a couple of times and quickly said, "Talk to George. He can explain."

I called George immediately. "Why can't I go back to the jail?" I demanded. "We were doing really well. I know the men were responding to me."

"Everything was fine until you started healing," he said. "Didn't you find it odd that all the men had pain in the same general area?" Silence on my end.

"Those guys have been in jail for a while, Noreen. A jail full of men and no women. You were turning them on."

"But I didn't touch them!" I protested. I was innocent! And mortified.

"I know you didn't touch them, Noreen, but your energy sure did!"

I thought that would be the end of my contact with prisoners, but I was wrong. One day, while I was doing my radio show, I had a call from a man who sounded distraught. "My initial is 'J,'" the caller said. "I listen to your show every week. I'm incarcerated in the local prison. Will you visit me? I need to talk to you."

Not on your life, I thought. But I asked, "Why are you in prison?"

"I was drunk; I hit my wife with a baseball bat, and she died," he answered flatly. I guess it wasn't the first time he'd told this story. I was not making any personal visits to a murderer, that's for sure!

"I'm sorry I can't visit you in prison," I said. "If I did that, then all the other men would want me to visit them too! But if you have a question, I'll answer that."

"Okay," he said, clearly disappointed. "When will I get out of here?" As I looked into his future, I saw nothing but the same walls he was looking at now.

After the show, I couldn't get the idea of visiting a prison out of my head. Maybe my old experience needed healing. This time around, I was older and wiser. I'd worked with the police and FBI, for goodness' sake. My work had contributed to putting some of these guys in there.

Once I get an idea, it's hard for me to let go. Finally, I called the prison. I was pretty well known in the area by then, and when I asked if I could visit and do a lecture demonstration for the prisoners, the warden agreed. With my vast knowledge of jails behind me, I insisted that I needed a raised platform or a stage-type structure. And no holding cells. And I made firm mental note to myself: *No healing.*

When it came time to go, however, I started getting nervous. I didn't want to go alone, so I asked my sister to go with me. She turned me down flat. "It's not my ideal way to spend an evening," she said. "I'd be too afraid."

Desperate to have someone I knew go with me, I asked my mother. She's an active and adventurous woman—in fact, she took up roller-skating at age seventy-three—and she always supports her children in whatever strange endeavors they pursue. "Sure," she said, "I'll go with you."

The sun was disappearing behind the rolling hills when we arrived at the prison, dressed in our Sunday best. My mother was relaxed, but I was frantic: Some of these guys were in there because of me. What would they think when I told them I worked with the police? Maybe they weren't my ideal audience after all.

As we walked through the first of many doors, we were greeted by a slim, easygoing young man in horn-rimmed glasses. When he introduced himself as the warden, I told him he wasn't at all what I had been expecting. "I guess I'm not the stereotype," he smiled, "but then, neither are you."

His casual chatter did a lot to put me at ease as we walked—again—through one steel door after another, down endless corridors, and finally descended into a dank, cellar-like room. The ceiling was so low I felt like I had to duck, and the room was dimly lit by a few scattered bulbs. It was a horribly depressing room. But, looking on the bright side, it wasn't a holding cell and it did have a raised platform. And no open toilet.

The guards soon ushered in an assortment of tough-looking men who sat down noisily in rows of folding metal chairs. These prisoners were light-years removed from the scared young men I'd visited in jail so many years ago. These were clearly hardened criminals, doing hard time for hard crimes. Many of them had ripped the sleeves off their uniform shirts to expose muscular arms covered with bizarre tattoos. It was a tense scene.

My mother, on the other hand, seemed to be having a wonderful time. The highlight of her week! She sat right down next to one of these scary individuals and struck up a chatty conversation. After a while, I had to tell her to keep it down. It doesn't matter how old you are, I guess, your mom can always embarrass you.

One big, burly guard was leaning against the back wall, holding a Bible firmly in his hands, staring at me. Other guards were standing around, keeping track of the prisoners. Nervously, I began my ESP presentation—by now, I'd done this quite a few times. Out of my mouth tumbled story after story about my work with the police. Naturally, the end of almost every story was "and then they caught the guy who did it." *Oh God*, I thought, *they're going to hate me.* But I couldn't seem to stop. When I did, I thought they were a little too quiet. Quickly, I asked, smiling brightly, "Does anyone have any questions?"

But it turned out that my concerns had been directed at the wrong audience—it was the guard who verbally attacked me. "You are an evil woman!" shouted the guard with the Bible. "Demonic!" And he started flinging Bible verses at me. Worse, no one came to my rescue. This was the main attraction for today, and even the other guards wanted to see what would happen.

I was in shock, but I was also getting madder and madder. I think my mother knew what was coming, because she was watching me calmly. "You are not only arrogant," I said finally, "you're ignorant, too." I knew you could find quotes in the Bible for or against anything, so I threw one back at him. It wasn't an exact quote, but it was the best I could do at the time: "Jesus, while healing the lepers, said to those around him, 'You too can do the things that I do and more, if only you believe.'"

We slung a few more quotes back and forth, and then I just couldn't take it any more. "This could go on all night," I said. "I'm sorry, but I didn't come here to listen to your disbelief about psychic phenomena. I came here to talk to these men." My arm swept out over the prisoners in the audience. I knew they were applauding me silently—they all wanted to yell at the guard too, I was sure, but he would be in charge of their lives after I left, so they kept quiet.

"I want *them* to ask questions, not you." All the prisoners began talking at once—even louder than my mother. "Wait a minute," I shouted. "You gentlemen were quiet while I answered the guard's questions. Let me answer your questions individually."

Another guard had already collected their jewelry for me to read, so I quickly picked up one of the envelopes that had been collected. I read the initial that had been written on the outside, R, and ripped open the envelope to touch the object. It was an earring! I tried to suppress my surprise—at that time, earrings for men had not yet become a fashion statement.

As I focused on the earring, I tried very hard to concentrate on its owner's good qualities. It was difficult—these men were murderers, thieves, and rapists. "R" was a very rough guy who had done a lot of bad things. Among other things, he seemed to be the ringleader of a prison gang who delighted in getting revenge on rivals who showed him and his men disrespect. "You're a leader," I finally said, putting a positive spin on it, "and you are very loyal to your friends." I asked him to stand up and confirm what I had said.

A giant of a man rose up. His eyes locked into mine for the longest second. Then suddenly he smiled and said, "That's true, all you said is true." As he spoke, some men behind him started talking. He whirled on them, towering over them: "Listen up," he said. Once was all it took, they shut up. He was a leader, all right. I glanced over at my mother. Her lips were sealed too.

After that, it was easy. The men were very open and honest—they told me when I got it right, and when I got it wrong—and I began enjoying myself again. This was a place where psychically locating body scars on a man was like picking daisies in a field of spring flowers. The men reciprocated the good feeling.

I read several more earrings, biting my tongue the whole time, and a variety of rings and watches. I described the men's tattoos, their physical scars and emotional scars, how they got caught, what they were in for. Like the prisoner who called my radio show, they had one thing on their mind—and it wasn't "When will I fall in love?" For these men, the most popular question was a bit more practical: "When am I going to get out?" They meant legally. And, like the radio caller, most of them weren't too happy with my answer.

Finally, it was over. The prisoners applauded, and the Bible-quoting guard was sullen and gave me a poisonous stare. I didn't think he'd be praying for me that night. My mother looked like she had enjoyed herself—it was certainly the most unusual evening out she'd had in a long time! As we left the cellar and slowly retraced out steps out through the corridors and heavy steel doors, I was glad to be out. I heaved a big sigh, and realized I'd been holding my breath the whole time I was in there. I was proud that I was an honest person—my mother had done a good job in bringing me up to respect the law.

The end result of my work as a psychic investigator sometimes means that a crime is solved. When that happens, someone inevitably ends up in prison. By now, after more than twenty years of experiencing the minds and feelings of murderers, you'd think I'd have some insight into their motives. But I don't. I think of these wasted lives often, and I am still bewildered that men and women would choose a life that causes others such pain and leads them to this dead end.

The feelings I experienced from my prison visits were harsh. Both times, I was terribly saddened by the aura of despair that hit me as soon as I walked in. I couldn't understand the point of it all, and I still can't. What is our society teaching—or not teaching—that leads these men to choose a life path that only leads to death and despair?

CHAPTER 14

The Professional:
The Client Was a Killer

Without hesitation or emotion he asked, "How close is death? Is it nearby?"

His question startled me—usually the first question is some varia-
tion of "When will I fall in love?" Intuitively, I knew he asked this
question not out of curiosity, but necessity. I normally would not answer
a question about an individual's death—despite the path my career has
taken, or perhaps because of it, I do not like to dwell on the negative.
But this felt different, urgent. I began my search for his death.

I didn't find his death, but what I did find was disturbing. I shook
my head as I answered, "No, I don't see your death in the immediate
future. But I do see guns around you, foreign countries, and death . . .
around others."

Stewart came into my life innocently enough, over the telephone.
In those days, I didn't have an answering machine, and I
answered every call that came along. I picked up the phone that

day as I always did: with the pleasant words, "Good morning, this is Noreen."

The man's voice came through the telephone with a demanding tone that made me sit up right away. "I must make an appointment to see you today!" he commanded in a strong British accent. The accent made him sound important in some indefinable way.

But I was busy. "No, I can't. I'm booked solid. How about ten tomorrow morning?" He agreed, grudgingly, and I told him to come prepared with ten specific questions.

So the next morning, punctually at ten o'clock, a well-dressed man knocked on my front door. "Call me Stewart,"[1] he said, locking his icy blue eyes with mine. He looked like a successful businessman in his forties, stocky and powerfully built. He tried to smile as he introduced himself, but his lips barely moved in his broad, chiseled face.

I led Stewart into my library, offered him a seat, and handed him a copy of my instructions about a "Psychic Reading with Noreen." I left him alone in the library for a few minutes to give him time to read my rules:

> The reading I offer is a personal one, which stresses a person's identity and potential for a more positive and fulfilling life.
>
> Help me to help you by doing your share to provide a positive, serene environment during the reading. I request you be alone for your psychic consultation so another person's energy does not interfere with yours.
>
> *Be prepared for your reading.* Send a list of at least ten specific questions you want answered. Do not ask "yes" or "no" questions. Send questions which require facts or information about concerns you have.
>
> The less you tell me before or during the reading, the more I will be capable of telling you. Give me first names of people and initials of companies or businesses you might be concerned with. You may mail me a recent photo of family or friends you wish to ask

about. *Do not mail me your photo.* I need a piece of your hair wrapped in aluminum foil.

I will start your session by describing you to some extent, including a few body scars. Your reading will last approximately forty-five minutes to an hour. Use your time wisely. We do not want to spend too much time on one area or one problem if you have several concerns.

I do not claim to be 100 percent accurate, nor do I claim to be capable of reading all people equally. A reading is a group of impressions that are merely possibilities at this time. You always have choices and are free to make those choices, which can totally affect anything I may "see" today.

Remember, your future is yours to decide.

I've done hundreds of private readings during my career, and most of my clients have been ordinary people who just want to know a little something more about their lives. Usually, as I found on my radio show, they have questions about the big three life questions—love, money, and health. Inevitably—though, thankfully, rarely—psychics attract some strange people. I think that if people are a little off anyway, experimenting in the psychic world, which has no boundaries and few safe places, can drive them a little farther over the edge.

Over the past two decades, I have been genuinely frightened by only three clients—but they were truly scary.

Ironically, they came to me in Virginia, at a time when my police work was really picking up. I hung out so much with the cops and the FBI that you'd think I'd have more sense about people—or at least known enough to call the police. But it seems that the same eager and willing openness to new experiences that allows me to go so readily into my psychic mind to help others also sometimes allows me to be hopelessly clueless when my own life is in danger.

People often think that doing psychic readings for a living is an easy and exciting life, but in my experience it is hard work that can take a real physical and emotional toll. Today, I've learned to protect my health by leaving enough time between clients and cases to allow myself to recover. But back in those days, when I was just starting out and trying to build a career—and make some money—I only left two hours between appointments. Afterwards, I would crawl under the covers and watch mindless television shows to calm me down, and then I'd go downstairs, eat, and start all over again.

I lived alone with my animals in my big old two-story farmhouse, with its wonderful circular driveway. I loved living alone. Some people need people all the time, but I seem to need that quiet space that is all mine. My office, where I would meet my clients, was very atmospheric. I loved this room, with its thick Oriental rug, big, old Chinese red trunk, and built-in bookshelves filled with books. My clients would sit on my wonderful old leather-covered theater chairs, and I would sit near them, but not quite facing them.

My Doberman pinscher, Tara, had come from the pound—I never get animals new. (I acquired Fat Cat when the police raided the home of a woman whose house was filled with neglected, underfed cats and kittens. Fat Cat's name was originally Sabrina, but she was a hungry, hungry cat and soon her new name fit much better!) Tara was a scary-looking black-and-tan dog, with clipped pointy ears and long sharp teeth, but in fact he was a real coward. He loved people. Still, lying outside the door he looked suitably ferocious.

Another thing that has changed over the years is my taping policy. In those days, I taped our sessions—and then I gave the client the tape! I didn't know how to copy a tape, and honestly it never occurred to me. When I worked for the police, they made the tape. Eventually, I learned to keep a copy of every tape for myself, and in some cases, I even had the tapes transcribed. Unfortunately, I hadn't learned this when I met Stewart.

Tara lay deep in sleep just beyond the door of my library, and I knelt for a while and gave him a good pat. Then I got a glass of water and returned to my office, and sank into my favorite chair.

I smiled warmly in my best professional manner, and asked Stewart for a personal object to hold. Slowly, he removed a very expensive watch from his wrist and gave it to me, his eyes never leaving mine. I touched it lightly with my fingertips, I closed my eyes, and took a few deep breaths to relax. Using the watch as a conduit into his psyche, I willed my mind to focus on his past pain and quickly entered the energy of his body. It was strong—he was in excellent physical shape for his age. I always began my readings by establishing authenticity. Usually, this meant telling the client about old or new injuries they had, so they would feel confident that I really did know what I was doing. So now I mentally began searching his muscular body for pains or scars.

Often, my body feels and experiences my client's discomfort. Whether the distress happened yesterday or twenty years ago, it will feel the same to me. At other times, injuries are mental images I see in my mind. When my mind sought and found the jagged scar on his right ankle, I moaned softly in pain.

Staring at me intently with light blue eyes the Englishman replied, "Yes, you are correct. I do have those scars."

Now it was time for his questions. Without hesitation or emotion he asked, "How close is death? Is it nearby?"

His question startled me—usually the first question is some variation of "When will I fall in love?" Intuitively, I knew he asked this question not out of curiosity, but necessity. I normally would not answer a question about an individual's death—despite the path my career has taken, or perhaps because of it, I do not like to dwell on the negative. But this felt different, urgent. I began my search for his death.

I didn't find his death, but what I did find was disturbing. I shook my head as I answered, "No I don't see your death in the immediate future. But I do see guns around you, foreign countries, and death . . . around others."

At that point he took control of the reading. Almost brutally, he began interrogating me about the movements of various people and the success of a forthcoming "business trip" out of the country. He was very concerned about whom he could trust, and gave me the initials of several business associates.

Stewart was definitely not an average client or an average person. Inside his mind, I was seized by an intensity and sense of discipline I have never experienced before or since. It was scary, but it was also exciting, in the way that an adrenaline rush is exciting, or perhaps a free fall from thousands of feet in the air. I fought to go beyond his turbulent mind and to keep hold of myself in the process. I held on to my concentration and focused, answering his rapid-fire questions for over an hour.

When the reading finally ended, I felt a surge of relief.

This was the first of many encounters over several years that I had with Stewart. He came to see me every two or three months. First he would give me feedback on my predictions from our last appointment—yes, this happened, just as you said—and then he had new questions. He always wanted information about his business trips, his safety, and his associates. He told me he owned an international construction company and traveled all over the world to supervise his company's projects.

We had many sessions before he ever asked me a question about love. Of course, being Stewart, he had separate questions concerning his wife and his mistress! Shortly after, both his wife and his mistress came to me for readings—separately, of course.

One day, Stewart called, but he didn't want an appointment. He wanted me to visit him in the hospital. As always, he sounded mysteriously urgent.

He was a good client, so I went. At the hospital I found him sitting on the edge of his bed, dressed in very expensive pajamas and robe and flirting with a young nurse. He greeted me warmly, and graciously introduced me to the perky young woman. After she left, I asked him why he was in the hospital "What's wrong?" I asked. "You look great."

His light blue eyes lost their flirtatious light and became glacially cold. The sterile white room grew even colder as he answered, "It's my stomach; I have a growth."

Intuitively I knew he was lying. But why? I couldn't imagine. Then, taking control of the conversation as usual, he abruptly changed the subject. He told me about his mistress—during one of our sessions, I had told him I saw her breaking up with him in the future. He went on and on. I nodded occasionally during his monologue, until finally the young nurse returned. My visit was cut short by hospital regulations.

What did he want from me? It seemed as if he had no one else to talk to. An indescribable feeling of foreboding overwhelmed me as I left his room and walked down the corridor of the busy hospital. Something was very wrong.

Three days later, Stewart called again. It was late at night and I was reading in bed. He told me he was out of the hospital. He was slurring his words, and I could barely understand him. He was drunk! I was aghast; I had never seen him without his shield of absolutely controlled composure.

"Why are you calling me at this hour?" I asked. I was annoyed and troubled. Incredibly, Stewart said he needed to read me his poetry. Why I did not hang up at that point, I don't know. Instead, I listened intently as he read me his poems about the Prince of Darkness and his poems about death. When he finished reading the poems, he began to tell me about his life and work. It was filled with violence and destruction, as I knew from the psychic readings. But I didn't know the details he was telling me now.

Stewart was an orphan, and his early life had been hard. When he was a teenager, he told me, he had been in a war and killed several soldiers. Surprisingly, he found that killing came naturally to him—it didn't bother him one bit. Soon after, he was recruited by the government and trained as a hired killer, an assassin, a career he had followed for the past two decades. He confessed that he had been seeking me out before each assignment to ask me carefully encoded questions about his targets and his chances of success. For the past few years, I had been an unwitting accomplice to murder.

I felt sick. Why was he telling me all this now? He was still babbling on about the Prince of Darkness, but I stopped listening to his words and tried to remember the images that had raced across my mind's eye during our sessions. But all I could remember was the feeling of dark turbulence. As often happens—and the reason I now keep a tape of every session—the information I had obtained for him had dissipated. I could not find any hard memories at all.

Now I really thought I was going to throw up. My head was throbbing and my heart was beating like crazy. I was panicked and looking wildly around the room. Worse, I felt violated on the deepest level of my being. This psychotic British assassin had taken advantage of my psychic mind.

But Stewart was oblivious to my turmoil—he was still rambling and raging on in his drunken monologue of death and destruction. He wasn't sleeping, he said. And when he did he had terrible nightmares. So he was drinking to kill the pain and talking his way through the dark night hours. It was obvious to me that his fear of his own death was all consuming. But I didn't want it to consume me!

Finally, I was able to break my own silence and force my words through his own barrage. "Stewart," I said in a loud, firm voice. "I do not want to listen to any more of your confessions. Goodnight." I placed the receiver into its cradle and unplugged the phone from the wall.

I wondered if I would sleep that night. So far, my chances didn't look good. I let out a long, slow breath—I must have been holding my breath for an hour—and managed to light a cigarette. I could feel the nicotine doing its work, calming me down ever so slightly. As I exhaled, I noticed the smooth cloud of smoke was disturbed by the uncontrollable shaking of my hand. I leaned back on my pillows and tried to make some sense out of what I had just heard.

Stewart wasn't visiting construction sites; he was flying around the world killing people. He had clearly been in a highly volatile, maximum-stress job for years and years, and now he was finally breaking down. Perhaps that had been the cause for his hospital stay. He was unloading all of his pent-up fears and demons.

That was the last time I talked to Stewart, and I never saw him again. Some months later, however, I was startled to read in the newspaper that he had been arrested in Egypt, with three other men, in an attempt to assassinate an important Libyan.

Perhaps, I thought to myself, you should have had a reading first.

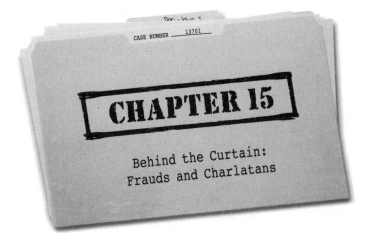

CHAPTER 15

Behind the Curtain:
Frauds and Charlatans

"How do you do your predictions?" I asked in my best innocent manner.

"I usually pick a place that's pretty far away, like Alaska, or I choose a subject most people won't read about. I try to say all the things I predict will happen in a year or two. By then they will have forgotten what I said."

I was aghast. He wasn't even lying to me. He was telling me how he faked his predictions. This is a terrible, terrible man, *I thought.* Does he think I'm a charlatan, too? *But I just kept smiling sweetly.*

A lot of people expect psychics to hit a home run out of the park every time. And when that doesn't happen, they're disappointed. Sometimes, they get suspicious. But even Hall of Famers have off days. I occasionally bat a thousand—as when I predicted the attempted assassination on President Reagan, or that another child in the Atlanta Child Murder case would be found on Easter Sunday. But these cases stand out because they are unusual. In fact, it's the people who score a hit *every time* you really need to watch out for.

In my work, I'm a bit like a radio receiver—the information waves are out there, and I need to tune in to the correct channel. When there's "interference"—if I am not feeling well, if there's a lot of hostility in the room, if many people came in contact with the object I am using to tune in to the person—this can get in the way. When I do private readings, with the person right there in the room with me, I have the best chance of establishing a clear connection. Even then, I'd say I'm about 80 percent successful. With police cases—trying to tune in over the phone to people who are dead or missing or both—I consider 70 percent accuracy a good day.

No one is right 100 percent of the time. You can bet that anyone who claims that kind of record is a fraud—and you'd win that bet.

Frauds exist in all professions—teaching, medicine, art, everywhere. But they seem to flourish in mine. Some folks think we're *all* frauds; others believe we're the devil's creation. Still others have blind faith and call us saints and miracle workers. Remember the Wizard of Oz? It turned out that he wasn't a real wizard at all, just a little man with a microphone hiding behind a curtain. A fraud. Real psychics aren't frauds or a saints, but just regular people who are using another part of their mind—like you, potentially, and like me.

Still, I think that everyone should have some skepticism. Some people do claim to be psychic when the only talent they have is the ability to dupe believing people out of their money. Even I—a born skeptic who should know better—was fooled early in my career. But not for long.

———◆·■·◆———

"What's a Psychic Fair?" I asked the reverend of the local spiritualist church in Orlando. She had asked me to do some readings for it, and I was mystified. I was brand-new at this psychic stuff, and I'd never heard of such a thing.

"It's a fair that the public comes to for mini-readings by psychics, astrologers, palmists, and card-readers," she said. I have to admit, I was slightly disappointed. I had been having fun picturing psychics dressed as clowns, operating Ferris wheels, and participating in pie-eating contests. Oh well, this would probably be better.

She explained that they were sponsoring an "International Psychic Fair" and had invited well-known psychics from all over the United States. They had even invited Cybil Leek, who was then a famous witch who had written a number of books. "The press is giving us plenty of coverage and we feel it's going to be a great success."

It sounded pretty interesting to me—I was still exploring—but a dark cloud soon began to form. A few self-righteous individuals, claiming to be Christians, picketed the mall. No way were they going to let a witch do her thing in their shopping center. The mall management caved in to their pressure, so I never did get to go to that fair. But one psychic had arrived early—and, like *The Man Who Came to Dinner*, he never left. He called himself Dr. Gills.[1] A press conference had been scheduled at the hotel where he was staying, and I wasn't going to miss him.

I arrived early, and was introduced to Dr. Gills—a small man with a beard. I wondered what kind of doctor he was. He was soon surrounded by reporters, and seemed to be giving one reporter a psychic reading. Naturally, I decided to eavesdrop:

"You have athlete's foot," Dr. Gills proclaimed.

"No," replied the reporter, shaking his head.

"Your sister is younger than you," he intoned.

"I don't have a sister," said the reporter.

"You have problems with your car," said Dr. Gills.

"Nope, it's brand-new and runs like a charm."

Oh dear, I thought, *the poor man must not be able to pick up well with all these people around. I'll send him some positive energy. Maybe that will help.*

Just then, Dr. Gills announced to the group of reporters, "When the camera crew arrives, I will demonstrate my abilities by shattering a glass with just the power of my mind."

Wow, I thought. *I can't wait to see that.* That was one Ellen and I had tried, but our glassware was still intact.

Soon the cameras were in place and he stood before them. On the table in front of him was a single glass. He picked it up, and barely got his hand into the air before it shattered into a million pieces. The small audience and large group of reporters applauded.

Dr. Gills bowed graciously, then announced that he was exhausted and needed to rest. Before he left, he invited us all to his performance in the hotel's nightclub that evening. I had never met another psychic who worked in a lounge, and I was curious. Maybe I could learn something.

I could hardly wait! I didn't want to go alone, so I called my favorite skeptic, Ellen. I knew she'd keep me from floating away with excitement.

We arrived early and got good seats near the stage. It was relaxing to be in the audience for a change, and I settled back to enjoy the show. A spotlight was aimed at a podium on the dance floor in front of the bandstand, and as the house lights dimmed, Dr. Gills walked confidently to the podium. I had to admit, he looked kind of seedy. His beard was neatly trimmed, but he was wearing a cheap black suit and his shoes looked scruffy.

He smiled, welcomed us, and passed out pieces of paper to the audience. Then he told us to write our names, addresses, and phone numbers in the designated spaces. In a large blank space, we were to write our question.

Ellen was already nudging me and whispering, "He's about as much a doctor as I am. He's a phony!"

"Hush!" I righteously defended the man and my profession. "Give him a chance." I wondered if people at the nightclub thought I was a phony too. It was not a pleasant thought.

Dr. Gills pointed to a woman in the audience and asked for a number between one and ten. "Seven!" she shouted out. Then he pointed to a young couple and asked them for a number. "Three," they said, after conferring. Two women in the front row gave him the number five, and he was ready to amaze us. "Look!" he said, and pulled from his pocket a piece of paper with all three numbers written on it. "I wrote these numbers down before I came down to the lounge—using clairvoyant telepathy," he added mysteriously. The audience—Ellen excluded—was clearly awed.

Next he held up two silver dollars and then placed them and a black blindfold on the podium. He produced some tape, which he cut up into specific lengths. This was a very labor-intensive activity, I thought to myself. Then he surprised me by asking me—by name—to join him on stage.

"Miss Renier," he said with a flourish, "I am going to place these silver dollars on my eyes and tape them into place." When he had done so, he said, "Please tie the blindfold over my eyes." As I did, he cried out that it was too tight, and put his hands to his face to loosen it.

He thanked me and I went back to my seat. Then he picked up one of the pieces of paper he had asked the audience members to full out, and placed it on his forehead. With a great show of concentration, he said slowly, "This is from Nancy Schultz. She lives . . . let me see . . . she lives at 737 Oak Street. Her telephone number is 783-6209. And your question is, 'Will I get married this year?' Is that correct, Nancy?" Loud applause followed Nancy's astonished confirmation.

How could he get those names and numbers? My abilities must be really bad, I thought. I couldn't get names and phone numbers psychically. After he did this trick a few more times, I thought, *Wait a minute. He didn't answer their questions; he just repeated them.* But I wasn't going to share my doubts with Ellen, who just kept repeating, "He's a fraud, he a fraud."

"No he isn't!" I insisted. "You don't believe in anything."

After his performance, I went up to the stage and gushed. I left thinking how much I had to learn: numbers, names, questions. I left the smoke-filled lounge with Ellen, who was shaking her head in disgust.

———————————•◆•———————————

A few nights later, my phone rang, waking me out of a deep sleep. It was the singer at the club, my old friend Mona. She was really upset. I told her to calm down and tell me what was wrong.

"He's a fraud!" she said.

"Who's a fraud?"

"The psychic who's performing at the nightclub, Dr. Gills."

"How do you know? Are you sure?"

"Yes. Every night while I'm waiting to go on, I watch him. I've seen him use his tricks."

"Tell me everything," I said, lighting a cigarette and settling in for a long night.

"Well," she said, "you know when he asks the audience for numbers, then produces a piece of paper with all the numbers on it and says he got them using telepathy?"

"Yes."

"He actually has a small piece of pencil lead stuck in the bottom of his ring, and he's writing down the numbers as the people in the audience call them out." *Damn*, I thought. *Ellen was right.* In my heart, I'd known it all along. But I had wanted him to be the real deal.

"Okay," I replied bravely, "but what about all the names and addresses he sees?"

"He cheats," Mona said flatly. "He reads them from below the blindfold. You know how he goes 'ouch' and says it's too tight? Well, when he adjusts the blindfold, he's actually flipping up the coins on his eyes so he can see the paper. The paper he holds to his head and 'reads' isn't the paper he's looking at."

Well, I felt like a complete fool, but I wondered why Mona was so upset.

"He knew I had a sore throat tonight—a singer's worst enemy. So he gave me a bottle of medicine and said it would fix me right up. I was so worried about my throat that I just swallowed the four tablespoons he recommended before I read the label. Noreen! It says to rub the stuff on your open sore or injured body. It's for external use! What's going to happen to my throat?"

"Relax, Mona. Be quite and give me a minute." I concentrated on Mona for a few minutes, trying to see if she was really in trouble. Finally, I said, "I don't feel what's in that bottle will help you, but it's not going to hurt you either. Just do whatever you usually do for a sore throat and go to bed. You'll be fine tomorrow night."

"Thanks, Noreen," said Mona. "I'm sorry I woke you up. Get some sleep."

But I couldn't sleep. Dr. Gills was a fraud—a magician pretending to be a psychic. Magic was so beautiful all by itself, why did he have to pretend to be something else? And how did he break that glass? (Months later, I learned the trick. The glass he used was specially made to break easily. Dr. Gills wore a small vibrator on his body that connected to his arm with a wire. You couldn't see it under his loose jacket, but when it came in contact with the glass, the vibration shattered it.)

I was furious. That afternoon, I raced to the spiritualist church to tell them all about it. But Dr. Gills was a good con. Like all good cons, his natural charisma and charm seemed to blind people to the fact that he was manipulating them. I've learned over the years that people will believe what they want to believe, and the people in this church had a lot invested in believing Dr. Gills. He had convinced the church's board of directors that he was a real psychic. On top of that, the wife of one of the board members had cancer, and he had promised to cure it. I felt terrible.

But they wouldn't listen to me. In fact, they thought I was jealous. They told me that the reverend was leaving, and they had offered Dr. Gills the position. They weren't going to change their minds; he was going to be their new minister.

I could accept my own naiveté, and I was willing to learn from my mistakes. But these people had been around psychics for years. How could they believe him? I was feeling pretty cynical and discouraged about the whole thing.

Just then, he walked into the church and asked for a ride to a radio show he was scheduled to appear on. Before anyone else could say a word, I volunteered. "No problem," I said sweetly. "I'd love to give you a ride." The church secretary, who'd been listening to my tirade, just rolled her eyes at me.

On the way, he gave me some money and asked me to run into the store to get him a pack of cigarettes. If I wanted to leave my purse in the car, he said, he'd keep in eye on it. Like a good girl, I trotted into the store. When I got back, he was making notes for his predictions that he planned to give on the air.

"How do you do your predictions?" I asked in my best inno-cent manner.

"I usually pick a place that's pretty far away, like Alaska, or I choose a subject most people won't read about. I try to say all the things I predict will happen in a year or two. By then they will have forgotten what I said."

I was aghast. He wasn't even lying to me. He was telling me how he faked his predictions. *This is a terrible, terrible man,* I thought. *Does he think I'm a charlatan, too?* But I just kept smiling sweetly.

I waited while he did the radio show and then I dropped him off at the cottage connected to the church. He invited me in for a cup of coffee. As he was busy heating water in the kitchen, I casu-ally strolled around the rooms and saw his magician's robes hang-ing in his closet. There was not one ounce of doubt left as to what he was or what I had to do. I drank my coffee and left, telling him that I'd be at the church tonight. "I wouldn't miss your perform-ance for the world," I said.

<hr/>

That evening, sitting with my girlfriend Suzie in the last row of the church, I watched Dr. Gills intently. But he wasn't doing his usual act. Instead, he told an assortment of folksy stories and jokes. He didn't talk about psychic phenomena until the very end, when he suddenly called out my name.

"Noreen, where are you sitting? Ah yes, I see you back there." *What the hell is he up to now?* I wondered.

"You drove me around town today," he said. "Did we discuss at any time your house being robbed?"

Suzie, who knew all about the burglary, screamed. Everyone turned. They thought it was me screaming. I poked her hard and she screamed again.

Smiling smugly, Dr. Gills continued. "Yes," he said, "I see a burglary. They took a carved ivory chess set, a Nikon camera, two tape recorders . . ." he continued reeling off the list of items I had reported to the police. I was really starting to hate that man.

Frantically, I rummaged through my purse, looking for my copy of the police report. It was gone! He had taken it when I left my purse in the car. He had memorized the list, exactly as it was on the police report. He hadn't even bothered to put it back. Did he think I was a complete idiot?

He asked for feedback, so I gave it to him. "Yes," I said, "those items were stolen." He was so happy with my answer that he started to make things up.

"You won't get your possessions back," he said. "The man that stole them is in Mexico." I thought I would get sick listening to him drone on and on.

What he didn't know was that it was an old police report. I knew who had taken my possessions—in fact, I had already gotten them back. But I said nothing—these people thought he was a god. They would never believe me.

"Tomorrow night," he was saying, "I want you on the stage with me. I want you to demonstrate your abilities." I just glared at him. I had no intention of joining him in his act. He left the stage practically bouncing with his success, and I went home more determined than ever to show everyone who he really was.

The church secretary befriended me. Apparently, she had already been suspicious of Dr. Gills. Together, we gathered all the information we could find about him, and she took it to a friend of hers in law enforcement. When he ran Dr. Gills' name through their computers, he found that Dr. Gills was wanted in several states for fraud, for practicing medicine without a license, and for being responsible for one death. I thought of Mona's close call, and shivered.

The secretary went to the church officials with the information, but one of them tipped Gills off. He fled before an arrest could be made. We never saw him again.

After that experience, I became more suspicious of people who claimed to be psychics. In a way, it made me feel more alone.

Dr. Gills was the first charlatan I ever met, but he wasn't the last. Wherever there is a lack of knowledge, be it ignorance or innocence, it's easy to trick and deceive. That's why one of my passions is to educate people about psychic phenomena. Early on, I educated myself through reading books and talking to people in the field, and I'm still learning.

Sometimes, like the people in the spiritualist church, we believe because we *want* to believe. We want good luck, money, a curse removed. We hope that if we send Madame Anna or Sister Mary or Reverend Bill $500 through the mail, all of our problems will disappear. A good dose of *healthy* skepticism—which really means keeping an open mind to all possibilities, including the possibility that someone is trying to pull the wool over your eyes—is never a bad thing. The next time you are tempted to give all your worldly goods to a charismatic holy man, or to believe predictions about your future that seem too good to be true, remember: No one can solve your problems or guarantee love will enter your life.

No one, that is, except you.

CHAPTER 16

A Doomed Flight:
A Missing Plane, A Brother Lost

"It's your brother . . . now he's walking away . . . he's survived the crash," I yelled, as I continued to watch him. After he took a few steps, he lunged forward. His leg buckled under him and he sank to a sitting position. "His leg is hurt . . . it's broken." As I felt Jessica's increasing excitement, my logical mind broke through my consciousness and I screamed, "No! He couldn't have. There is no way he could have survived that crash."

<hr />

January 28, 1984. A small chartered plane carrying four passengers had mysteriously vanished from the sky somewhere over rural Massachusetts or New Hampshire. The Civil Air Patrol and the U.S. Air Force had searched diligently for ten bone-chilling winter days before giving up the grueling hunt. They had a limited budget, and they'd come to the end of what they could do. But Jessica Herbert, the sister of one of the missing passengers, didn't want the search to end. When she asked an official from the Civil Air

Patrol what he would need to start up the search again, he replied, "The location." In February, she called me for help.

———————·—•—·———————

"Good morning, Ms. Renier. My name is Jessica Herbert. I need your help." The woman on the other end of the line was clearly upset, and she wasted no time in getting to the point. "My brother has been lost in a plane wreck and they can't find him. It's been days. You've got to help me. I'm at my wit's end. I don't know what to do."

A plane wreck? Why was she calling me? Yes, I had located people who were missing. But an airplane? I wouldn't know where to begin. She sounded worried, and I didn't want to waste her time, so I explained that I had never been asked to find an airplane. "I honestly don't believe I can help you," I said. "I don't find things, I describe murderers. I work with the police on unsolved homicides.

"Usually, I touch something the victims were wearing when they were killed," I told the distraught woman. "I just can't do this in your case." But she was not going to let me turn her down.

"Ms. Renier," she pleaded, "you have been highly recommended by my ex-husband, Mark Babyak, an FBI agent. You were also validated by Special Agent Ressler," she added.

That stopped me. What could I say? Robert always backed me up, especially in the face of skeptics, and recommended my services to the police. Now it looked like I had impressed at least two people at the Federal Bureau of Investigation, and I was flattered. But I still didn't think I could help this woman find a missing plane.

"I'm so sorry your brother is missing," I said more firmly, waving my cigarette in the air for emphasis. Too bad she couldn't see it. "I understand your urgency, but I don't normally find airplanes." I started repeating myself. Maybe she just didn't hear me the first time. "I work on homicides. Usually, I touch something that was on the victim when he or she was killed. We can't do that with your brother. He's missing, the airplane is missing. I don't think I can . . ."

"Please! You're my last hope. Don't you understand?" I could hear the woman's desperation, and my heart went out to her. "They are all giving up trying to find him. The officials have stopped searching. I must find my brother. He's eats health food and he's into physical fitness—he's in great physical shape. He played professional hockey. *He could still be alive.* Please try. He's my only brother."

I gave up. "Okay," I agreed reluctantly. This was beyond my scope, I knew, but I just could not say no. "Can you drive out to see me tomorrow? And bring me something your brother touched or used a great deal before he disappeared."

It was about a two-hour drive from where she lived in Washington, D.C., to my rural home in Virginia. I gave her directions and hung up.

As I stubbed out my cigarette, I thought, *What the hell have I done now?*

Late the following afternoon, as the sun was lazily sliding down toward the Blue Ridge Mountains, I greeted Jessica Herbert at the door. She was beautiful—beauty-queen beautiful—with a perfect oval face and warm, intelligent brown eyes that smiled as she introduced herself. She was expensively dressed in a cream silk blouse and dark slacks with her jacket draped over her arm. The outfit looked good on her model-thin figure. She was clearly exhausted, and not just from the long drive down. Her brother's disappearance had grabbed her and wouldn't let go.

I led Jessica down the entry hall to my combination library and office, and she sank gracefully into one of theater chairs. I told her that I made no promises or guarantees, and it would be up to her to recognize and follow up on any clues I produced. As I explained how I worked, I slipped an audiotape into my recorder, which sat next to my ashtray on my old red trunk. She gazed around at the bookshelves that lined the walls, crammed with books about metaphysics and psychic phenomena. The smoke from a stick of night jasmine incense curled upward in circles, filling the room with one of my favorite scents.

Jessica handed me an expensive billfold that had belonged to her brother, and began to tell me about him. I interrupted, reminding her that I preferred not to know any details or personal background. "Strange as it may seem, the less you tell me the more I will be capable of telling you."

I spoke slowly and soothingly and gave her my entire attention. The room was still. In a private blessing, I envisioned a light-like energy moving from me to her, removing the hysterical edge I felt within her.

I pushed the record button on the tape recorder and leaned back in my chair, lightly stroking the wallet in my hand. I explained what I was doing. "I'm going to try to describe your brother to see if I'm tuning in to him. Then I will ask you to confirm or deny my impressions."

"All right," answered Jessica, "I understand." She seemed surprised at the authoritative tone my voice had suddenly assumed.

Surrendering to the soothing jasmine scent, I closed my eyes. Breathing deeply and exhaling slowly, I began my usual warm-up period, trying to see what her brother looked like. I do this for two reasons. First, to make sure I am correctly tuning into the target and checking to see if my psychic ability is working. Second, it gives my clients confidence in me as a psychic. If this part is at least 75 percent successful, I continue. If not, I call it a day and stop.

I sat quietly for a time before speaking.

"Okay," I began, "I want to see this young man. I want to see Jessica's brother. Let me see . . . yes, I see a young man. His hair is medium length, light brown. He is not quite six feet tall. He's good-looking. I see some sort of space in his front teeth . . . no, I'm wrong, something happened to that space. He must be very nervous because I can see he bites his nails . . ."

I paused for a moment; my eyes opened. "Am I there or not?" I asked Jessica.

"Why, yes. That was very good," Jessica smiled in amazement.

"Could you give me specifics? What did I say that was right?"

"Well, all of it. You got his hair and his size right, and the space in the teeth. He had a large space in his front teeth, but one year earlier he had gotten braces fitted, and the space closed, and it was also right that he bit his nails. He just started doing that recently."

Satisfied, I closed my eyes again and focused my attention on the other three people in the small plane. I described the two men sitting in the front seats, and the pretty young woman who sat in the back of the small plane who was sitting with Jessica's brother. Their faces entered my mind so easily that I felt confident I was connected. At the time, she could not confirm my information because she had never met the other passengers. It turned out later, however, that my descriptions were accurate.

Jessica was impatient. She wanted me to see the airplane. "Where is it? Where is the plane?"

The clock on the mantel ticked loudly in the stillness of the old farmhouse. I was deep inside the world that had opened to me through her brother's wallet, calmly abiding in a place outside of time and space. Reaching into the unknown, I began searching for the airplane.

I saw the downed plane immediately. In fact, I found myself almost on top of it. I was on the side of a hill, but all I could see around me were trees. I felt walled in by them, and I knew no one could see me. This was no help. Suddenly, I remembered the advice of my early mentor, Dr. David Jones. He once told me that if a particular image was not clear, I should try changing vantage points.

I had no one here to direct me, so I had to direct myself. This was turning out to be quite an experience. Seeking a new angle, I asked my mind to go higher. Now I was above the trees. I had a panoramic view! In an instant, my perception changed and *I was the plane*. It was an impossible, exhilarating feeling.

The night was black, and I was circling a small, dark, deserted airstrip. Without warning, beams of lights flooded the sky, disorienting the pilot.

As the plane, I turned sharply left, veering toward towering hills. The area looked primitive, undeveloped. I caught glimpses of rocks below, and sensed quicksand and big gorges underneath me.

I was flying very low, too low. Suddenly, I felt a pulling sensation and made a sharp turn toward the right, but it was too late. A down draft was sucking me into the hills. As I plummeted out of control, trees rushed to greet me. I was swallowed and concealed by their thick foliage.

The next moment numbers began to enter my mind, and I knew I was no longer the plane. I saw two sets of numbers. Breathlessly, I repeated them to my client. I could feel they were important.

Now letters came into my head. "I see three letters." I said. "G, T, and O . . . they are significant . . . they could be initials of towns . . . they definitely have something to do with the location of the missing airplane."

Unexpectedly, the skyline of a large city filled my mind's eye. I told Jessica the approximate number of miles the plane would be from "the big city."

The images changed again. I was back in the sky, hovering over the crash site, but I was no longer the plane. Now I was pure consciousness. I could not see the plane because of the thickness of the trees. So I began searching for something I could describe to my client. As I flew over the area, a dirt road came into focus, and I followed the thin yellow thread of a winding road down the mountainside. I told Jessica, "There is an old dirt road near the crash site, and at the bottom of it . . . is an old-fashioned house. The house has been turned into a gas station . . . it's rickety . . . I see old rusting sign . . . it looks like a Texaco sign."

An old woman's face came into my mind. Encouragingly, she smiled a toothless grin and then vanished. I said, "There's an old woman who runs the gas station. She doesn't have any teeth. She sells a lot of junk."

I told Jessica how confused I was about the old woman. It felt as if she was there and not there at the same time. Later, we learned the toothless old lady had died the year before.

My body jerked suddenly, startled by the sound of barking dogs. "She has lots of hunting dogs, I can hear them."

I opened my eyes, exhausted. I looked at Jessica as I dragged deeply on my cigarette. She gazed at me, her dark brown eyes full of hope. Her unspoken enthusiasm recharged my psychic energy, and I continued.

"When you reach the gas station, take the dirt road up the mountain. You don't need to go all the way to the top. The plane will be found to the right of the road. It didn't explode."

I pressed the thin billfold against my forehead, slowly exhaling a cloud of smoke. I was still hovering over the scene, an uninvolved observer. I looked calmly at the two dead men in the front seat of the crashed plane. Their necks were broken.

Then my attention focused on a well-built young man in the back seat. Even though my eyes were closed, I could feel Jessica growing more intent. I saw the young man lifting something with great effort and carrying it out of the mangled plane. After a few steps he placed it gently on some dark flat rocks, under a tree.

"It's your brother . . . now he's walking away . . . he's survived the crash," I yelled, as I continued to watch him. After he took a few steps, he lunged forward. His leg buckled under him and he sank to a sitting position. "His leg is hurt . . . it's broken." As I felt Jessica's increasing excitement, my logical mind broke through my consciousness and I screamed, "No! He couldn't have. There is no way he could have survived that crash."

I was afraid Jessica's desire to find her brother alive had affected the images I was receiving. Maybe I was reading *her* mind, seeing what *she* wanted me to see.

Opening my eyes, I was almost yelling at her. "It's you, you want me to see him alive! I'm afraid I'm telling you what you want to hear. I can't do any more. I have to stop. I'm exhausted."

Jessica, showing more hope than when she arrived, reassured me. "It's okay . . . it's all right, Noreen. Go rest." Gratefully, I relaxed a bit and told her that the information I had given her was just visions. Everything I saw would fall into place in the end, but it would be up to her to figure out how to put it together.

"I'll take this new information back to the officials in charge," Jessica said, gathering her belongings. "Hopefully, we'll search again." She thanked me, paid me, and took the audiotape. After she left, I walked slowly upstairs to bed and fell into a deep sleep.

Two days later, Jessica called me. They had found the plane! My clues had been accurate. Sadly, her brother and the other occupants of the plane were dead, just as I had seen them.

With deep emotion, she told me what had taken place. She and Mark had taken my information to the head investigator of the Civil Air Patrol in the area—the crash had already been narrowed down to a rugged area in western Massachusetts—who was pretty skeptical. Information from a psychic did not impress him, and they had called off the search two days ago. But when he heard about the abandoned Texaco station and the old woman, he got a lot more interested. In fact, there *was* an old combination gas station–dry goods store nearby, with the rusting metal sign hanging in front. The woman who had owned it had died about a year ago—which jibed with my feeling that she was both there and not there—and the place was abandoned now. So much of my information was accurate that he felt he couldn't ignore it. In fact, the numbers I had given Jessica turned out to be longitude and latitude of the downed plane. And the letters? They were the initial letters of the names of two towns, Gardner and Templeton, whose outskirts connected in the area marked by the longitude and latitude. The "O" turned out to be the first letter of the name of the river that runs right next to the crash site.

Now everyone was interested again, and the search resumed.

Jessica, Mark Babyak, and off-duty FBI agent Jim Crouse rented a small plane and flew from Virginia to Massachusetts to the general area where it was believed the plane had crashed—near a town called Gardner. They followed directions I had provided when I was the plane—landmarks, speed, sharp turns, longitude and latitude, and they saw what I had described. But the weather worsened, and they had to return to the airport.

Agent Babyak decided to go after the ground crews, and he and a friend got into a car and began the search. Meanwhile, Jessica and the FBI pilot returned to the sky, now heavy with storm clouds. Babyak and his friend had a difficult time tracking the plane from the road because they were unfamiliar with the area. But just before they reached the abandoned gas station, they encountered the dogs, which barked so much they decided not to get out of their car.

Soon, the clouds erupted into a snowstorm. Despite the weather, the searchers persisted for several hours, but eventually the Civil Patrol canceled the search for that day. They would resume when the weather improved. It was agonizing to be so near, yet not near enough.

But this was not the end of the story. Residents of the area couldn't help notice the planes that had been circling overhead, and the following day, a man and his daughter who lived in nearby Templeton decided to take up the search. Carl F. Wilber, forty, and his eighteen-year-old daughter, Cheryl, chose an appropriate vehicle for the winter search: a snowmobile, which allowed them to explore the woods unhindered. Following some deer tracks, they soon found the crashed plane. Cheryl actually tripped over the body of Arthur Herbert.

The crash site was exactly the way I had described it. Thickly forested and rocky, with quicksand and big gorges. The hill the plane had crashed into had created a strong downdraft that had likely sucked down the low-flying plane—just as I had felt as I plummeted out of control in my vision.

When the authorities arrived, they found the plane intact. All occupants were dead. The two men in the front seat had been crushed by the impact, their necks broken. Sitting on some flat rocks under a nearby tree, as if someone had placed her there, they found the headless body of a young woman. They found the body of Jessica's brother a few yards away, sitting on the side of a hill, his leg broken, a torn piece of his sweatshirt hanging from a tree branch above him. It was clear to everyone that he had been alive when he left the plane.

The following are excerpts from a telephone deposition by Jessica Herbert; she testified on August 28, 1986.

Q. Did you have a brother who was involved unfortunately in an airplane crash sometime back?

A. Yes . . . we'd been working with the Civil Air Patrol
and the air force searching for the whereabouts of
the plane in January of 1984. January and February
I should say. After approximately ten days of
extensive searching, the air force made a decision
to cease any further operations mainly for mone-
tary reasons as they have fixed budgets . . . and I
spoke with a captain in Illinois who was in charge
of this particular case, and asked him what I might
do to have them continue the search and he said
they would need much more information and I said
what type of information and he said well, basically, more specific . . . the location of the plane.

Q. Could I ask you whether or not at that time you
were married to a person connected with the FBI?

A. Yes, Mark Babyak.

Q. Did you contact Noreen Renier then?

A. Yes, I did. She first described my brother. She had
no information there, nothing written in the
papers about the crash, up here anyway and even in
. . . I should say Washington . . . there had been
absolutely no information anywhere about my
brother, no description of any kind, so she proceeded to describe him. . . . Then she proceeded to
describe the four people in the plane which (after
the session) I had gotten more information about
the woman and then two other men besides my
brother . . . and described them incredibly accurately . . . she described the area as being almost
primitive with gorges, quicksand, and all this. Well,
that in fact, I didn't even know. This is the western
part of Massachusetts and it is like that, but I had

no knowledge of that and I lived all my life in Massachusetts except for five years in D.C. . . . And she said that in the area where the crash occurred that there was an old woman . . . lived in a house but it had been a gas station . . . vision of general store type of thing. It had a Texaco sign, rusting out in front of it. She described a lot of stone fences, foundation . . . and she mentioned dogs. Dogs barking everywhere in the area. . . . She also described where the plane went down . . . it was a junction of three letters and she gave me those letters . . . she kinda rambled and she said, "It'll be 175 miles from the big city. . . ."

Q. Jessica, I'm sorry but I'm going to have to ask you if you ever came to any conclusion about what the large city was?

A. Oh, yes. New York. Because that was the only large city from Gardner that happened to be the exact miles she gave me.

Q. Now, one last question about that. Do you recall today whether it was 175 or are you using that as . . . ?

A. I'm just using that. I don't remember, but whatever number she gave me was the exact as the crow flies miles from Gardner to New York City . . . she felt it was very, very close to the airport, so were . . . and she also described how the plane had taken off, how it had been flying over the airport and had accelerated and made a sharp left and a right, so that's what we did, we took off, made a sharp left, a sharp right, and she'd given us a certain number of seconds before the crash, so we were trying . . . you know, basically to replay this crashing, getting to this area, the weather got worse and we had to come in. The one other piece of information was at the same time we were flying, my husband's cousins were in a car sitting from where we were, trying to drive to that area, and they got to more or less a dead-end street which abutted a forest area. They couldn't go any further and they tried to get out of the car and when they did, there were all these dogs coming from almost nowhere, barking and so forth and they couldn't get out of the car.

Q. Had she told you that there would be . . . ?

A. She had told me that in conjunction with this woman, old cabin. . . . That existed also in the area, that's what the colonel of the Civil Air Patrol . . . why he got very interested in putting some of the other clues together. . . . The colonel of the Civil Air Patrol was talking to a couple of state troopers and explaining that a psychic had given some information that might be helpful to the case and they were very skeptical and so forth and then he divulged some of the information including the old woman, the cabin, the gas pumps, and so forth and all of a sudden their whole attitude changed because there was in fact an old woman who had this cabin with a dry goods store–gas station type of thing and there was a rusting, old type of sign hanging outside. She had died about a year previously, which went back to what Noreen had said about this old woman being there, but she wasn't.

Q. Let me ask you this question. Was the plane found where she had described it?

A. Yes.

Q. Was it . . . how precise was it in terms of being where she had described it?

A. Well, it was in an area exactly the way she had described it. . . .

CHAPTER 17

Murder Times Two: Jake and Dora Cohn

"He's got something in his hand. I think I dropped the phone. I might even stand up. No . . . stay down. Stay down. He comes fast. I'm on the phone. I hear . . . I keep hearing two voices at the same time.

"I know this person. I know this person. Common name. The gun is there. He looks mad. He's upset. He's talking emotional. He looks taller. He's up there. He's up there. He's up there."

"Now, what, Dora?"

"'Jake!' I yell, 'Jake!' He shoots me." I suddenly became quiet and relaxed. In a whisper, I continued. "I can hear him. He acts like he is mad at me." I slumped into my chair and wanted to fall on the floor, but Roehr's voice took on a sharp edge.

"Don't die on me, Dora! Listen to me! What's he saying to you? Tell me what he's saying to you?"

But I was Dora now. I could only answer, "I'm shot, I'm hurt . . . I'm hurt."

After the case of the downed plane, I was tired. Not just so tired that I had to sleep for a day; so tired I wanted to sleep for a week.

I'd been working as a psychic nonstop for about five years without a real break. Psychically, I was depleted. I was so excited about my work that it was all I wanted to do, but no one had explained to me the toll this kind of work can take. As a single mother, I'd been running hard for years to keep up. Now my daughters were grown, but I still hadn't learned to pace myself and replenish my energy.

I was also financially depleted. I had started out charging $35 per case (and a case sometimes took two sessions), and now I was up to $40. So to make enough money to survive, I took a lot of cases and clients and lectured as much as possible. And I still wasn't making it. Charlottesville then was a small town, and I'd probably done a reading for everyone in town a couple of times.

I knew I didn't have enough money to last much longer. The only way I could think of to get money was to sell my house. Much as I loved it, I was ready to move.

My father and my brother and his wife were living in southern Oregon at the time, and I thought a change of scenery and a chance to rest would be just what I needed. So I took an inventory of everything I owned, made a list, and told my daughters to check off what they wanted. Then I put everything I owned in a truck and drove down to Florida to see my girls and drop off my furniture. After a few weeks, I flew to Oregon to see what the West would bring.

Like a bird, my dad always migrated out of Oregon for the winter, looking for a warmer climate, so I stayed by myself at his trailer for a while. With the money from my house, and no mortgage to pay, I had enough to live on for a while. I decided that what I really wanted to do was write. I had a lot of stories to tell. I felt that it was so important not to forget the beginning, when you learn something new, and it was all still fresh in my mind. I was also ready to use my rational mind for change. I'd learned that when the right brain was tired, using my left brain was a vacation. Even today, one of my favorite ways to relax is to get in an absorbing chess game—I just concentrate on the next move and everything goes away.

But after a few weeks of not working, just relaxing and breathing the fresh air around Ashland, I was still tired. I mean *really tired*. I was so exhausted that it was painful to walk across the street for a pack of cigarettes. As any dedicated smoker knows, that's tired! I'd go to the typewriter every morning at nine o'clock, write for about two hours, and then collapse in bed. Looking back, I can see that I was more than tired; I was depressed.

It took my daughter Reené to figure out what was going on. "Mom," she said, "I think you're going through menopause. You need hormones." Well, *this* was not something I had considered. Who thinks about menopause in their early forties? Not me. And nobody talked about menopause then. But then I started to think about it. I'd had a partial hysterectomy when I was around thirty-eight. Maybe that had kicked my body into overdrive.

I'd already complained to my doctor about being tired and depressed, but I looked so young (and had been knocking a few years off my age for so long) that I guess he didn't think about menopause in connection with me. And I certainly never brought it up. So I went back to the doctor demanding hormone pills, angry and yelling, and he said he wouldn't give them to me until I gave up smoking. I went home and thought about that for while, and tried, and then I decided to *tell* him I'd given up smoking.

Those pills had a miraculous effect on me. I felt like I had come out of a fog into bright sunlight, and now I was rested, too. Life was good again.

When my father came back in the spring, I wasn't ready to leave. It was beautiful in Oregon. I love the cold and beauty of the mountains, and the crisp air was a welcome relief after Florida's unrelenting heat and humidity.

So I found another place to live: a little baby brick building in a trailer park. It was tiny—really tiny; you had to turn around sideways to enter the bathroom. And it was also cheap—very cheap. I stayed there for about eight months. I finally bought my own typewriter and continued typing up my stories. I wasn't much of a typist, so I gave them to a typist who would correct my spelling and transcribe them onto her computer. That way, when I made changes it wasn't so much work retyping the whole thing.

I was happy and started to work again. I love my field. I love talking about it. I love working with the police. So I gave a few lectures at the University of Oregon in the afternoon, and afterward I would pass out my literature (which consisted of my brochure and a few newspaper clippings about my work). I even got a couple of small police cases. And in May 1985, the *Ashland Daily Tidings* published a front-page article about me, with my picture, that discussed my work. A few months later, in October, the paper published another, smaller article that said I was thinking of leaving the area.

It was true. I was feeling much better and, as much as I was enjoying Oregon, I felt the restless urge to move south again. Yes, it was time to move on. Florida was beckoning again.

On the evening of May 15, 1986, Margie and her mom, Dora, were talking about having dinner together soon when Dora suddenly broke off the telephone conversation and screamed, "Jake! Jake!"

"Mom, are you all right?"

And then Margie heard a scream, a shot, a thud, and silence on the other end of the phone. What had happened to her mom and dad? In a panic, she called 911 and told them that something terrible had happened to her parents. Then she called her son, James, and together they rushed to her parents' house to find the retired couple dead, both shot in the head and lying in pools of blood in their two-story frame home in the suburban town of Colonie, New York, spent .25-caliber cartridges scattered on the floor.

After almost three years of rigorous investigation, the brutal double murder of the retired couple was still unsolved: no murder weapon, no fingerprints, no motive, no clues. Dora and Jake, both seventy-two, were ordinary, everyday parents and grandparents— no one could come up with a motive for their murder. Every single person on the list of suspects had provided a seemingly sound alibi for the night of the murders. Everywhere they turned, Detective Lieutenant Raymond Krolak and his team reached a frustrating dead end.

Margie, however, refused to give up. She was determined that the person who was responsible for their deaths would be caught and punished. But what more could she do than the police had already done? Then she read a story about my work on cold homicide cases in the *National Enquirer.*

Right away, on October 17, 1988, Margie visited Detective Krolak and told him that she wanted the detectives to work with me. I'm sure his first thought must have been *A psychic? I don't think so.* But the department had placed a top priority on solving this case, and he had run out of leads. He called me right away and asked how I worked. I explained that I did not want to know anything about the case except for the first names and ages of the victims. If they sent me something from the bodies, I could work with them over the telephone.

The first thing I did was send Lieutenant Krolak a copy of my instructions for working with the police and the names of some detectives at police departments I had worked with on homicide cases. He spoke to several of the detectives, and apparently they all stood by my psychic ability and claimed they had great success working with me.

He also contacted ex-New York Detective Vernon Geberth, the author of *Practical Homicide Investigations.* This textbook, which is used at police training schools and the FBI Academy, includes a chapter discussing psychics and my achievements with law enforcement agencies.[1] Geberth told him that I would be the only psychic he would consider using. I guess that did it, because Krolak called and asked me to take the case. We agreed on a time to speak, and I waited for the personal items to arrive.

A few days later, a package from Krolak arrived in the mail. I opened it to find Dora's bloodied eyeglasses and a belt that Jake was wearing at the time of the murders. I would have preferred metal objects, but Jake wasn't wearing any rings or his watch, and Dora had been buried with her jewelry.

Krolak called me on the phone at the time we had agreed upon, and I settled into my red leather armchair. My black cat jumped up on my lap, and I stroked her as I tried to relax and get into a receptive frame of mind. I wondered what this no-nonsense cop would say if he could see the psychic with the black cat—what a picture he would have! Krolak told me that another officer, Detective Roehr, was also listening in on his end.

Krolak knew that I like to establish that we're all on the same page by confirming some things about the victims, so he first asked me to describe Dora. I closed my eyes, holding the bloody glasses in my hand. As I gripped the glasses tightly, sometimes brushing my hands through my hair, I spoke about the impressions I received. This would be the first of several sessions.

Lieutenant Krolak, of course, was taking no chances. He taped our conversation and later had a transcript made of our first session. From the transcript, he prepared these notes about my accuracy. I always find it strange to see the foggy, dreamlike impressions I experience as real pain and suffering in my own body translated into police-speak on a piece of paper:

1. She gave a general description of what the victims looked like. Note: Fairly accurate. Short hair, gray, older, and was shot.

2. Dora. Maybe expecting someone . . . newspaper sack. Note: The paperboy came and Jake was expecting him.

3. Noreen states wherever this happened would be close to the street. It was an older structure. Note: Accurate.

4. Describes floor. Different texture that Dora feels on her feet. Note: Floor tiles were coming loose.

5. Describes hallway . . . Accurate.

6. Describes Jake . . . prominent nose, facial features. Accurate

7. Money deals were important to Jake . . . True . . . he was always changing his CD accounts to where the best percentage would be.

8. Jake gagging from blood. True . . . shot in face, blood running down throat.

9. Noreen discusses surroundings outside. Secluded . . . another building made of old stone. Note: This describes the garage.

10. Noreen starts to describe the killing . . . Dora turns, her back hurts, tall killer, damage done, momentary struggle, they didn't have a chance. Jake is killed looking at the killer, victims knew this person. Don't see a car close by for killer. Killer left door open when he left. Killer goes out door, goes left, walking on something bumpy. Note: All the above fits.

11. She describes the door in the back of the house and the door where entrance was made . . . wood . . . window to right of door. True.

12. Jake is in the living room when he hears Dora called his name twice. Accurate.

13. Note: At this point Noreen tells me to stop analyzing everything she says. She is right, that's what I was doing.

14. Noreen is now Dora . . . she hears a noise, something is happening. Dora starts to do something but does not get a chance, she thinks someone is right there, she says a name or word "Oh Dam[n]." She says a lot of words quickly. She sees this man with blue on him. Noreen is then asked, "Is this while you were talking?" She replies, "I'm on the phone." Noreen then stops and tells me I'm only telling you what you already know. Note: she is correct and also very accurate about the phone. I advised her I was just trying to establish the correct crime scene.

I was getting cranky—why did he want me to tell him things he already knew? Krolak responded, "You did fine. I'm just trying to establish the correct crime scene. Would you mind if Detective Roehr puts you into a hypnotic state and questions you some more?" It turned out that Krolak's silent companion, Detective Roehr, was a forensic hypnotist. *Why not?* I thought. *I'll try anything once, and this could be interesting.* "I'll try it," I told Krolak, "but I don't know if it will work. I've never been hypnotized before."

15. Noreen is asked to go back to being Dora and on the phone. Who is she talking to? She replies, "A female relative" . . . Accurate. Sees a gun, not a

rifle. Heard something breaking before he came
in. She hears Jake's voice, she want[s] to fall down,
she is hit and hurt. Her back hurts. Note: Autopsy
report shows bruises to upper back area. She has
pains in her stomach, lower feel[s] like it's burning, then asks, did I have a hysterectomy?
Accurate . . . Dora did have one.

16. Now Noreen goes back to where she recognized
the killer that comes to dinner. A family member
brought him, she describes a male in his late 20s,
5-11, then describes his mental and physical problems. She then says, the police know this person
and he was questioned by police.

17. Killer knows how to use a gun and that it would be
effective at close range. Brutal killing intentional,
had to kill Dora 'cause she knew who I was.

18. Jake prior to his death is in living room, he is reading or working on figures, relaxed, hears a noise,
gets up, takes a few steps towards room. Killer is
coming quick like "in, boom, boom, quick." Jake
recognizes him, calls him a "bastard" . . .

19. Killer left, took something he could carry, something unusual shape. Look around but did not
search.

20. Killer doesn't have steady employment. On
parole.

21. Noreen states that she has to stop, she wants to
drop the phone and lie down, and she is really getting deep into it. She felt that she can see a lot
more during this line of questioning but was afraid
that she may become too relaxed and too deep

into a hypnotic state. All agreed that it would be extremely beneficial to combine hypnosis with the psychic mind. Arrangements are being made to travel to Florida and do this in person with Noreen.

I went so deep into a trance state I dropped the phone and almost fell off the chair. That hypnosis was really something.

Detective Krolak later told me that he found my information so compellingly accurate that he had my phone logs checked to see if I had contacted anyone in the area. Of course, I hadn't.

After reviewing the taped session they were excited and decided it might work even better if they came to Florida and had another session in person. As long as I didn't have to travel, I was up for it.

———————◦◦◉◦◦———————

A few weeks later, on December 6, I answered the knock on the door and met the men connected to the two voices I had heard over the phone. Alan Roehr was tall, thin, and wiry, with receding brown hair and large brown eyes. His energy was intense, and he looked as if he enjoyed kicking down doors. Raymond Krolak was also tall and older than Roehr. He was solidly built with light hair and blue eyes that emanated warmth and intelligence. He had a likable aura, someone you knew you could trust.

We began a series of intense meetings that combined hypnosis with my psychic abilities. These consultations, held in my home, lasted four days with two interviews daily. Each day, after the morning session, they would go back to their motel and listen to the tape, take notes, and return for the afternoon session. They were always well prepared, and the three of us turned out to be a good team.

In the first, session Detective Roehr pulled up a chair to sit directly in front of me while Lieutenant Krolak sat at a distance, notepad in his hand.

Roehr told me that he wanted me to become Dora, the murdered woman. I smiled at him and nodded my head, indicating that I was ready to begin. He told me to focus on a spot in the distance and count from one to twenty, relaxing with each count.

Throughout all of the hours of interviews, Krolak always stayed outside the interaction, only offering structure and suggestions from time to time. It was Roehr who was always in command, and he established his role quickly. During the hypnotic sessions he would bully, cajole, or pacify me to get me to reveal information that could aid the investigation.

If I started to be scattered, if I went off into directions that were not relevant, Roehr gently but firmly turned my attention back to Dora, at the same time assuring me that I was doing very well. He was a natural at working with a psychic.

At these moments, I would breathe deeply and settle myself down again. Even when I was focused, however, my impressions were often fragments. "Okay, I want to be Dora alive. I have a car. If you go out the side door . . . the kitchen goes down. Maybe have a little step down. There's a kitchen over here, I'm sitting down at a table. Then silence."

The hypnotist entered the silence. "You're doing all right, Dora. That's very good. What are you doing when you're killed?"

"I am on the phone."

"Who are you taking to, Dora?"

"I am taking to a woman. I hear a female voice," I continued in a husky whisper, a worried expression on my face. "I don't know what she's saying, I don't know . . . I don't know . . ."

Roehr sensed that I was stuck on the issue of the phone conversation and urged me on. "Don't worry about that, Dora. Just tell me what is going on." He was right in there with me. Perfect.

I looked to my right. "I think I hear some noise over there. I'm here," I motioned. "I'm talking on the phone. This person is coming in. Let me see what he looks like. What does he look like?" Eyes closed, I was peering into the distance. " I'm sort of surprised. I'm not off the phone. I'm still on the phone. I'm surprised that this person is here."

Krolak leaned forward as Roehr bore down. "Do you know the person, Dora?"

"I've seen him before, but he is not supposed to be here now. Why is he here? What do you want? What are you doing? Why are you here?" My voice was rising.

Detective Roehr didn't let up. In fact, he became more insistent. "Dora. What is he saying to you?"

I looked quickly to the right, then back to the left. "I'm confused. The woman on the other end of the phone is talking at the same time he is saying something. He is saying something to me. What is he saying? What is he saying?"

Roehr softened his voice. "Go past it, Dora. Don't worry about what he says. What happens? What's he doing next?"

"He's got something in his hand. I think I dropped the phone. I might even stand up. No . . . stay down. Stay down. He comes fast. I'm on the phone. I hear . . . I keep hearing two voices at the same time.

"I know this person. I know this person. Common name. The gun is there. He looks mad. He's upset. He's talking emotional. He looks taller. He's up there. He's up there. He's up there."

"Now what, Dora?"

"'Jake!' I yell, 'Jake!' He shoots me." I suddenly became quiet and relaxed. In a whisper, I continued. "I can hear him. He acts like he is mad at me." I slumped into my chair and wanted to fall on the floor, but Roehr's voice took on a sharp edge.

"Don't die on me, Dora! Listen to me! What's he saying to you? Tell me what he's saying to you?"

But I was Dora now. I could only answer, "I'm shot, I'm hurt . . . I'm hurt."

Krolak signaled to Roehr, and the hypnotist brought me slowly out of my trance. I was clearly exhausted, so Lieutenant Krolak suggested they stop for the day. He was very supportive of my work, and I appreciated it. "What you're seeing is correct," Krolak said. "Just about everything you said so far is accurate. You described Dora, and you also have the crime scene right." I smiled with appreciation. I need that kind of affirmation to continue a case as draining as this one.

In the next session, Krolak gave me Jake Cohn's belt to hold as Roehr put me under.

"I want you to be Jake now," Roehr began. "What time is it, Jake?"

I swallowed several times, sighed, and sat quietly before I spoke. "I'm Jake. It's about 9:05 p.m."

"What do you hear, Jake?"

"I hear some noises. I hear Dora scream. I put away my newspaper and I get up. Going to get something. Got to get a gun. Got to get something. A weapon." My voice became a low whisper as I repeated to myself, "A weapon. A weapon. A weapon."

"Why do you need a weapon, Jake?" Roehr's voice was loud and sharp. He was trying to keep my energy up. He knew that if he released his control, I would simply fall deeper into trance and finally into sleep.

"Because I heard a shot and a crash. I heard Dora scream. Heard a shot and a crash in the other room. Got to get something. Maybe in the hall, near the door is something I can get. There's something long. I don't know if it's a gun or a stick, something long so I can go toward him. I see him there."

Roehr raised his voice slightly. "Who is it, Jake? Do you know who it is?"

"Yes," I responded.

"Do you know his name? Is he a friend of yours, Jake?"

"Not a friend of mine."

"Is he related to you?"

"I know him through the family. He's been here for dinner."

Detective Roehr slowed the pace of the exchange, encouraging me to relax. "Go out in the hallway, Jake. What do you see?"

I shuddered. "I can see Dora on the floor. She's got blood all over her. She's been shot . . . I came toward him. I've got something in my hand. I think I get shot, once."

The interview slowly ended. I was Jake, and I was dying. As I died, I could no longer respond to Roehr's insistent questioning. The session ended soon after.

I shook myself out of the trance, bone tired. I was back in my in house with these two solicitous men. No blood, no bodies. We arranged to have dinner together later. Maybe we would even shoot some pool.

The four days I spent with Krolak and Roehr were intense and powerful. The three of us spent a lot of time together, working hard during the day and relaxing in the evenings. One night, while eating dinner at a restaurant, I became upset with Roehr. The lights around us flickered, although other lights were unaffected. Several times, when the three of us were together in my home, doors would shake and rattle, thumps could be heard in the walls and ceilings. I attributed these manifestations to the high level of energy the three of us generated when we were together.

One afternoon following a session, I received a call from Krolak. He and Roehr were coming right over again, he said. They had discovered something on the morning interview tape.

"Noreen," Krolak said, "We're New York cops, we have guns, the sun was pouring into our motel room as we listened to that session. But what we heard on the tape made the hairs stand up on our arms. Noreen, we are used to listening to your sessions, but have never heard this before."

We gathered around their tape player in my living room and listened. I heard my voice repeating a series of numbers that had to do with the license plate of the killer's car. As I said a number, I paused, and then I said the next number. But *in between* the numbers, during each pause, we clearly heard a male voice moaning, "Noooo, nooo." We were all a little freaked out. The detective had tested the new body microphone both before and after the incident, but could find nothing wrong. I had never experienced anything like it before and had no explanation. Later, when they went back to the police station, they had experts listen and test the tape. They never did find an explanation.

During our last session together, Krolak told me they had ten photographs of ten suspects for me to look at. I told him that I did not want to see the faces, in case they would affect my decision. So I asked him to place the photos face down in front of me on a table. I closed my eyes and made a few passes with my hands, and with little hesitation I discarded all but three photos. Touching the back of the photos and lingering over them, I told the detective, "These three are involved. I picked up one, showed it to them, and said confidently, "This one is the shooter."

Based on information gathered from hours of our taped sessions, and the photo IDs, the detectives tore into the Colonie double murder investigation, reviewing some old leads with a new eye. Commenting later to reporters, Krolak said, "Noreen never could have known this stuff beforehand, and she was so accurate, it was chilling. She is extremely credible and has a great reputation for accuracy. This case shows me how she earned it. Her information caused us to take another closer look at Robert Skinner and the victims' grandson. They had alibis and we had checked them out. However, Noreen's information made us look again, and we discovered their alibis were not that good. It took us another year to build a case around this new information and to arrest them."

They arrested three men. The shooter was Robert Skinner, the man I had picked out as the shooter. They also arrested the man in the second photo: the Cohns' grandson, James Mariani. They had plotted the murder with another friend, Keith Snare. In October 1990, after a year-long grand jury investigation, all three were charged with murder.

Two years later, Detective Krolak told me the rest of the story. Skinner had entered the Cohns' house alone through the side door. He surprised Dora, who was sitting at her desk off the kitchen talking to her daughter on the telephone. Immediately, he shot her in the neck. Jake Cohn, hearing the shots, left the living room and entered the hall carrying a baseball bat. He was shot once in the face and fell to the floor.

And the motive? Money. James Mariani thought he would be left a fortune in his grandparents' will. As it turned out, he was wrong.

CASE NUMBER __13701__

CHAPTER 18

The Swami Team and Me:
The New York Zodiac Killer

"Mr. Z," the detectives asked, "why did you select the name
Zodiac?"

"There was an old book, I found it, that was written about the West
Coast Zodiac. I didn't buy it; I think I found it and I think it's been
out of print for a while . . . or it was published a while ago. I think to
find this book and decide under evaluation I would be considered
insane, but I'm sane enough to know I want to do this. Your sanity,
your question of sanity is for me to believe. I think these men should die.
I think I should have this attention. I like this game. It's going to go on
longer."

———————◆•◆———————

"Detectives scratching for leads in the Zodiac manhunt have enlisted the
help of the psychic who predicted an assassination attempt on former
President Ronald Reagan three months before he was shot, the Daily
News has learned. . . . The Zodiac shooter has shot four people, one
fatally, and has left taunting notes at the scenes of two attacks, threatening

to kill 12 people based on their horoscope signs. The psychic, Noreen Renier, was scheduled to meet with Zodiac task force detectives. . . ."
—New York Daily News, July 17, 1990[1]

It was July 14, a hot Sunday in New York, and I was scheduled to appear on *The Joan Rivers Show* the next day. Right now, however, my air-conditioned Park Avenue hotel room was filling up fast with police. Then one of the detectives called the captain, who was jogging in Central Park, a few blocks away. He came up to my room too, still in his jogging outfit. I guess they were wondering what to do with me now that they were all here.

"What's your sign?" By the end of eighties, this pickup line was so clichéd that it usually got a laugh. But by July 1990, no one in New York City was laughing. For months, a copycat killer who called himself Zodiac had held the city hostage. During the preceding eight months he had already shot four people, and one was dead. No one could predict whom he would shoot next, or when, or where. They just knew it was inevitable.

The Zodiac had written his first chilling but puzzling note, covered with astrological and satanic symbols, on November 17, 1989:

> *This is the Zodiac.*
> *The First Sign is dead.*
> *The Zodiac will Kill the twelve signs in the*
> *Belt when the Zodiacal light is seen?*
> *The Zodiac will spread fear*
> *I have seen a lot of police in Jamaica Ave and Elden*
> *Lane but you are no good and will not get the Zodiac.*
> *Orion is the one that can stop Zodiac and the Seven Sister*[2]

The city went into action, committing a task force of two hundred officers to hunt down the Zodiac. They knew they had to capture him before more people died.

The original Zodiac was a notorious serial killer who had been responsible for a series of murders in the San Francisco Bay Area in the late 1960s and early 1970s, murders that remain unsolved to this day. The NYPD was determined that this killer *would* be caught, and they were willing to try anything—including venturing into the psychic realm. That was the birth of the "Swami Squad," or the "Swami Team," officers whose job was to interview "psychics, seers, and Satan worshipers and consulting astrologers in an effort to peer into the mind of the Zodiac gunman."[3]

The detectives were in my hotel room that day because my new assistant was very enthusiastic. Without my knowledge she had called the police, told them I was in town, and suggested they interview me for the Zodiac case. Around this time they were getting a lot of bad press for turning away tips, so they said yes.

In fact, they got right on it. The cops came to our hotel right away, immediately separating me from my assistant so we couldn't talk to each other. Then, separately, they interrogated us about what it was I thought I could do for them and what I was going to do on Joan's show. "Wait until after you do the show," they said. "We'll talk to you then."

After the show, I called the Swami Team and said I'd be glad to help them now. I told them I would waive my usual fee, which was then $200, but I had to check out of the hotel, which had been provided courtesy of Joan Rivers. We would need a place to stay. "No problem," they said.

Under police escort, my assistant and I moved into our new digs: a rundown little motel across the street from NYPD headquarters at 1 Police Plaza, way downtown. It wasn't Park Avenue.

When they led us to our room, I couldn't help noticing that the cops both kept looking nervously at the smoke detector on the ceiling. As soon as they left, I hastily wrote a note to my assistant: "Watch out what you say, we're being bugged." I guess this was more than she had bargained for.

"I can't handle this," she said in a panic. "I'm going shopping."

So there I was, alone in my room, waiting for the police to come back and say it was time for the interview. But an hour passed, and another hour passed, and nothing. I figured they must be waiting for conversation to come out the other end of their listening device, to make sure we were on the level and weren't trying to put anything over on them. By nine o'clock, my assistant had returned, with full shopping bags. I was getting tired by then, and frustrated. I said in a loud voice, "If they don't come soon, I'm going to bed!"

At about eleven, they finally showed up. When we walked across the street to the police station, it was almost empty. I guess they had been waiting for people to go home from work before they interviewed me—I think they were already embarrassed enough to be on this detail without getting more flak from the other cops. Even with the more relaxed atmosphere, however, I needed to relax. No problem, they said, and provided me with a bottle of wine and a glass to go with it. Whoever said there's never a cop around when you need one never had the pleasure of working with the NYPD.

We started working, and we worked all night long. These men may have had their reservations about being on the Swami Team, but they were serious about their work. They were good questioners, and they drilled me. The detectives were very good at addressing me as "Mr. Z" when I was in trance and speaking as the Zodiac. They weren't put off by my moaning and groaning and changes in voice tone, like so many detectives were.

My assistant was good too: She took down more than thirty-two pages of notes on the interview, in longhand. Robert Ressler was quoted in the *Daily News* that day as saying, "A psychic's batting average ranges from hot to cold. I know of cases where [Renier] has been extremely accurate and where she's bombed." Well, I'd say that night, I was pretty hot.

I spent the next hours inside the killer's skin, and the first thing I noticed was that his skin was a different color than most people thought it was. The police had gotten information that the killer might be African American, but I was getting a different message. "What do you look like?" they wanted to know.

"A strong, rounded chin," I replied, ". . . I have black hair, it's curly . . . I feel I have dark skin—I don't think I'm 100 percent a black person, I just don't feel I have all black in me and . . . I speak Spanish well. . . . I speak with an accent. . . ."

Of course, the police were interested in where the Zodiac lived. "What do you see in your neighborhood?" they asked.

"I feel brick, old brick. . . ." I couldn't give an exact location, but I felt that he lived outside Manhattan—he had to take the subway under a river to get into town—and that he lived in inexpensive apartments in an ethnic area. The direction east kept coming up, and a high metal bridge nearby.

"Mr. Z," they asked, "why did you select the name Zodiac?"

"There was an old book, I found it, that was written about the West Coast Zodiac. I didn't buy it; I think I found it and I think it's been out of print for a while . . . or it was published a while ago. I think to find this book and decide under evaluation I would be considered insane, but I'm sane enough to know I want to do this. Your sanity, your question of sanity is for me to believe. I think these men should die. I think I should have this attention. I like this game. It's going to go on longer."

So far, the Zodiac had shot his victims on Thursdays, every twenty-one days. So on the preceding Thursday, July 12, about two hundred police officers had been put on patrol. But on that Thursday, no one had been attacked. "I want you to ask me why I didn't kill Thursday," I said tauntingly.

"Why didn't you kill Thursday, Mr. Z? Tell me."

"I was out there; I was walking, looking. Seeing all of you."

"Why are you fearing to be caught?"

"Not fearing to be caught. I like this game. I want to win. If you win fine. It's a game. Not going to turn myself in."

"Who got in your way on Thursday?"

"The police, the City of New York. All were expecting. All your men, all your women on television talking about me. I listened. I listened to the late night show . . ."

"Mr. Z—"

"No," the Zodiac said through me, "I don't want him to be Mr. I want him to be Z. No I don't even want him to be Z. . . .

"What do you want me to call him?"

"Stupido. Never does anything right. Never will amount to anything. Never can amount to anything. Stupido! Stupido! . . . I want to give him a name. Eduardo."

"What weapons have you used in the assault of your victims?"

"Ah hah! My talent is being appreciated. Man has great dexterity with fingers. Man has gun . . . that has been worked on, simplified. . . . Not difficult to shoot gun. More difficult to change gun's identity."

"You're wonderful," the detective said. I guessed I was getting some things right. "Tell me," he asked again, "what does he fear?"

"Not caught too soon. Man realize he will be caught. Not soon. How long game play most important. Must pass, go past astrologer in West. He must kill more."

I came out for a second and asked, "Does anybody know how many he killed in the West? . . . I want to say eight, that's his goal."

The interview went on, and on, and on. I drew a map, trying to pinpoint his location. Finally, it was over. I was dead tired.

The next morning, they gave us a police escort to the airport because they didn't want us to talk to anyone on the way out of town. As a final caution, they asked me not to talk to the press, and I didn't.

But someone had talked, because as soon as I got home I started getting calls from TV shows like *Good Morning America*, asking me to appear to talk about my work with the Swami Team. True to my word, however, I said, "No comment."

———————•◆•———————

They finally caught the Zodiac six years later—on June 18, 1996. It wasn't because of my information, or anyone's information: In a rage, the Zodiac shot his own sister in the back while aiming at her boyfriend. After his arrest, the police found a stash of homemade zip guns in his room—the kind of guns involved in the Zodiac shootings. They joked, "It would be a pisser if this were the Z-Man."[4]

And looking back, the clues I had provided six years earlier about the man who wanted to be called "Eduardo" seemed to fit. The Zodiac turned out to be a twenty-seven-year-old unemployed man named Heriberto Seda—but everyone called him "Eddie." He was a good-looking, dark-eyed Latino man, curly black hair, with a strong, rounded chin, who lived in an old red brick apartment building in East Brooklyn. He used zip guns, which he modified himself. In his room, the police found a number of books on serial killers, including a well-thumbed copy of *Zodiac* by Robert Graysmith, which detailed the crimes of San Francisco's unknown Zodiac killer.

It seems I *was* in touch with the Zodiac that night. I had a name, I had a description. My clues were good ones, but unfortunately the police had no context for them. A lot of people live in Brooklyn. Seda lived a quiet life under the radar, with his mother and sister. I can get under a killer's skin, I can speak the killer's thoughts—but it's the police who have to solve the crime.

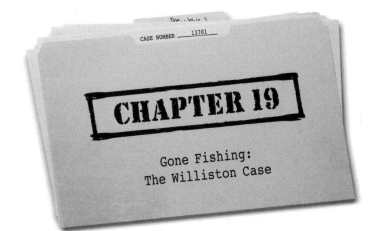

CASE NUMBER ____13701____

CHAPTER 19

Gone Fishing:
The Williston Case

Suddenly, something happened. "I'm driving for a short distance, and then something happens and I'm going down. I feel metal around me. I feel plants." Very clearly, I saw that truck going off a cliff into still water. How could that be? I opened my eyes and looked at Hewitt. "What state is he in?" I asked. I had thought he was in Florida, but Florida is very flat—we don't have cliffs.

—————◆—————

Nothing much ever happens in the small central Florida town of Williston—a tight-knit town that bills itself as "the Gateway to the Nature Coast." Just twenty-five minutes from Gainesville, this rural community is surrounded by miles of scenic back roads, green woods, lakes, and streams. It's a heartland town of just twenty-four hundred people where everybody knows everybody else, and they care about them. So in April 1994, when one of their own disappeared, everybody knew. But nobody knew where he was.

Sixty-seven-year-old Norman Lewis—a Navy veteran, enthusiastic fisherman, and good guy—had vanished, along with his truck. He had left behind his wallet, his identification, his medication for glaucoma, his inhaler for asbestosis, and pretty much everything else he owned. Right away, his brother, Joe, was worried. They were close, and he usually knew where Norman was. It wasn't unusual for his brother to take off on a whim to go fishing, but this just felt different. Why would he leave without his wallet and medications if he was planning to be gone a long time?

The Williston police jumped on the case with everything they had. They searched everywhere, circulated flyers, and put out national bulletins. They compared Norman's dental records with those of every unidentified male body in the United States. But despite all their efforts, he was still missing.

After seven months of fruitless searching, Williston Police Chief Olin Slaughter refused to give up. He put Sergeant Brian Hewitt in charge, and Hewitt hit the ground running—even though, he says, "There wasn't much to go on." He started over as if it were a new case. He questioned everyone who knew Norman or might have seen him. He visited all of Norman's fishing sites around Williston. But he was not going to give up. As he put it, "Every case is solvable. It's just a matter of the right things coming together at the right time."[1]

"Noreen? This is Brian Hewitt. I have a case for you." Hewitt and I had met recently when he attended one my lectures at a police conference in Orlando. I always say that the police shouldn't contact me, or any other psychic investigator, until they have exhausted every avenue of police investigation, and I know I repeated that at the lecture Hewitt attended. This case was a perfect example of that sort of timing.

With the blessing of Chief Slaughter (who took it on himself to reassure the churchgoing townspeople concerning the validity and moral safety of calling in a psychic), Hewitt asked Joe Lewis and his wife, Virginia, if they would be willing to pay my fee. A bit skeptical at first, they soon agreed—they'd already tried every other avenue. Hewitt called me—he said he could make the two-hour drive to see me in Orlando right away.

On a murder case, I like to work with something that was on the body at the time of the murder. But when a person is missing, it's a different story: The person is missing, and so is everything that's on him. I've found that the next best thing is to work with items that the person used a great deal, such as a toothbrush or hairbrush. In this case, Sgt. Hewitt drove to my house and brought me Norman's wallet and a couple of pairs of well-worn shoes.

Hewitt and I settled down in my library. Holding the wallet in one hand, I closed my eyes and focused in. Right away, I started getting images. But, as happens sometimes, none of them seemed to make any sense. I saw him driving in his truck, going down a road that seemed like it used to be important, but wasn't any more. My rational mind was back there somewhere saying, *Huh? That makes no sense at all.* Then, as usual, my right brain just took charge.

"I'm driving for a short distance, and then something happens and I'm going down," I said in a rush. "I feel metal around me. I feel plants." It seemed as if I was buried in plants. Very clearly, I saw that truck going off a cliff into still water. How could that be? I opened my eyes and looked at Hewitt, all left brain for a few seconds: "What state is he in?" I asked. I had thought he was in Florida, but Florida is very flat—we don't have cliffs.

A lot of people assume that psychics know everything. In a murder case, they think, I should be able to tell them the murderer's name and address. In a case like this, I should be able to tell them why Norman took off that day, where he was going, what he was thinking, and exactly where and how to find him. But it just doesn't work like that. Sometimes, the images come into my mind like a movie someone took scissors to and taped back together. I'm watching the movie, but it doesn't make sense because some scenes are missing, others are complete but out of context, and the plot is not always completely clear. Other times, I'm one or more of the characters in the movie, feeling their pain, knowing their thoughts, and as much in the dark as they are about what's happening.

Now I was out of the water and hovering above the crash site. I saw bricks, an old bridge, railroad tracks that seemed to go nowhere. And strangest of all, I saw three numbers very clearly: 45, 21, and 22. At the end, Hewitt thanked me, and I wished him luck. I hoped my clues would help, but I couldn't imagine how.

What Sgt. Hewitt did with those clues is a perfect example of what I say over and over again—"I don't solve crimes, the police do"—and something I always hope will happen: The investigators will use their own intuition. In this case, Hewitt put together the numbers and images that made little sense to me with his intimate knowledge of the Williston area and came up with an answer his gut told him was right: Norman must have somehow driven his truck into a water-filled quarry.

Hewitt threw himself into the search, walking around every quarry in the area. In the end, he searched thirty quarries, sometimes cutting his way through the underbrush. Virginia Lewis said that he took so many chances, scrambling around the loose rock quarries, that she worried he would hurt himself.

Finally, maybe inevitably, he found the quarry where all of my clues came together. It was a lime rock pit right outside town, exactly 2.1 miles from Norman's house. So that's what the 21 clue meant—not twenty-one, but two point one. You never know.

And the quarry was just off old State Road 45, which ran right by Norman's house. Years ago, this *had* been an important road, a main route.

When he got to the quarry, my vision of "cliffs" made perfect sense. The whitish edges of the partially filled quarry did look cliff-like, rising above the still blue-green water.

The banks of the old quarry were overgrown with tall weeds, like the ones I'd seen around myself when I was Norman driving his truck.

As he walked the area, Hewitt found old bricks there, and an abandoned weigh station that looked like a bridge. He even found railroad tracks that had been buried in the muck and brush for years—a railroad that went nowhere.

Now he was certain: Norman was right here, under the still blue-green water of the quarry. It was just a matter of finding his truck. Sgt. Hewitt called in some local divers, and they went to work. But the vegetation was so thick down there they couldn't find anything, not even something as large as a red and gray 1985 Chevrolet S-10 pickup with an extended cab.

But Sgt. Hewitt wasn't giving up—he knew he needed better equipment to find that truck. Norman was an ex-Navy man, so he contacted the Navy. They were more than willing to send a team of Navy SEALS to find a Navy vet—although they later said that if they had known they were following a psychic's tip, they would have refused.

After two days of searching with sophisticated equipment, however, they came up empty-handed. But Hewitt refused to believe that Norman wasn't there, and the SEALS gave it one more day.

On April 3, 1996—two years to the month after Norman had disappeared—they found the pickup in tall grass under almost twenty feet of water along a sheer cliff wall and pulled his truck out of the watery depths. Inside, Norman was still behind the wheel. And on his wrist, the calendar setting on his dive watch was stopped at a familiar setting: 22.

When the case was reported solved, the Williston police were gracious. "I don't think we ever would have found him without [Noreen's] help," Chief Slaughter told the papers.[2] "She led us to the site. She gave us a lot of clues."[3] I even got to go down and walk the site myself, and I was amazed at what I saw, especially those "cliffs"—they were just like the ones I had seen in my mind.

I was glad to learn that my information helped them solve the case. Most of the time, the police take what I give them and I never hear anything again. Unless it's a big case that makes the papers, as this one was, I sometimes feel as if my work has disappeared off a mysterious cliff—just like Norman.

CHAPTER 20

The Killer Calls Ahead:
The Murder of Debi Whitlock

"I just want to stop," I pleaded.

But they weren't going to let me off this time. "You want to be calm, you want to be relaxed, just relax," said my assistant, Jo.

I was Debi again, crying. "He hurt me so much."

"Move past the killing," Jo urged.

"He hit me, he hit me."

"Can Debi tell us about this? When Debi tells us, there will be no more pain. Let Debi tell us, as she tells us, the pain will go away. . . . Has this man hurt Debi?"

"I didn't want to die, I didn't want to die."

"Beyond the death. Debi goes beyond the death," she instructed me. "There's no pain."

But now I was sobbing, almost uncontrollably.

———————◆———————

Jacque MacDonald called to tell me her daughter Debi had been murdered. "I need your help," she said, in her soft British voice. Right away I stopped her. "Please don't tell me any more. I

don't want to know anything—the police have to talk to me." It
was only later—after I had experienced Debi's violent death and
her killer's twisted thoughts—that I would learn the facts of this
brutal case. Debi's murder, like most violent deaths, was not simply the death of one woman. It changed forever the lives of her
mother, her husband, Harold, and her young daughter, C. J. And
it would be years before justice was served.

The Modesto, California, police had been working on the case
for four years and had eliminated scores of suspects. But Jacque
had the passionate determination of a mother who would not let
her daughter's murderer rest. Driven by her love for Debi, she was
trying everything she could think of: She moved to Modesto from
her home in Minnesota to be closer to C. J. and the scene of the
crime. She rented billboards pleading Debi's case. She offered a
cash reward for information. She even started a cable TV program
and support group for the families of crime victims. Then, when
Jacque saw me on a segment of *48 Hours* about the murder of Jake
and Dora Cohn, she saw new hope.

Harold Whitlock made this frantic 911 call early in the morning of March 24, 1988:

"I need the police."

"What happened?"

"I just . . . I just came in. My wife . . . I think my wife is dead.
Oh, God. Hurry please!"

"Okay, I want you to stay on the phone with me, okay?"

"Oh, God, my little girl's back in the bedroom, okay? I gotta
go check on my little girl."

Whitlock had come home in the early morning hours from a
bachelor party to find his thirty-two-year-old wife, Debi, sprawled
in the hallway of their Modesto, California, home. Her throat had
been slit; she had been stabbed to death. Down the hall, in her bedroom, their three-year-old daughter, Courtney, was safe—she had
slept through the whole thing.

Four years later, after investigating twenty-seven suspects, Modesto Police Detective Ray Taylor had reached a dead end. The murder of Debi Whitlock, a vivacious wife, mother, and successful businesswoman, was a cold case. When Jacque MacDonald asked Detective Taylor to give me a call, he did.

We agreed that we would do a phone session, and Detective Taylor sent me three pieces of evidence: Debi's wedding rings, a bloody kitchen knife, and a set of car keys. Taylor was impressed. He later told John Walsh of *America's Most Wanted* that I gave "an eerily precise description of the murder. . . . Of the twenty facts or specific details she provided, sixteen of those were right on the money—and that's a pretty stunning record, actually." In fact, Taylor was so impressed that he decided to fly all the way across the country to Orlando and pay me a visit in person and continue our conversation.

The television show *American's Most Wanted* followed Detective Taylor to my house that day. The crew was only three or four people, and they set up quickly. The most wonderful part is that I go out of the room while they set up, they turn on their bright lights, and then I just sit down and close my eyes and start being psychic. The cameras don't bother me. I know they're there, but I just go into my mind.

As I held the various pieces of evidence in my hands, I became by turns myself watching and describing the murder scene, Debi experiencing the murder, and the murderer himself, gloating about his brilliance. I know it can be disconcerting for people to watch me when I'm being psychic, especially when I am the killer or murder victim. My face takes on expressions that I never use in normal life, and my voice can become very menacing or terribly frightened. It's especially hard on people when they see me being killed. Here I was, sitting in my library in Florida, a middle-aged woman nicely dressed in a burgundy jacket and slacks, getting ready to turn into a vicious killer. I know Detective Taylor, a thin, studious-looking man, had seen a lot—but he had never seen anything like this before. Fortunately, my assistant, Jo, would help question me, and a police sketch artist would draw the face I would describe.

"It's 1988 and I'm in California. And I'm Debi," I began. There's always a danger that I will go too far into the murder, but Jo knew how to guide me and keep me calm.

"And you're alive, you're well, this is before the incident. Debi's fine, there's no pain." Her voice was a low, soothing purr. "Debi is going to recall calmly . . . with whom did Debi last talk before this incident?"

"I'm on a phone, I'm talking to a male . . . I feel male, and I feel hanging up abruptly or some anger involved." I later learned that the Whitlocks had been getting late-night hang-up calls for months before the murder. This night, it turned out, the killer had finally connected.

"Is this person involved in Debi's death?" Jo prompted.

"I cannot think other," I replied.

"And how does Debi feel about this?" she asked.

My voice became tense, constricted, almost crying. "I tried to prevent it. I really took a lot of precautions and did a lot of things that were supposed to not make this happen. I really didn't want this to happen but I knew it was gonna happen but I really tried! I did what people told me to do and I know I shouldn't have talked to him at all, I know I shouldn't have spoken to him. . . ."

I felt that Debi hadn't shared this information with anyone close, because she didn't want to worry anyone, especially her mother. Then they asked if Debi had had a sexual relationship with this man.

"I think someone did something to me after I was dead," I said, puzzled.

Jo continued, trying to get a fix on the murderer, yet still calm and soothing. "We want to move closer and closer, calmly, closer, and then past Debi's death . . . there's no pain, it's done, now Debi looks back."

"Can I look at him at this point?" I was slipping back and forth between being Debi and being Noreen.

"Yes," she replied.

"First let me see how Debi sees him," I said, "and I'll do the man then, and then I'll switch." And then suddenly I was Debi again. "He had strong features. I thought he was so handsome and rugged." And then back to Noreen: "He had worked out or been conscious of his body . . ."

"Distinguishing characteristics?" asked Jo.

"I see something on his chest, a cross, perhaps this person has strong religion around him, stocky, I feel more stocky, short man. Stocky." I stopped, my voice sinking almost to an inaudible whisper. I was drained. "Okay. I need a cigarette. Okay." I lit up and took a drag, and felt the nicotine coursing through my bloodstream almost immediately, calming me down.

I think my assistant and Detective Taylor must have been getting worried about me. I must have looked like wreck. "You're doing fine," said Jo. "You're doing so good," echoed Detective Taylor.

I was grateful for the support. "Thank you for not letting me hurt. I appreciate it. I'm still a little cautious. I do hurt a few places . . . bad man." And then it was time to go back in.

"Debi wants to see the murderer now," Jo began. "She wants to see him clearly and calmly." It was always a danger that I would get too caught up in the emotion of the killing. That's why I always need someone to keep me on track.

My voice became a low, menacing hiss and my face assumed a chilling smirk. I was the murderer. "I feel comfortable with knives," I said. "Hate. Anger. I've gotta mess her up some way. I've gotta mess her up some way good. Yeah. There's not any way they're gonna find out who did this." And in a flash I was Noreen, explaining what I saw. "I look just like the man that Debi described—strong bone features . . . I feel strong in my body . . . a vainness . . . not that tall, more broad . . ."

"Look at him clearly," my assistant pressed. "Feel his anger . . . his motive . . . why has this man killed Debi?"

"She's not gonna leave me and get away with it," said the murderer, with venom in his voice. "She stays with me till *I* say it's over. I know she's in love with someone else. I can just tell." And then back to Noreen: "I feel a lot of paranoia around this man . . ."

The questioning continued. "Has anyone else put this man up to doing this?"

"I like doing this," the murderer said with a horrible pleasure. "I enjoy, I enjoy, I'm enjoying this a good deal."

"Why is he enjoying this so much?" asked Detective Taylor.

My voice became a low and menacing whisper again. "I'm in control. I can make it go fast or as slow as I want. . . . I'm strong. Yeah." I saw him picking out a kitchen knife, making his move. "I'm gonna cut. A hit. Oh! . . ."

And then, breathing hard, I asked, "Could I just know if I'm in make-believe land, if those things happened to her or not?" I really needed to know if I was on the right track; otherwise, why did I need to experience this horror?

"You're doing fine in regard to her," Taylor assured me. "I can confirm a lot of those things." Taylor sounded calm, but afterward he told me a different story. "I had so many chills during the conference I thought I was getting sick. More chills have followed— every time I find something else that matches."[1] That was good to hear later. But at this moment, I was ready to flee the room.

"I just want to stop," I pleaded.

But they weren't going to let me off this time. "You want to be calm, you want to be relaxed, just relax," said Jo, my guide through this journey.

I was Debi again, crying. "He hurt me so much."

"Move past the killing," Jo urged.

"He hit me, he hit me."

"Can Debi tell us about this? When Debi tells us, there will be no more pain. Let Debi tell us, as she tells us, the pain will go away. . . . Has this man hurt Debi?"

"I didn't want to die, I didn't want to die."

"Beyond the death. Debi goes beyond the death," she instructed me. "There's no pain."

But now I was sobbing, almost uncontrollably.

"Relax, just relax," said Jo.

"I'll be all right." I said. But I was still crying. "I want to stop. I want to stop. I want to stop."

"Okay," said my assistant. "Take a little break."

But I was still sobbing. "She was really upset that she died, I'll tell you that. . . ." And now I just went stream of consciousness. "Why did she want to live so much? Was she in love again? Why did she want to live so much? I guess everybody wants to live."

Detective Taylor stepped in. "She may have been in love again. . . . You said two more things about the scene that were very accurate." He really wanted me to continue.

But I felt lost in all this. "Where am I going? Is there a place I'm supposed to be going? I don't want to keep hurting all the time." I meant the actual murder. "Emotionally, it's even more painful."

So Detective Taylor changed tack and asked me if the murderer was the same person she had a happy sexual time with "just a few days before."

I had no idea. "I don't normally know where in time I have landed," I tried to explain. Normally, when detectives ask a question to establish a time frame, I'll go right to the strongest reaction the person had—not the most recent experience. Maybe it was two weeks or two months earlier—I just didn't know.

I did know that I didn't want to be the murderer any more. "His emotions were just horrible," I said. "I hated that. I hated that. It got me so upset. I had so much anger and hate. I don't want to do that either." I saw him leaving out the back door, going back into the dark night the way he had come. They wanted to know if he left anything around the house, and I told them I had the feeling he was handy—he might have done some repairs to the house.

"Before he leaves—" Jo began

"I'm not into it. I think we need to take a little break."

"Just relax and be Noreen for a little bit," she relented.

This was brutal stuff, and it was having an effect in the room. I am always so thankful that, exhausting as the experience is for me, I am able to let go of these vivid and horrifying emotions and scenes. With the smoke from my cigarettes filling the small room crammed with people, I think some of them would go outside just to breathe fresh air.

Detective Taylor, of course, had been around murders and murderers. I was sure he had heard similar things before, although not quite in this way. I think I scared him—I'd scare *myself* if I hadn't been through this so many times before.

He told me that he wanted to question me as the murderer, just as if he had a suspect in the interrogation room. As I became the murderer again, I taunted him.

"You don't know anything," I said mockingly.

Calmly and evenly, Taylor replied, "We know the truth."

"You don't."

"We know there were a lot reasons for it. What were the reasons?"

"The reasons? Doesn't matter."

"Did you plan it?" Taylor asked.

As the killer, I replied with extreme satisfaction, "It was orchestrated with my usual genius."

Following my description, the police artist drew a detailed picture of the murderer.

Eventually, they all left the house, and Detective Taylor said that he now had at least three leads to follow up.

———•●•———

I rarely hear the outcome of cases I work on. This case, however, stayed in the news for the next ten years, thanks in large part to the efforts of Jacque MacDonald. She had never given up hope of finding her daughter's killer. In fact, as the years passed, her resolve seemed to get stronger. During all that time, many people suspected Harold (who died tragically after falling asleep at the wheel of his car in 2001) of having murdered his wife. "My son-in-law went through hell," says MacDonald. "People called him on the phone and called him a murderer . . . C. J. was told at school that her daddy killed her mummy."[2]

After years of following every lead, the case was finally broken in 1999 when a police informant, a former drug dealer, came forward in response to Jacque's billboards—she had never stopped hoping someone would see them and tell what they knew. On his information, a twenty-seven-year-old day laborer from Arkansas named Scott Avery Fizzell was arrested and convicted of Debi's savage murder. A drifter, he had lived in Modesto when Debi was killed. He was eighteen years old at the time of the murder. Just as I had seen and lived it, he had stabbed Debi repeatedly and slashed her neck. After she was dead, he raped her. In a plea agreement, he pled guilty to burglary and murder and was sentenced to thirty-one years in prison.

He comes up for parole in 2017.

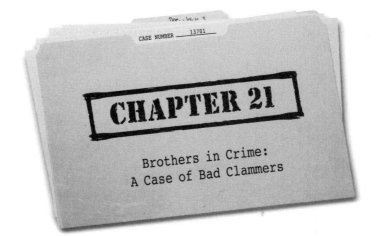

CHAPTER 21

Brothers in Crime:
A Case of Bad Clammers

I saw her face, wide-eyed and full of fear, and then I was inside her—I was her—trembling with anger and fear for my life. The barrel of the gun was huge, black, and pointed right at my face—and then I doubled over in pain. He shot me! At the same time I could feel the young woman dying, the shooter's face began forming in front of me, feature by feature. First I saw his right eyebrow, then his left. Mike was drawing madly as I talked. "He's got a long thin nose . . . I see a full beard, dark brown or black, long straight hair around his head . . ." When I had finished, Mike stopped drawing. We had a face.

It was a cold afternoon in March 1991 when our plane landed in the little Tennessee town of Ransome,[1] near the Tennessee River. As soon as we got off, I had a bad feeling. And I wasn't the only one. "What the hell have you gotten me into now?" whispered my sketch artist, Mike, as we shook hands with my new clients.

Uh-oh. My new clients were two big, beefy, middle-aged men who looked like TV gangsters. They weren't young, but still guys you wouldn't want to meet on a dark street. The older brother, Stoney Stallworth, had an unlikely halo of gray curls framing the broad, flat face and hard eyes of a gangster. He was heavy and muscular but expensively dressed, like the wealthy businessman he was. His younger brother, Mickey, was short, stocky, powerfully built but gone to fat for quite a while. His hair was also gray, like his brother's, but the similarity ended there. His pudgy face was round and pouty. Unlike his brother, he was dressed like a working man, with a newsboy's cap pulled down over his eyes. And no one had to tell me he had been a boxer—his nose was, to put it kindly, "different": flattened, bulbous, and all over his face.

No polite conversation for these two. Abruptly, Stoney said, "It's getting dark. Let's go down to the site right now and see what you can pick up." So we all piled into Stoney's rented van and started driving. It was getting colder, and Stoney had the heat on and the windows rolled up. Between my cigarettes and his cigar, it was a wonder he could see where he was going. I was supposed to fly to New York to appear on *Geraldo* in three days. I hoped I'd make it.

———————————

Stoney had hired me to find out who had killed Jimmy Jameson and his wife two months earlier. Stoney owned a shellfish business in Ransome, but he lived out of state. Mickey lived in town and ran the business, but Stoney came to town to check up on things regularly. Over the years, he'd become friends with Jimmy, a young clammer, and he'd come to think of Jimmy as a little brother. So when the police couldn't seem to make any headway on the case, he decided to take matters into his own big, beefy hands.

From the beginning, everything about this case was just a little bit off. First, even though I had been working by phone for some years, I agreed to travel from Florida to Tennessee out of necessity:

He had nothing to send me because everything belonging to the victims had been burned to the ground. He assured me that I would be working with the police, so, reluctantly, I agreed. That's all I knew about the case. If I'd known anything about the cast of characters in this story, I would have stayed home and rested up for *Geraldo.*

Here's the story I didn't know: What was left of the bodies of young Jimmy Jameson and his wife had been found in the smoldering ruins of their house, which had burned to the ground. But they didn't die of smoke inhalation: Postmortem examination showed they had been shot to death, and the house was likely set on fire to cover the murders. The Jamesons lived way out in the country on a narrow road, and their nearest neighbor was more than five miles away. No one could have heard the shots, and the fire went unseen and unreported.

The Ransome police searched what was left of Jimmy's house and property. They questioned his friends and the people he came in contact with at work. Jimmy hauled clams to market in his truck. Because he was paid in cash, he usually had a lot of money on him and in his home. Robbery seemed like a good motive—but for whom? It was a small town, and there were a lot of rumors, but no one they questioned would admit to knowing anything. Finally, the local law enforcement brought in the Tennessee Bureau of Investigation. Still, the case went nowhere.

The central problem was three mean brothers. Over the years, Bobby, Gene, and Billy Mackey had intimidated everyone in town—even though they still lived with their mother. Most folks in town just assumed the Mackeys had something to do with the murders. These three were always in trouble with the law. They got into drunken brawls, committed petty thefts, and were generally bad news. No one dared to argue with a Mackey—they supported each other with their fists. No one wanted to call down the wrath of the Mackey brothers.

Of course, I didn't know any of this—just that the bodies had been found in the ruins of the house, and the police had run out of leads. When we got there, it was a desolate site. Nothing was left except the concrete steps that used to lead to the front door. The detective who met us there was quiet, a friendly, good ol' country boy who kept to himself and deferred to the Stallworth brothers. I thought that was odd—in my experience, cops like to take charge of a case. But then everything about this case seemed odd, so I just got to work.

I had nothing to hold that belonged to the Jamesons, so I had to look for a link that would allow me to tune in to the young couple. I started walking. I walked around the rubble, circling the grounds several times. Finally, I returned to the front of the house. Nothing. But when I stood on the cement steps, I began to see the young couple in their home that night. I was in.

They were having dinner. Someone knocked at the door, and Jimmy got up to see who it was. Suddenly, three men charged in. One grabbed Jimmy and wrestled him to the floor. Another one grabbed his wife and put a revolver to her head. The third man began waving a rifle, swinging it back and forth between Jimmy and his wife, yelling that he was going to kill them both. He was wearing a black cowboy hat. "Where do you keep the cash?" yelled the man holding the terrified young woman.

I saw her face, wide-eyed and full of fear, and then I was inside her—I was her—trembling with anger and fear for my life. The barrel of the gun was huge, black, and pointed right at my face— and then I doubled over in pain. *He shot me!* At the same time I could feel the young woman dying, the shooter's face began forming in front of me, feature by feature. First I saw his right eyebrow, then his left. Mike was drawing madly as I talked. "He's got a long thin nose . . . I see a full beard, dark brown or black, long straight hair around his head . . ." When I had finished, Mike stopped drawing. We had a face, and Mike showed it to the brothers.

Mickey looked troubled as he narrowed his eyes and squinted at the sketch. "He looks familiar," Mickey said, grudgingly. "I've used him a few times to dig clams and load 'em into trucks to go to market." Then Mickey got quiet. Anxiety was just oozing from his pores—you didn't have to be psychic to feel it. I figured the stress must be getting to him. I knew I was ready to call it a day. It was almost dark, and with the sun going down, it was even colder.

We piled back into the smoky van and started driving back to town. Stoney dropped us off at our motel, which didn't do much to take the chill off my mood. It wasn't quite the Bates Motel in *Psycho,* but it was a collection of down-at-the-heels, 1950s stucco cottages. It was located on the outskirts of town, right across the street from a graveyard. "See you in the morning," I said. I hoped that would be the case.

The next morning we all got together for breakfast at my motel. The weather was even worse, and a cold rain was beating down on the pavement outside the restaurant. Stoney decided we needed to go see the sheriff, so we piled back in the van. When we got there, Mike very wisely declined the offer to go in.

We were in and out of there in two minutes. The first thing I discovered was that the police hadn't hired me at all. The good ol' boy detective *was* a local cop, but Stoney had paid him with his own money to be on the case. The sheriff just yelled at me. He said he wanted no part of what he called my "strange ritual." He was sure it would just be a waste of time. He stopped just short of calling me evil. "The police can solve this case without the help of a psychic!" he said, and showed us the door. When we got back to the van, Mike's expression said it all: *I told you so.*

The rain was still pouring down, and the Jameson property would be a mud hole today, so we decided to meet in my motel room and continue. The rented policeman was there, and we all settled into chairs. As I closed my eyes and visualized myself back on those concrete steps, I went easily into a trance. I began to take long, deep breaths and rub my forehead rhythmically. I could hear Jimmy screaming, "Don't shoot! Don't shoot!" as his wife fell to the ground, motionless. Then I became the gunman wearing the black hat. He was yelling at Jimmy. "I want all the cash you have. I know you keep a lot of money around here!" My arms rose up to shoulder level and tensed, pointing the rifle at Jimmy. Jimmy led me into his bedroom, scooped up some cash from his top dresser drawer and gave it to me. "I'll make sure you don't tell anyone about what happened here tonight!"

Abruptly, I was Jimmy—looking down the barrel of the rifle, just as his wife had. "No! Don't shoot me! Take the money and go. Please don't shoot." I was pleading for my life. I was too young to die! Then I heard a loud blast and felt a searing pain in my chest. I heard a couple more blasts, felt the pain get worse. Then I slumped back and closed my eyes. In my mind, I was watching the face of the killer take form.

Mickey was staring at me in something akin to horror. Stoney was watching me closely. Mike was used to this. He already had his sketchbook out. I opened my eyes and said to Mike, "I can see his nose. It's long, thin, with a small bump on the side of the bridge as if it had been broken in a fight." He began sketching as spoke.

"His face is long and narrow with hollow cheeks, high cheek bones. He's wearing a black cowboy hat, low brim, and he has long, stringy, black straight hair." It was nearly an hour before the drawing was completed.

"This is crazy," said Mickey, shaking his head and staring intently at the drawing. "This guy's one of my part-time clammers. He works for me once in a while. Something strange is happening here," he said, giving me a cold stare.

This had been an intense day. I needed a nap. "Gentlemen," I announced, "I am exhausted. Can we get together tomorrow morning and continue then?" It looked like I'd be in Tennessee for at least one more day.

The next morning we decided to head for Jimmy's clam truck, which was now in police custody. The truck had been stolen from Jimmy's house the night of the murders, and the police believed it had been driven by one of the murderers.

I sat in the truck and touched the steering wheel. As I did, I began to see another face taking form, and I described it for Mike: "Round, smooth, young, large eyes, pencil-thin eyebrows . . . short straight hair. Very young man." Mike began sketching the portrait of a man in his early twenties. Again, Mickey knew who it was. "This guy drove this truck," I said.

Meanwhile, Stoney had a question: "*Why* were Jimmy and his wife killed?" I concentrated on the sketch of the third suspect and said, "I'm getting an input that he knew too much and had to be silenced." I wasn't getting any more information. This case was over for me. I told them I was going home, and wished them luck.

But it wasn't over yet. Later that evening, as I was packing up to leave, the hired detective called. He had taken an interest in my information and wasn't afraid of my ability, as the sheriff had been. "Noreen," said the policeman, "can you meet with me and Agent Conroy of the Tennessee Bureau of Investigation?" Agent Conroy told me that the three men I had described as the killers were the Mackey brothers. They had all worked for Mickey at one time or another, and they all knew Jimmy. Now the Ransome rumor mill, which had suspected the Mackeys for some time, was saying that Mickey was involved too.

"I don't know anything about that," I told Agent Conroy. "I just don't know what more I can do here." It was past time to go. I just about had time to catch my flight from Tennessee to New York City and make the *Geraldo* show to talk about the Dora and Jacob Cohn case. When we landed, I grabbed a cab and told the driver to hurry. We made it, but just barely. When I got there, I looked in the audience and there was Detective Krolak, all made up for the show and ready to go. He smiled. I barely had time to get into makeup. Soon, the two sets of Tennessee brothers were a dim memory.

When I got home, I didn't give the case another thought. It's unusual for me to learn what happened after I finish my work—if the police arrested suspects based on my information, and if they landed in prison for their crimes. So six months later, when my phone rang, I was surprised to find out who the caller was.

"Noreen, this is Agent Conroy from the TBI. Remember, we met in Ransome? It's been wild here since you left. First, the detective you worked with has received death threats. I've been threatened twice myself. All because of our involvement in this case against the Mackey brothers." He paused. "Everyone in this town is afraid to tell us anything." I was sorry, but what could I do?

"I have one question," Conroy continued. "We just don't think these brothers were smart enough to have planned this. Since you did such a good job identifying the Mackeys, and with the other details you shared with us, I wonder if you could identify the person who hired the three brothers to kill Jimmy?"

"If you could get something from one of the brothers for me to hold and touch, I could do that," I replied.

Agent Conroy sent me a lock of hair cut from the head of Billy, the youngest brother, who was in jail on a disorderly conduct charge. As I held his hair in my hand, I saw his dark, pulsating aura surrounding him. He was talking to a man about murder. "It's a short, stocky man." I waited as the face slowly formed. "A gray eyebrow, another gray eyebrow . . . full round face, double chin, pouty lower lip . . . sad, slanted eyes . . . a large, bulbous nose." Agent Conroy and I recognized the man at the same time: It was Mickey Stallworth. I couldn't believe he'd been with us the whole time, acting so innocent and surprised. No wonder he was oozing anxiety. He had good reason to sweat.

<hr />

The police finally arrested the Mackey brothers on suspicion of murder. Once they were safely behind bars, several witnesses lost their fear of reprisal and came forward to say they had heard the Mackeys bragging about killing Jimmy and his wife. At trial, the three men were found guilty. Momma Mackey was found guilty of perjury—she lied under oath many times, swearing her boys were home at the time of the murders. The oldest brother, Bobby, escaped from jail, but was captured a few weeks later and returned to prison.

It was more than a simple murder to cover a robbery. Billy Mackey told several people that Mickey had hired the brothers to murder Jimmy Jameson because Jimmy had found out that Mickey was stealing thousands of dollars from the clamming business. In the end, though, Billy refused to testify against Mickey. Mickey was never brought to trial. Stoney fired Mickey, and as far as I know, the brothers never spoke to each other again.

About five years later, I got a call from Stoney. He told me he'd been in prison for something, but wouldn't tell me what. "I was framed," he said. His girlfriend had left him, he'd lost his business, and he was broke. Would I give him a free reading? He wanted to know what the future held for him.

But all I could really see when I looked into Stoney's future were more bad clams. I was pretty sure he already knew that.

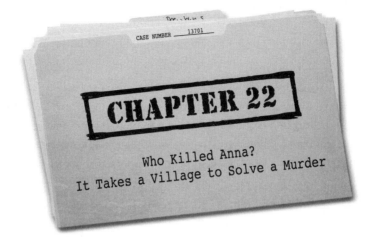

CHAPTER 22

Who Killed Anna?
It Takes a Village to Solve a Murder

"We're all set," I began. "I'm gonna put you on a speaker and let everyone introduce themselves, okay? Can we just call you by your first name?"

"My name is good for me," said Sgt. Marvin Dudzinski. "We're here with Kathy, and we've got you on a speaker phone and we're taping you then, okay?"

We all introduced ourselves to Marv and Kathy, and then Jo began. "Marv," she asked, "have you ever used a psychic before?"

"No," he replied, "we never have. This is a whole new experience for me."

"Well," Jo laughed, "it will be a whole new adventure."

And with a little explanation, we began.

As I've made clear, I have never claimed to have solved a crime. In fact, the opposite is true. As I have said many, many times: *I don't solve crimes, the police do.*

Often, a team of detectives is assigned to a case. Law enforcement officers are primarily trained to use rational techniques in conducting their criminal investigations, such as DNA analysis, fingerprint identification, and autopsies. However, some crimes resist solution by traditional means. In such cases it is possible for investigators to seek new approaches. I am just another tool for them to use, one that complements their other traditional investigative methods. The intuitive mind as an investigative tool can provide clues, information, and perhaps a new angle to an unsolved case.

Just as each member of the detective team is following up on a different lead, my input is just one more piece of the puzzle. Sometimes my information helps the police pinpoint a location, decide to look more closely at a particular suspect, or find a new way to connect the dots they already have. Sometimes, as in this case, the input of family members also plays a part.

It's also true that although I often work alone, I am sometimes helped by a team: a person who acts both as my "guide" through a case and as an interpreter for the police; and a police sketch artist, who translates the images I see and describe into a drawing that materializes on paper.

Just as it "takes a village to raise a child," it often "takes a village" to solve a homicide. That was certainly the case in the murder of Anna Turetzky.

It was one o'clock in the afternoon of November 4, 1992. I sat by the speaker phone in my Florida home, relaxed and ready to go. With me were my assistant, Jo, and Mike, a police sketch artist. At the other end of the phone sat Sergeant Marvin Dudzinski of the Woodhaven, Michigan, Police Department, and a young woman named Kathleen Turetzky-Caurdy. Working together—the detective, the victim's daughter, the psychic, the artist, and the guide—we were hoping to shine some light on the puzzling murder of Kathy's mother, Anna.

Nine years earlier, in 1983, Anna Turetzky's four children were frantic: Their mother had been missing for four days. Her body was found in her car, in the parking lot of the Best Western Woodhaven Inn. She had been strangled to death. Anna, a successful businesswoman, was the co-owner of two Michigan medical clinics with Dr. Jasubhai Desai, with whom she also had a sometimes violent romantic relationship. The police questioned her friends, family, and business associates, and had developed some promising leads. But after nine frustrating years on the case, all they had were dead ends.

Anna's daughter, Kathy, would not let go: She needed to see her mother's death solved and the murderer brought to justice. When she read about my work in a women's magazine, she begged the Woodhaven police to work with me. Very reluctantly, the lead investigator, Sgt. Dudzinski, agreed. "I thought it was a waste of time," he said later. "I did not have much faith in psychics."[1]

On this afternoon, however, I didn't know any of these things. I just knew there had been a murder, and the police needed my help. A set of keys, a gold pendant-type charm, and some eyeglasses were all that would connect me to Anna, but they would be enough to convey some startling information. What follows in this chapter is taken from a direct transcription of the tape we made of our session that day. It shows very clearly how everyone played a part in the success of my psychic investigation.

———————

"We're all set," I began. "I'm gonna put you on a speaker and let everyone introduce themselves, okay? Can we just call you by your first name?"

"My name is good for me," said Sgt. Marvin Dudzinski. "We're here with Kathy, and we've got you on a speaker phone and we're taping you then, okay?"

We all introduced ourselves to Marv and Kathy, and then Jo began. "Marv," she asked, "have you ever used a psychic before?"

"No," he replied, "we never have. This is a whole new experience for me."

"Well," Jo laughed, "it will be a whole new adventure."

And with a little explanation, we began.

"The first thing that we're going to do is have Noreen become very relaxed and tune in to the victim," Jo began, "back to the time when the incident occurred." She explained that I would first describe the victim's physical and personality traits—things that they could confirm for us so that I could be certain that I was tuned in to the right person. Then we could move on to questioning. "Now at this time, I would ask that you simply say the victim's first name and the year of the incident which occurred."

"Okay," said Marv, "the victim's name is Anna and it's 1983."

I began to tune in immediately. "I'm a little stout, my hair is more short . . . maybe sometimes I get a perm or there's some curl in it. I seem to have some eye surgery or some problems with one eye itself. . . . I feel a short neck, a little fullness in the body . . . uh, good smile, nice smile. Didn't trust a lot of people. I don't know if she was just a little paranoid or if she had reason to really . . . distrust. Anna. I'm an older woman, not really young. I think she might look good for her age, but I don't feel that young of a person. . . ."

I stopped, and Jo prompted, "Her type of work, or something she's involved in."

I mentioned her grandson, and a job with a lot of repetition. "I don't know if I actually wear a uniform. I consider it a uniform on her . . . I don't know if she works in a hospital or not."

"Okay, Marv," said Jo. "I presume Kathy must be a relative. Is that right?"

"Yes," they affirmed.

"Could either of you confirm the general description that Noreen feels from Anna at this time?"

"I think that we've located her, yes," said Marv.

After a while, Kathy spoke up hesitantly. "Do you want to know what you did say that, um, is . . ."

"That's correct?" I asked. "Yes, just . . . don't tell me anything more than I've already said to you."

"As far as wearing a uniform," said Kathy, "that's true. As far as her working in a place that could be a hospital, yes, that's true. . . . As far as her body . . ."

"Yes," I said, "nice smile?"

"Nice smile," Kathy said.

"Paranoid," Marv put in.

"Paranoid," Kathy affirmed.

"Okay. Yes. All right," I said. "So I guess we should go get killed." That's what we were here for, after all. And now that I knew I was locked on to Anna, I was ready to get started.

But it turned out that the murder wasn't going to be the focus of this session, which was fine with me. I don't need to experience anyone's death if I don't have to. "No," said Marv, "what we're interested in is the perpetrator and the motive."

"Let me draw the face from my mind then, okay?" I asked. And we got started.

Jo's soothing voice started me off. "We go back to 1983 with Anna . . . very calm . . . let Anna be very calm, but very clear in remembering. Seeing the person causing her death."

When I'm psychic, the whole face doesn't appear at once. Like the Cheshire Cat in *Alice in Wonderland*, whose smile hung in the air without him, faces come together like pieces of a puzzle—a nose, eyes, skin color—until suddenly it begins to take shape. "Would be younger than me," I began. " Would live in the same complex or work in the same area as me, Uh . . . maybe a little . . . darker in the skin . . . dark hair . . . a more square face . . ." I stopped and explained, "Any time I'm describing Anna, please interject, because I only have Anna's stuff." And then back I went. "Okay. . . . My hair seems to be curly, dark black . . . It's sort of all over the place. It's not neat. It's not organized. . . . I would feel a medium to low forehead . . . I feel eyebrows that go out of thickness in the eyebrows arched out. I feel more round brown eyes. . . . I definitely feel an imperfection in the upper part of the face . . . Man, short nose, a little wide to the nose. Looks to me like he would have some Spanish in him. Might work as either an orderly . . . uh . . ." I was drifting.

"Let Anna see him clearly, staying with his face," said Jo, bringing me back.

As Anna, I said, "Short, he's maybe a little higher than me, but I'm short. So I would say maybe 5'8" to 5'10" in height. I don't feel thin . . . maybe 150 pounds. I feel more boxy or not fat but I feel more strong, like a bull . . ."

Now Mike, drawing madly all this time, asked, "Okay, you said that you were younger than Anna. Can you determine how old Anna is?"

"Anna," I began, "I feel like is in her fifties . . . give or take a few years. I feel this man would be younger than Anna, maybe late thirties . . . thirty-eight. . . . Can you give me Anna's age?" I asked Marv.

"Forty-seven at time of the incident," he replied.

"Okay," I said, "this guy's a little younger than Anna. I would say late thirties. I'm getting a little bit of a Mexican look to him. I don't know why."

Mike wanted more specifics. "Go back to his hair. What about the length of his hair? Does it come down over his ears?"

"Well," I said, suddenly in the mind of the killer, "They have a rule I can't make it too long, but they didn't say how thick I could do it. They're always telling me to get a haircut. They're always telling me to get a haircut."

"Is it tight?" asked Mike. "You said it was curly?"

"It's fullness," I repeated, "it's wildness . . . but I do feel not below the ear. We do have a dress code. A hair code. I wear green . . . uh . . . I wear green a lot."

"Does the hair come down his forehead at all?" asked Mike.

"Well, I see during the struggle, it getting in more disarray, but before that I can push it back, but I still have a short forehead, but even if I push it back it still can be curly, more full here on the sides."

"What about facial hair, do you see any facial hair?" We were really working together now.

"I don't at this moment . . . uh, there would be some strength to the chin, maybe a square strong chin . . . maybe a cleft or a scar in the chin itself. . . . I don't know if she was suspicious of him taking drugs." I was off on a tangent, but Mike pulled me back to the face.

"Can you describe his ears for me?"

"A little out . . . not totally close to the head . . . a little out."

"Stay with his face," said Jo, keeping me on track. "It's becoming more and more clear,"

Mike asked, "What about his mouth?"

"First I want to put some lines across the forehead," I said, "and . . . uh . . . then let's see the mouth . . . Anna . . . Yes, his mouth would have an overbite. Uh . . . a shapely upper lip. I don't feel real broad, but I feel more shape and fullness to the mouth. Medium mouth, full upper lip and full lower lip. Slight overbite. Had a lot of dental work done."

"Okay," said Mike, "Go back to the eyes. You described his eyes as being round and brown. What about the size of them? Large eyes, medium eyes, small eyes?"

"The eyes . . . the eyebrows are what I noticed first about him, so I would say medium-large eyes. Round, more open. Uh . . . wide apart, a little broadness in the nose, but the nose is not long. It's a short nose. He is short, maybe I've got him too tall."

"Cheekbones," said Mike. "Are they prominent cheekbones, average, or not bony at all?"

"The thick, sweeping eyebrows and the eyes are what I first see," I said. "There is some highness in the cheekbones, but then it would go straight down and would be more of a squareness there. Could have some Indian, Mexican Indian . . . light-skinned, but he's not real dark-skinned . . . light-skinned." I stopped and suddenly changed direction. "I know. Okay. Motive."

"Go ahead," said Jo.

"I feel the guy was . . . stealing from the hospital and she was becoming more suspicious."

"Had Anna told someone else of her suspicions at this time, of this person?" asked Jo.

"She was the type that would give people two or three chances or really make sure," I explained. "I don't think she would really leap to conclusions. So she would take her time on making a decision, not an emotional leap . . . logical person." And now I was back in Anna's head. "Just felt creepy in the end. I don't know if someone was following me or seeing where I lived. . . . uh, I do feel she was killed in her home."

"Marv, can you confirm that?" asked Jo.

"No, we can only confirm where she was found."

"Oh, okay," I said. "Where was she found?"

"In her car behind a motel," said Marv. "Can we get back to the eye again?"

"Yes," I replied.

"The eye, could the eye be cut?" asked Marv.

"Her eye?" I was trying to get a clear picture.

"Left eye," Marv clarified.

"Yes," I said, suddenly Anna. "It could be cut 'cause I just hurt. I felt my eye . . . one of my eyes was injured."

"Left eye," pressed Marv.

"I never know," I explained as Noreen. "I do mirror vision sometimes, so it doesn't really matter. If there's one eye that had an injury to it, we'll take it."

"It does appear like a recent injury, right?" said Marv.

"Well," said Jo, "we're taking Noreen back to 1983 . . . the energy from the items is a 1983 residual from Anna. . . . So that's why we'd asked . . ." I wondered why they hadn't confirmed anything about the eye injury back at the beginning of the session.

"There was slight cut to the eyelid," Marv conceded.

"Okay," said Jo. "Thank you."

"Okay, good." I was relieved. "So that's good. I wasn't reading their minds. So they weren't thinking about it, but I was off on where she was killed. She was found in a car by a motel?"

"Yes," said Marv, "Yes, we have no idea where she was killed."

"That motel was not someplace Anna would have gone," I said, feeling very confident now that I was with Anna's energy. "It's just not . . . let's see, where was I killed? Let me see. Okay. We gotta find out where I was killed."

Jo stepped in to help. "Be with Anna just before her death . . . she is to be alive . . . remaining calm and remembering."

"I still feel he came to my house . . . I feel like I wasn't in my nurse's outfit. I just feel there was change in my clothes. Uh . . . took me someplace . . . there were several injuries . . . it was pretty quick. I think that I died pretty quickly. I don't know if my throat was actually cut, but I feel I died quickly. I feel like from the motel, I—for some reason want to go to the home. Either he got her out of there or picked her up. I just . . . I want to go to the home. I want to see a '4.' I don't know if it's four miles. I don't know what the 4 is, but I see a 4."

"Is Anna expecting him to come to her home?" asked Jo.

"No, not really. No. No. No."

"Is she taken by surprise then?"

"Yes."

"Let Anna listen as she first sees the killer arrive. Let her listen."

"Well," I said, "Anna was the type that if you needed me, I would help you, and he might have played on her goodness and said, 'Please, I must show you this. You must come with me. This is important.' Anna couldn't drive, wasn't killed there."

"Let Anna move . . . beyond any pain," guided Jo. "Then let Anna look back. Let her see the killer. He's finished. Let's watch the killer as he leaves Anna."

"Leaves my car . . . leaves me."

"Go with the killer," said Jo.

"I can catch a bus close by," the killer said. "There's a bus stop close by. For some reason I can still wear my green, but I had clothes that I could peel off. His shoes were covered up for sanitation," I explained, moving back to myself. "They . . . like . . . plastic cloth booties over the clothes. I see those on him, unless it's her . . . unless she was in operations or things like that."

"No," said Marv.

"Okay," said Jo.

"Let's give it to him," I said, "'cause I see those shoes covered up and I see green on him. I see, you know, how the orderlies wear the loose-fitting green little short-sleeve cotton outfits?"

"Like a smock, maybe?" asked Marv.

"No," I shook my head, "it wasn't a smock. It was pants and a shirt."

"Okay," said Marv.

Jo said, "As you go back and review these things, Marv, remember not everything is exactly literal. Okay?"

"Okay," he agreed.

It was important to help the detective understand how to work with my information—it certainly wasn't the usual type of black-and-white facts he was used to seeing, but it wasn't that different from any eyewitness account. "Pants and shirts that are green," said Jo. "If the hospital type idea doesn't fit, maybe some type of a green jumpsuit. Okay? You've got to play with it as you work the case through."

"Okay," he said, "I understand."

"I'm gonna asked Noreen again to tune in," said Jo. "Anna knows who this person is. It's been since 1983. . . . Is this killer still in the same area where Anna was killed?"

"I feel like he might have stayed there a while longer, but then maybe transferred or moved to another side of town. West side of town. Can get jobs easily. Would have stayed a short time after her death . . . not a long time."

"Have the police spoken to this individual about Anna's death? Looking back."

"Don't think that I was a prime suspect. I think they just did a general canvassing of a lot of people. My accent can get stronger in . . . uh . . . not comprehending for some reason. I can have a stronger accent and not understand English as much when the police are questioning me."

"Has the killer been in trouble with the police before?"

"I feel like there is a record. I feel like there would be some record to him, maybe going two years prior to the killing . . . maybe he was out in January. . . ."

"Anna knows this person," said Jo. "Anna wants to be helpful now to the police and the family and tell us more about this killer. This person that did this. Any family ties or any hobbies that Anna knew the killer had."

But right then I really needed to take a break, and said so. As I left the room, Jo told Marv that this would be a good opportunity for him to acknowledge how things were going. "Are you following along okay?"

"Yes," Marv replied, "we're following along okay."

"I know it's probably unusual and kind of weird compared to the typical interrogation, but it gives you something else to work with and that is the whole idea," Jo said.

"Well," Marv asked, "what's the possibility—or what can we find out of maybe two perpetrators?"

"Okay. When Noreen comes back into the room, that's something we'll go into."

Then Kathy spoke up. "Could she tell us how she"—meaning Anna—"knew this person?"

"Well . . ." said Jo, "we'll see if we can get something a little bit more specific when she comes back in."

When we started up again, Jo began, "I understand from what you said a moment ago that your concern is . . . how Anna would have known this killer."

"Through work, our work," I said right away.

"And if it is possible someone else was involved."

"More than one person," I replied.

"You want to be very calm," said Jo. "Very relaxed. Let Anna remember. Just let her remember. Look back on the incident. She sees a man that we've described. Let her look around before her death moving closer to the incident, but remaining calm."

"I feel the individual that we have been describing would be more looking for a person a little bit higher up. Okay, if he's in a supervisory capacity or not . . . I get a more wiry, older person . . . wiry, thin."

"Is this the other person with the killer when Anna is killed?"

"I don't feel like the person I described is who killed. If somebody else has masterminded it, it would be more the short, wiry old . . . more an older man, maybe because the hair is receding on him and he would have more wiry hair . . ."

"Does Anna know this other person?" asked Jo.

"Anna knows them well," I answered with certainty.

"And how would Anna know the person?"

"We have to go to his area to get certain things from the hospital. He dispenses something. He's in his little place there . . . very insecure, very insecure."

"Okay," said Jo, "take this with a grain of salt, Marv. It could simply be someone that's very strongly associated with Anna that's coming through here. . . . We don't want to point the finger too strongly the wrong way. It could just be somebody that Anna was close to—but don't discount it either."

"All right," said Marv. Then, "She said wiry, thin, receding hairline?"

"Yes," I replied. "Wiry, thin, his eyes . . . he looks very thin. His face looks almost skeleton-like to me in some ways . . . and he has, like, little wiry hair. But it seems to be thinning and he has some jutting . . . some juttingness with the jaw and some prominence with the nose. His eyes would be small, more close together . . . very. It's funny, I'm seeing his elbows. I don't know why . . . maybe the thinness."

"Okay, Marv," said Jo to the detective. "You've heard how I've asked the questions, putting Noreen in Anna's position. Are there things that you would like to ask Anna directly? If so, Marv, just pretend that you're talking to the victim now."

I broke in. "Did the bad guy drive her car? Touch these keys?"

"We think so," Marv replied. "We think the bad guy touched the keys."

"Okay. That's why I could get the guy in the green so strongly. Okay. One of the bad guys, he drove the car there."

"Somebody did, yes," the detective confirmed.

"Yes," I was on a roll now. "It was the guy in the green, and this is why you found almost no evidence in the car, because, remember I said I keep seeing those little booties on him. . . . I feel like whatever I had I could take it off after and it could be almost like paper . . . and throw it away. So I feel like you found very little, like, fingerprints or there was just . . . Where there should have been stuff, there was nothing."

"Right," said Marv. "You're very right. There's nothing there to tie anybody together."

"Yes, right," I went on, "because he wore all that protective stuff from the hospital." We were closing in on him now.

Around this point, I saw that she had been taken to a cold space, possibly in a trailer. I spoke as Anna, and then as Noreen. "I really do believe that they're gonna let me go. Anna is used to being in control. She's not used to somebody having control over her, so it's almost like 'I don't believe this is happening.'" Then I said that I would be Anna when she disappeared and try to locate that place on the clock.

"Anna, when you disappeared," I said, and then I was there. "Okay, I'm inside. Let's make where she is inside the clock. . . . Trailer park would be at . . . I want to go to 5. I'm pointing 7 . . . I'm seeing 5, but I'm pointing to 7. That's where they actually found me from where I was. My home from the place where I live—and I don't think I live very far from the center. That would be more at two o'clock. I feel like two o'clock would be more east." I stopped.

"Go ahead," urged Jo.

"Miles," I said. "I want to go 4.2."

"Put the clinic, the place where Anna worked, in the middle of the clock," Jo suggested.

The image of the clinic started me off again. "We were gonna make an addition, or considering building on, or maybe there has been some start of some addition to the center. I feel some construction going up there. Let's see the center. We would call it the north side of town, or more north."

Jo guided me. "Broaden the view . . . rise above and see fully."

"We could go towards the airport road or the old airport road. I think there is a new road now, but remember back when. The old airport road. We could go in that general direction."

"The clinic's in the middle of the clock," Jo reminded me. "Stand in the middle of the clock. The direction that Anna would be taken to the place where she was kept."

"Southwest 14," I replied promptly. And then, "I'm not really seeing as good. . . . This is old. Anna's gone on. It's hard getting Anna here."

Jo could tell I was getting tired, and she really wanted to get Marv in on the interrogation before I gave out altogether. "Keep your questions kind of quick," she told him. "Don't pause too long."

"Okay," said Marv. Poor guy, I knew he'd never had an interrogation quite like this one.

"Just pretend you have the killer here," Jo explained. "He's going to be truthful with Marv." That was for me. "Marv is going to ask the questions."

"Okay, Marv," I said. I'd never be more ready—and very soon I might be a lot less ready. This had already been a long session!

"Ready?" said Marv.

"Yes," I replied. I guess I was going to have to step in. I saw a scar on the killer's hand. "Ask him where he got the scar on his hand. Ask him how long he has had that scar on his hand. Ask him about that."

"He has a scar on his hand?" asked Marv, still trying to get up to speed on the long-distance interrogation technique for psychics.

"Yes," I said, "right hand . . . my right hand, unless I'm doing mirror vision."

"Where did you get that scar?" Marv finally asked.

"A knife fight from the past," the killer replied. "It was a knife."

"You know Anna very well?"

"I've been working for her two years."

"Two years. . . . Is she your partner?"

"Anna would not really consider a whole partner, although on the books I was a partner, but Anna still ran everything."

"Do you owe Anna any money?"

"I paid most of the money back. There is some outstanding money, but it's not as much as it was. There has been money paid back."

"Was it a lot of money?"

"Yes, it's a lot of money."

"Did you just give it to her today?"

"No, really Thursday or Friday."

"Did you give her money Thursday?"

"Uh huh."

"Have you seen her since Thursday?"

"No one has really seen her since Thursday. We thought somebody called in and told us not to be concerned. I feel like there was some reason why we were not as concerned as we should have been. Somebody misled us."

"Somebody misled you?"

"Well, I could have been part of the misleading, but we misled people so they wouldn't worry about her so much."

"Okay," Marv finished, "I've run out of questions."

"Yes," I said, back to myself. "I think that we need to just evaluate this tape."

"I think we've done pretty good," said Marv.

"Yes, yes. Mike will send you the faces," I said. I wondered if the drawings Mike made, or anything I'd said, would have any meaning for Marv and his team of detectives. I figured I'd never know. But I was wrong.

———————•◦•———————

We faxed the sketches to Michigan. One bore a startling resemblance to Anna's father, to whom she was very close. But it was clear to everyone that Anna's father had nothing to do with the murder—perhaps the energy of her love for him had permeated the objects. The other was someone they all recognized: Anna's business partner, Dr. Desai, as he had looked so many years ago.

Then the case started to break. Some years earlier, Kathy's brother had found a tissue in Anna's car with the letters "S. A." written on it. They felt strongly that their mother had been trying to tell them who the killer was. But they hadn't been able to connect it with anyone. Now, suddenly, a clinic employee was pointing the finger at Stephan Adams—S. A.—a former medical assistant and X-ray technician at the clinic. The friend told police that Adams had told him all about Turetzky's murder. This was the break the police had been waiting for, and their suspect matched my description of the man in green: He was a slight man, with a receding hairline, who had moved west soon after the murders—all the way to Denver, Colorado. And he wore green scrubs because he was a hospital employee. Dudzinski knew in his gut that this guy was connected with the murder. There was just one problem: when he traveled to Colorado to give Adams a polygraph test, Adams passed. Without any other evidence, they had to let him go.

Dudzinski and his team looked again through Desai's financial records, trying to find something to connect the two suspects. Finally, they found what they were looking for: a canceled check from Desai to Adams for $2,018. It was his payoff for the murder.

The police never discovered exactly what happened on the day of the murder, but they figured that Desai probably lured Anna to a meeting to talk about business, and she was killed at some point afterward. With Anna out of the way, Desai was the sole owner of a business worth more than $2 million—a lot of money now, and even more in 1983. Adams got paid for the killing, but he had another motive: Anna had fired him for stealing from the clinic. In the end, Desai and Adams were each charged with three counts, including first-degree murder and conspiracy.

Our "village" only came together for this brief time and purpose, but it got the job done. The case was finally put to rest: Eighteen years after the murder of Anna Turetzky, Steve Adams—who police felt actually strangled Anna—was convicted of solicitation to commit murder and got only ten months in jail. Dr. Desai didn't fare so well: He was found guilty of first-degree murder and sentenced to life in prison, where he resides today.

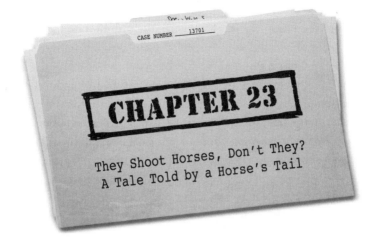

CHAPTER 23

They Shoot Horses, Don't They?
A Tale Told by a Horse's Tail

A murdered horse!

Immediately, I was intrigued. I loved animals, but I'd never worked with them. Could I see into a dead horse's energy as I did with humans? Could an animal see his murderer? And if he could, would I be able to interpret an animal mind? It was worth a try. I decided to work the same way I did on my homicide cases, asking to touch an object that was on the victim when he or she was killed. But I never expected a horse's tail!

I have to admit, I felt slightly ridiculous: I was sitting on a large bale of hay in an empty horse stall. I held the tail of a dead horse in one hand and its bridle in the other. The hay itched. But I knew I had to concentrate on discovering who had killed my client's favorite horse.

He'd called the day before, angry and sad and out for blood. "Noreen," he said, "some maniac put two bullets through Dandy Dancer's[1] head. I want you to find out who did it!"

A murdered horse! Immediately, I was intrigued. I loved animals, but I'd never worked with them. Could I see into a dead horse's energy as I did with humans? Could an animal see his murderer? And if he could, would I be able to interpret an animal mind? It was worth a try. I decided to work the same way I did on my homicide cases, asking to touch an object that was on the victim when he or she was killed. But I never expected a horse's tail!

My client, Ted, raised thoroughbreds out in the Virginia countryside. A trim man in his forties, he was frantically pacing up and down the almost spotless barn when I arrived. Nearby, the other horses were safely tucked in their stalls, where I could hear them crunching grain in their buckets. The local sheriff, whom I had worked with before, was leaning up against one of the stalls, sucking on a piece of straw. It was like a scene out of a movie.

We had decided to hold the session right there at the scene of the crime, and we had a full house: Ted, the sheriff, two of his deputies, my sketch artist, and all those horses. As I settled onto the bale of hay, they waited patiently for me to begin the session. I nodded to one of the deputies, and he turned on a tape recorder. I took a deep breath, inhaling the hay and horsy smells. No smoking allowed in the barn.

Feeling like a witch doctor, I closed my eyes and gingerly put the long, coarse tail to my forehead. Right away, one face after another swept into my mind, lingering only for a moment. I couldn't slow the swirl of images. I described several of those faces I saw, speaking as fast as I could before another image came in.

I saw Ted's face and lots of other male faces. There were too many, and they came too fast. It looked as if a whole gang was involved. But the parade of images didn't feel right to me. When I opened my eyes, I looked at the artist. She rolled her eyes, her pencil still. I could tell she had stopped trying to draw. How could she? I could barely find words to describe all these faces!

Frustrated, I expressed my dilemma. The sheriff nodded, and asked Ted if he recognized any of the faces I had seen.

"It looks like you're describing everyone who was close to Dandy Dancer," he said. "I recognized a couple of the farm hands, the handlers, and the horse's trainer."

This just wasn't working. "Look," I said. "I don't think the horse fears the same things we do. He did not fear the gun when he saw it, and he didn't fear the person who fired it." I thought about this problem for a few moments.

Suddenly, I had the solution. Who had carefully loaded each bullet into a chamber? Someone with a mind for murder. "Do you have the bullets that killed the horse?" I asked the sheriff.

"Yes, we have the projectiles," he corrected me.

"Would you let me hold them?" I asked. "There's a chance I could focus in on the person who touched them."

"I'll send someone back to the station to get them for you," he said, and dispatched one of his deputies right away.

Then I started to fret. I knew the forensic people had touched the bullets. Did they contaminate the projectiles with their energy? Still, from experience I knew that the energy emanating from killers was powerfully enduring and could overshadow the others. Could I pick up the energy left from those hands and interpret it correctly?

Hell, it was worth a try.

We took a short break. The artist sharpened her pencils, and I meditated outside the barn under an ancient oak tree. I guess the sheriff's office was pretty close, because the deputy quickly returned with the fatal bullets in a plastic evidence bag. I got up from under the tree and walked back to the barn, ready to be the horse again.

I selected one piece of a fragmented bullet, sat back down on my bale of hay, and held the projectile in my hand. As I closed my eyes and tuned in to the bullet, an image collected in my mind like the Cheshire Cat in *Alice in Wonderland*. First the eyes emerged, then a small nose, and a delicate mouth. Feature by feature, the face evolved and took form as I verbalized what I saw to the artist. When I opened my eyes, she had the face of a small, attractive woman in her forties.

"Oh my God," Ted blurted out, "It's my ex-wife!"

The divorce had been Ted's idea, and in the months and years that had passed his ex-wife's hatred toward him had grown stronger. His recent marriage to a younger woman didn't help. His ex-wife wanted revenge. She wanted to cause him pain in return for the pain and suffering she felt he had caused her. So she chose what he treasured most: his prize racehorse.

The sheriff acted on the information and confronted the woman. They found the gun, and she willingly confessed to the crime.

But Ted, shocked by her destructive act, wasn't out for revenge anymore. He didn't want any more violence, he just wanted to end the acrimony between them. In the end, he refused to press charges.

He did, however, pay for her psychiatric treatments.

According to Joe Uribe, Montana MCI Agent, retired: "Noreen's incredible insight helped close our case by providing the macabre details of our victim's murder, which when presented to our suspect, caused him to negotiate a confession. She also identified two other accomplices to the crime."

———————◆◆◆———————

A government employee working in the tiny border town of Shelby, Montana, is found dead, the victim of an apparent car accident. However, upon a closer look, detectives determine that this was no accident—he'd been shot. When the ensuing murder investigations hit a wall, detectives hope psychic Noreen Renier can give them a lead.
—Court TV, Psychic Detectives

I was on the phone with my artist, Barbara Tiffany, confirming the upcoming police session.

"Yes, they are coming all the way from Montana to work with us. They don't want to mail the evidence. So come a few minutes early, okay."

Barbara and I were used to working over the phone with law enforcement agencies all over the country. The detectives would usually mail me something from the homicide victim that would not be important to their case: a ring, watch, glasses, or a small piece of clothing with blood. It was imperative that it had been on the person when the individual was killed. The heightened emotions can cause the experience at that time to be imbedded into objects, and I am able to pick up that emotional memory from the victim's items. Barbara draws the face on paper that I see in my mind so that the police can have a better process of elimination of their suspects.

My cats scattered when the doorbell rang a few minutes before our scheduled appointment. Undersheriff Dave Robbins introduced himself and Agent Joseph Uribe. Undersheriff Robbins was very tall and nice-looking. He wore a white shirt with his sleeves rolled up, blue jeans, white socks, and loafers.

What I first noticed about Agent Uribe, from the Montana Criminal Investigation Bureau, were his large dark-brown eyes that you knew would not miss a thing. He had a mustache and a quiet demeanor; I thought he was cute in a conservative way. He wore his business suit well. Much later, I found out he had seen me on television and was the one who suggested hiring me.

After I introduced them to Barbara, the men set up a video camera in the middle of the room, and I put an audiotape into my tape recorder. I wasn't used to having a video camera film me as I worked and was a bit nervous, but not as anxious as Barbara.

Barbara hated being on camera, and she sat as far to my right as she could so she wouldn't be picked up by the camera. Undersheriff Dave Robbins sat to my left and Agent Uribe stood behind the video camera that was aimed directly at me. I sat on my theater chair next to my red trunk and took a big sip of wine. I asked for the name of the victim. I never ask for the full name prior to my sessions; I don't want the detectives to think I do any checking before our appointment, like the skeptics always claim psychics do.

Undersheriff Robbins dug into his large box and handed me a man's jacket and watch, and told me the individual's name was Walter Sullivan; then he sat back, crossed his legs, put his crossed arms in his lap, and waited for me to begin. They had told me absolutely nothing about the case except that it was a homicide. I closed my eyes and began describing Walter; I saw that he had facial hair, was short and stocky, and had a short neck. I also saw numbers around him and felt he worked in financial matters and traveled a lot. I felt he was a disciplined man who was very organized and had sons. Something seemed to be wrong with his leg and he had a limp.

I opened my eyes and asked for feedback, but none was forthcoming; I asked for the date that Walter was killed so I could go back in time. I was told it was December 1989. That was six years earlier, as it was now December 1, 1995.

I was now holding his belt and the key to his vehicle. After a few minutes I was handed a bullet. I took a few deep breaths and began to describe the features of the murderer, one by one, to my artist, Barbara. A long oval face emerged, the high forehead, then the deep-set eyes, which were close set, then the thin mouth came into view. The nose was large, with a bulbous tip on the end. His skin was fair but very weathered, his hair was thinning, and the chin was square. As Barbara drew, she asked me several questions about the face I was seeing and then concentrated on drawing.

Undersheriff Robbins was not asking me questions and there was almost no feedback in the beginning. I do understand that there is no manual about working with a psychic and every psychic works differently. Nevertheless, I would have liked to have confirmation on my description of the victim, just so I would know I was on the right frequency and picking up correctly. I liked to be asked specific questions, but that was not happening and I didn't know what they needed to know. I had to ask myself the questions aloud and in my mind. I took another long drink of my wine. This was going to be tough, I thought.

Once again, I went back into my psychic mind asking for a name and suddenly a name was in my head and I spellled C-L-A-R-K. And then I said, "Clark . . . I see the name Clark." Of course, it didn't make any sense to me. I had no idea where the name fit in. My job isn't to make sense of the information that comes through me. My job is to get the information. Putting it all together is the detective's job.

Robbins wanted me to see the vehicle. I was holding both the bullet and Sullivan's personal effects, so I didn't know whose vehicle I was seeing as I described the large tires and how high off the ground it was. It looked like I was describing a truck.

The next scene in my mind was a license plate and I could see a government sticker on it. I tried to get numbers but could see only a few. Then my psychic mind, without directions, started to wander off on a different path. The next thing that came out of my mouth was, "I'm becoming very Indian and I see graves." Uribe later confirmed that Shelby is by an Indian reservation with a very large grave site.

Agent Uribe saw that I needed questions that were more specific and began helping Robins by asking questions that were more precise. Occasionally, they would ask me what I thought about what I had just described. I tried to explain that I don't analyze my information, I just try to describe the images I'm seeing as best I can.

"Describe how he was killed," Agent Uribe asked. Suddenly I was in my logical mode and thought, *Why are they asking me that? They have the bullet, they found the body . . . why are they asking me that?*

It's always a very bad idea for me to be in my logical mode. My job is to be psychic, not question their questions. But I did.

"It's very important," Agent Uribe said.

Agent Uribe wanted to know how Walter Sullivan was killed, so still holding the projectile, I became Walter. I was in a blue metal building when men jumped out and started beating me on my head; I knew it was an ambush, but couldn't protect myself. I could see glimpses of three men. Suddenly, I felt the most horrific pain in the back of my head and cried out as my hand reached out to grab the back of my lower head. The pain broke my psychic trance and I was Noreen again. As I took another sip of my wine, my head was still hurting—badly.

Undersheriff Robbins wanted me to tell him about the other two men. I noticed he was now taking notes on a yellow legal pad. Agent Uribe was silent again, observing me from behind the camera.

After another sip of wine and a few deep breaths, I went back into my psychic trance and focused on the two men. I knew they had the same blood and were of Mexican descent. I also got a first name, José or Joseph, and I felt they were Catholic.

Lots of information poured forth: It was premeditated and the shooter, whom Barbara was drawing, was mentally unstable and very angry—not running-through-the-streets crazy, but emotionally unstable. Sullivan knew his killer.

Next, they asked me to describe the gun. I knew I needed two hands to hold it. However, they couldn't relate to what I was telling them, so I grabbed a pad and pencil and drew a picture of the gun I was seeing in my head. My artistic skill is limited, but I did my best.

The next question they asked was, "Where is the gun, who has it?" I felt that it was with the individual's other guns and that he had a collection of guns. [Note: In the fall of 2007, I asked Joe Uribe if he remembered what I had said about the gun. He wrote: "The gun you drew was known as a Tech 9, a high-tech, Uzi-type, black semi-automatic handheld machine pistol. You described it as having two (2) grips, one you held with each hand ahead of the other with the trigger in between. You said it was black and had a large, round barrel with holes or vents in it. I then asked you to draw it and you drew an exact depiction of a Tech 9, which also matched your description. The relevance of this weapon is that it is very unique and very few are around today. During the search of Eugene Moore's truck stop, two Tech 9s were discovered, one under the sales counter and one hidden away in a file cabinet in the office. The weapon also tied Moore to the two Mexicans."]

After that, I was up in the air looking down. I could see the blue metal building close to railroad tracks and then three towers came into my sight. I drew a circle on my pad and put NW on the top of the circle, the blue metal building in the middle, and drew where the tracks and towers should be. I felt a running stream or river close by, and later, they did confirm there was a river that flowed in that area. I had also drawn where two small lakes were situated on my map. I felt a border was close by.

At one point, I saw a woman, and Barbara drew the face. There was no look of recognition when they were first shown the sketch. At the end of the session, they said it looked like the suspect's wife. That was the first time I was aware that they had a suspect.

After an hour and fifty-one minutes, we stopped. They both gave me feedback on most of what I had said. I was exhausted, as I usually last only an hour. After our goodbyes, I fed the cats and went to bed.

I didn't hear from them again until Storyhouse, a film company working for Court TV's *Psychic Detectives*, asked me for several of my cases to follow up in order to see if the cases had been solved. I had given them the Montana case, explaining that I didn't know if I was able to help them or not.

Soon I found out my clues had helped, and I flew out to Montana to film the case for *Psychic Detectives*.

A few years later, in 2007, The Biography Channel's *Psychic Investigators* wanted to film the same case. The following are transcripts from the Dave Robbins and Joe Uribe interviews with Nextfilm Productions, Inc.

> *Interviewer:* What did you think when you first met her?
>
> *Joe:* Well, I talked to her first on the phone, and again I was still skeptical. And, after talking to her a while, we decided to fly down to Florida because we had some evidence and she wanted us to mail the evidence to her and we didn't want to do that; so we, we flew the evidence down to her, and I was still pretty skeptical. I'd never worked with a psychic before, nor had I ever dreamed of working with a psychic. And Dave Robbins, my partner, he was even worse skeptical than I was and, I have to say that she was pretty incredible. Some of the . . . we told her nothing about the case, and some of the things she said was just

incredible. She was on the money. She gave us details that how she knew the things she knew we just couldn't believe it.

Int.: What did you think when it was suggested that you go and see a psychic?

Dave: When Agent Joe Uribe brought . . . brought up the prospect of talking to a psychic in regards to this case, I was very skeptical. And honestly, I thought it was just a waste of time. But in doing so, I believe that we did have some information that was corroborated. Obviously, she saw some things that . . . that we already knew . . . but which I found to be very interesting, that it . . . that she saw what she did see. But, honestly, at the onset I thought we were just wasting our time.

Int.: At first you must have felt that she was being lucky, but then it must have seemed like there's something to this. Was there a turning point?

Joe: There was a turning point in talking with her. One of the things she told us to bring is . . . she wanted some items from the victim's body. In our case we brought several pieces of clothing and we even brought the bullet that was in the victim's head. The moment she touched these items she started talking about the case in such detail that was unbelievable . . . it was very consistent with the investigation we had done. And the information she provided continued to be credible to the point where we were just amazed . . . we couldn't believe it. In fact, the hair was standing on the back of my neck a time or two in talking with her, and she just . . . the more she got into it, the more detail she gave us.

Int.: I was talking about Walter Sullivan having facial hair. She told us that he had facial hair, and you can say well Walter Sullivan had a beard. So, Noreen told us that Walter Sullivan had facial hair, or a beard, can you comment?

Joe: Well Noreen started by describing the victim first. She told us that she could see the victim and that he had facial hair. Walter Sullivan had a beard. She told us that he was short, stocky physique . . . short neck . . . basically described Walter to the tee . . . She, she, I felt she was pretty well tuned into him by the description she gave. She then told us that he worked in financial matters. Walter Sullivan was an auditor for the State Workers Compensation Bureau, and he dealt with finances. She said he was a traveling person that went around with some official business . . . well of course he was a Government auditor . . . just the things she said were very consistent with what we felt was consistent with Walter.

Dave: Noreen asked us to bring some items from the victim's body . . . some items associated with Walter. We brought with us a jacket, a watch, a shoe, a belt, and we actually brought the bullet from Walter's head that he was killed with. And, once we handed them to her one at a time, and once she started touching these items she immediately started describing the chain of events that happened at the Moore residence.

Int.: Now one of the things that she talked about was the property, the nature of the property. Can you describe what she saw in regards to the physical layout of the property?

Joe: Well we had a, a suspect in the case, and with the information Noreen provided us, we actually went out to his residence and we started looking around. And the physical features that Noreen described, such as a, a blue metal building . . . there was a blue metal building on the property. She said there was a railroad track close by, well right across the road from him was a railroad track. She drew a picture and a layout of this whole area, and in the picture she used, she put three towers on a hill, and in Shelby at the top of the hill there are three radio towers just in the location that she said they would be. And, just below that, she said there was water or a river, and of course the Morias River is just right over the hill from those towers. And it was strikingly accurate.

Int.: What happened when Noreen touched the bullet?

Joe: The moment she touched the bullet, she had a vision of the attack on Walter Sullivan as he entered this blue metal building. We knew that Walter had been beaten, and we knew that he had been shot, but we told her nothing about where he was wounded, if he was wounded, or anything in that nature, but she starts telling us about the scenario of what happened. She says that as Walter went into this building he was ambushed . . . she said there were two men [who] jumped him and . . . they beat him about the head and suddenly she gets a pain at the side of her head, which is exactly where Walter had a wound from being struck. It was pretty dramatic what she told us about the rest of the beating, and finally, she indicated by having a sharp pain in the back of her head that . . . something went in her head there, or some pain in her head, and that was exactly where Walter was shot. So by the time she got done, we knew all of these things but she basically laid out the scenario of what we believe is the actual fact of what happened with Walter Sullivan.

Int.: Had you known anything about that before, about those other two men being there?

Joe: Well, we did have a suspect, but we didn't know how many people were involved with it or what the circumstances were. Noreen started laying out the details of the assault; we had knowledge of possibly two other people being involved, and the way she laid out the story . . . put everything together for us, and . . . and we believe to this day that that's exactly how the assault occurred.

Int.: Did the word Clark have any meaning in this case?

Joe: Definitely. Once she said the word Clark, it came out kind of spontaneously that she said this word Clark, and . . . incidentally the body and the car were found on the Clark ranch, about nine miles southwest of town, in a deep ravine. And, by giving that name that was a direct link for us to the case, and it came out of the blue.

Int.: Now in this event, there was the presence of a video camera and an artist. Was there anything done with the artist? And, if so, what did they reveal?

Joe: We asked Noreen if she could visually picture the people that were involved in this assault, and, and she said she could, she could see the actual events going on, and the actual assault. So, we asked her if she could describe it to an artist. She has an artist that does work for her, and was present during the day that we were there. Noreen gave details . . . [interruption]

Int.: Tell us about the pictures she had done.

Joe: We asked Noreen if she could accurately describe the suspect for us, and she provided information to her artist, which very accurately depicted our main suspect and his wife.

Int.: Can you explain what Noreen did for you in respect to putting this cast of bad guys together?

Joe: We knew that these two brothers were possibly part of . . . of this assault on Walter, but it was Noreen who actually put them in the blue metal building during the assault on Walter Sullivan. And, through further investigation, we were able to show that they were in fact in town at the time and could have participated just like Noreen said.

Int.: Talk to us about getting a confession, what it takes to face them and make something happen.

Joe: Well, Noreen provided us with enough information that when we walked into that room we knew what happened in that building. And, we were able to tell Eugene Moore what happened in that building, and it shook him so much that he finally cracked and started co-operating and started admitting to some of the things that he had done, and it was enough for us to get an arrest warrant for him, which we later did.

Int.: What did you get from Noreen that emboldened you and enabled you [for] that confrontation with Moore?

Joe: We got enough information from Noreen about what happened in that building that when we walked in the room to interview Eugene Moore again, we were able to really rock him. And, we had enough information where we could tell him we knew what happened in that building. And, he knew at that point that we knew what had happened, to the point where we got enough information out of him, where we got our arrest warrant, and later tried to arrest him.

Int.: Could you see that of being any use with Joe in his subsequent interview with Moore?

Dave: Well that information that we received from Noreen really corroborated a lot of things that we knew and, it would help in substantiating, you know like when Joe interviewed Gene Moore . . . him and another agent interviewed him later on . . . which precipitated us getting a warrant. And, I assumed that it probably helped Joe in . . . in knowing that the information we had, had been corroborated and . . . and so it would have armed him with that much information in the interview.

My understanding is that after listening to my taped interview and reading the earlier interviews with Eugene Moore, they felt they knew more about what had happened and wanted to confront Moore with his inconsistencies, contradictions, and what they now knew about how Sullivan was killed. They met with the suspect, who now lived in Joplin, Montana, on April 17, 1996.

Moore said he would not speak with Undersheriff Robbins, so Agent Uribe went to the interview with Agent Ward McKay. They were not allowed to tape-record the session, so detailed handwritten notes were taken by the agents.

Moore told the agents about the circumstances surrounding his last meeting with Sullivan. The agents noted discrepancies between the details in previous statements given by Moore.

Moore was visibly shaken by what they were telling him about how Sullivan was killed and began smoking heavily, his voice went very low, and he avoided eye contact with the agents.

The agents told Moore they believed his account of his last encounter with Sullivan appeared to be untruthful.

Moore stated, "If I confess to this, what will happen to me?" He also asked how much time he would spend in prison and expressed concern about facing the criminal justice system alone and expressed concern for his family and business. Moore asked if he could go home, eat, and think about his situation. Moore agreed to return in approximately thirty minutes and speak with the agents.

About forty-five minutes later, Moore contacted the agents by telephone. Moore stated he had considered the previous conversation with the agents and wanted the agents to provide written guarantees about what would occur subsequent to his arrest. He asked how many years he would serve in prison and what types of homicide charges he might face. The agents advised Moore he should reveal any accomplices to the crimes.

Moore, however, was reluctant to return to the agents' location to make a list of his concerns. Moore said he needed time to be with his family and to put his affairs in order. He stated he would talk again with the agents and he would not run.

On April 23, 1996, the agents attempted to contact Moore on several occasions, leaving a message with the Moore's wife to return the calls.

Meanwhile, the State of Montana had filed felony charges of deliberate homicide against Eugene Harrison Moore.

On the afternoon of April 23, 1996, Agent Uribe telephoned Agent McKay in Helena, Montana, and requested investigative assistance for a post-arrest interview on Moore.

Undersheriff Robbins met with Agents Uribe and McKay and deputies from the Toole County Sheriff's office who would be participating in Moore's arrest. The officers discussed the necessity of getting close to Moore without alerting him of a law enforcement presence. An important consideration was to capture Moore in an area away from Moore's home or business due to concerns of armaments and the safety of the Moore family members and other citizens. The officers believed that to surprise Moore would have the highest potential for preventing a violent response and would provide a minimal level of exposure to others. A primary consideration was not to act until Moore's children had left the residence for school.

Three possible scenarios were discussed for the upcoming arrest. At 9:24 a.m., Agent Uribe and Undersheriff Robbins decided to terminate the arrest operation. They had been observed numerous times by local citizens and it was believed their presence had been revealed to Moore. The order was given by Undersheriff Robbins to return to the Liberty County Sheriff's Office to begin a telephone negotiation with Moore in an attempt to arrange a peaceful surrender.

But it was too late. A spotter team had seen Moore enter his bulk-fuel truck and he was observed traveling north at a high rate of speed. Agent Uribe and Undersheriff Robbins discussed by radio Moore's prior history of running from law enforcement and it was determined Moore was attempting to flee to the Canadian border.

In the events that followed, Moore's vehicle was stopped a short distance from the Canadian border, and a shootout ensued where Moore was shot and killed, and two deputies were wounded and had to be taken to the hospital in Shelby.

Agent Uribe knew who the two Mexican brothers were who has assisted Moore in the murder of Walter Sullivan in 1989. In the fall of 2007, he wrote to me:

José and Richard [the two brothers] were over-the-road truck drivers from Texas (at the time). Richard routinely left firearms at Moore's Husky Truck Stop in Shelby, MT, prior to crossing the border into Canada. He also ran guns up north from Mexico, which the Canadians and other truck drivers routinely purchased from Moore. On November 14, 1989, the day Sullivan was murdered, Richard and José were in Shelby on one of their trips hauling produce north, then grain to the west coast, and a final haul back to Texas. When questioned about their whereabouts that day by Undersheriff Dave Robbins, Richard Delafuente stated they were at the Moore Husky Truck stop early that morning to have breakfast. Richard stated he saw Sullivan come in and have a conversation with Moore about conducting an audit, then leave following Moore, presumably to Moore's residence, where Moore allegedly had his business records. Richard also told Robbins that he and his brother left Shelby that day to haul a load of wheat to Portland.

But after the death of Eugene Moore, the two Mexican suspects had fled to Mexico and were never seen in Shelby, Montana, again.

CHAPTER 25

I Never Hired Her!
The Laci Peterson Case

Oh, my gosh, I thought, never expecting Scott to pick up the phone.

"Mr. Peterson, my name is Noreen Renier and I'm a psychic detective. Your mother has hired me to find your wife. I'm so sorry your wife is missing; I hope I can help. I can't make any promises but I'll do my best."

I expressed my sorrowfulness again, but there was no reaction—emotional or verbal—that I could pick up. So I continued my monologue.

———————◆———————

It was late December 2002. I remember watching the evening news about a pregnant woman named Laci Peterson who was missing in Modesto, California. Never suspecting that I would be involved in this case, I silently prayed that she and her unborn child would be found.

In January of 2003, I started to get e-mails asking me if I would find Laci. I responded to them all by saying that I appreciated their concerns, but it was a police case and I would have to be invited to work on the case by either the family or the police. The truth is, the police don't really want to work with psychics on high-profile cases. The cases I am hired to work on are usually several years old, when all else has failed; they call me as a last resort.

I never expected to get a call from Jackie Peterson, and was excited that she wanted to hire me to find her daughter-in-law. I readily agreed to accept the case and even lowered my fee from $650.00 to $450.00. Working in the field of psychometrics, I told her that I needed to touch something that Laci had worn or used a great deal just prior to her disappearance. I also asked her for the name of the detective who was working on the case.

While watching the evening news a few days later, I saw the Modesto police taking a wrapped package from Scott Peterson's vehicle and whisking it away. A few days later, I got a call from a Modesto police officer asking me why, in a package they found in Scott Peterson's vehicle, was a check made out to me for $450.00? I told the officer on the phone that I was a psychic detective and Jackie Peterson had hired me.

Soon another package arrived with a college sweatshirt that said "CAL POLY" in large bold letters across the front and with small letters below which spelled out "San Luis Obispo." It looked brand-new and I doubted that it had ever been worn. I was disappointed; I thought I had explained to Jackie Peterson that I needed something her daughter-in-law had worn recently or used a great deal. The families usually send me the items from the missing person and it helps me connect to the individual who is missing.

Thinking perhaps she had misunderstood, I dialed the number she had given me. I was leaving a message on the answering machine for Jackie Peterson when the machine was cut off, and a male voice said, "This is Scott Peterson."

Oh my gosh, I thought, never expecting Scott to pick up the phone.

"Mr. Peterson, my name is Noreen Renier and I'm a psychic detective. Your mother hired me to find your wife. I'm so sorry your wife is missing; I hope I can help. I can't make any promises but I'll do my best."

I expressed my condolences again, but there was no reaction—emotional or verbal—that I could pick up on. So I continued my monologue.

"Unfortunately, the sweatshirt I was sent is too new and doesn't look like it has been worn. Could you send me her hairbrush, toothbrush, or something more personal?"

"No," he said abruptly, "the police have all those things." After requesting other personal items, I could almost hear the clinking of his privacy shield going up as he kept answering "no" to my requests.

Finally I said, fibbing outrageously, "How about a shoe? The police said you had plenty of her shoes."

At that time, I was sure the Modesto police were tapping his phone, and I wondered what they thought about his unemotional reaction to a psychic joining the search for his missing wife.

But after talking to Scott Peterson, I did something I had never done before. I made a copy of Jackie Peterson's check before I deposited it into my bank account. Much later she denied to the *National Enquirer* that she had hired me and the copy I had made of her check proved she had.

This was not the first time I had worked with the Modesto police. Eleven years earlier in 1992, I had worked on a homicide case with Detective Ray Taylor for *America's Most Wanted.* (See chapter 20, "The Killer Calls Ahead: The Murder of Debi Whitlock.")

The next package arrived with one Tommy Hilfiger shoe, size 6 medium. It too looked unworn. Scott had handwritten his return address, along with mine.

I called Detective Craig Grogan. I told him that I had been hired by Jackie Peterson to work on the Laci Peterson case and wanted to set up a time to work with him. He politely explained that because it was a high-profile case, he was concerned about other psychics contacting them, and I'm sure, although he didn't say so, skeptics as well. However, he said that I should e-mail him the information and gave me his e-mail address.

I was confused as to how to continue. The police always questioned me, and in this case, I didn't have anyone to ask me questions while I was in my trance state. After thinking through my options, I decided to call Joanne McMahon, PhD, a parapsychologist I had originally met at a conference in 1995 in Durham, North Carolina. Joanne was a pretty blonde with plenty of smarts. She had a long-standing interest in parapsychology, which included a master's degree in Consciousness Studies and a PhD in Human Science from the Saybrook Institute. She had also been the director of the Eileen J. Garrett Library of the Parapsychology Foundation. McMahon was a natural choice, since she was familiar with my work, having interviewed me for one of the chapters in the book *Shopping for Miracles,* authored by her and Anna Lascurain in 1997. She wrote in chapter 2, "Superstars," which profiles two psychics—Lenora Piper and me—"Noreen Renier will forever be remembered as a superstar." I thought that was nice!

I called her and explained my dilemma. She graciously agreed to question me and we set up an appointment for March 2. We had never worked together, and I was a bit anxious. Joanne was in New Jersey and I was in Florida. Hoping that it would help her, I sent her the basic rules (see chapter 9, "Lost . . . and Found"). I explained to Joanne that since Jackie Peterson had hired me to find her daughter-in law, Laci, that's exactly what I wanted to do, focus on where Laci was, not who killed her.

Our sessions together were tough on me. Joanne, like so many of the detectives I've worked with, would cross-examine me about what I had just seen, and that doesn't work very well. I see images and get impressions and then they are gone. I always think of the sessions as fact gathering; get as much information from me as possible and later separate the wheat from the chaff. But we did the best we could under the circumstances.

The following is a copy of the e-mail Joanne McMahon sent to Detective Grogan at the Modesto police department a few days later.

To: GroganC@modestopd.com
Date: Tuesday, March 4, 2003
Subject: Laci Peterson Case

Dear Detective Grogan,

Attached please find my report on a session with Noreen Reiner. On March 2, 2003, I had a phone meeting with Ms. Reiner on the case concerning the disappearance of Laci Peterson. This report was compiled from my notes taken during the meeting and are not the exact transcripts of the session. Though possibly useful, the statements are in no way to be seen as a clear, concise roadmap. I say this since I am not sure if you have worked with psychics before. The information they impart is not designed to solve the case but provide useful clues that may help you.

Should you have any questions please do not hesitate to contact me.

Respectfully yours,
Joanne D. S. McMahon, PhD
Shopping for Miracles: A Guide to Psychics & Psychic Powers
www.DrGhost.com
<http://www.drghost.com/>

REPORT ON LACI PETERSON:
A SESSION WITH NOREEN RENIER

The following is based on notes taken by Joanne D. S. McMahon, PhD, on March 2, 2003, at 1:00 p.m.

Introductory statements:

Laci was greeted by an uncle and grandfather (both of whom are deceased). The uncle was much closer in age while the grandfather is distant and possibly from the maternal side.

Important to the investigation are two missing items: a missing or different rug that anyone coming into the home would see and a club of some kind. The club could be a golf club or a baseball bat; it was not clear exactly what it was but was seen as "something that could be used to hit someone in the head."

Specific information:

Laci is in a vehicle. She has something covering her face and is probably already dead.

The number 4709 is in some way connected to the vehicle, either miles or tag numbers.

The vehicle pulls out of the driveway and goes straight. *(JM: When questioned how this was possible, Noreen said that there is only one way for the vehicle to go, since going in the opposite direction "makes no sense"; it sounded like the house was either on a dead end street or on a cul-de-sac. According to Mapquest, 532 Covena Avenue hits a dead end at Thousand Oaks Park, so going in the other direction makes no sense.)* The vehicle continues through a major crossing and turns right past a large billboard. It moves through an "older" section of town. It is dark and the number 3 appears. The vehicle continues moving west on state highway 14 or 41; there may or may not be the letter "B" in it. They make a right-hand exit and seem to go into a U-turn and are now facing water. *(JM: The exit sounded like it could have been a jug-handle, though that was not specifically mentioned. As one comes closer to the Marina, the instructions are to make a U-turn at 7th street onto University Avenue; then, straight onto Marina Blvd.)* When questioned about the length of time the vehicle was in motion Noreen responded "4 hours."

There is a campground or a park of some sort that's near the water. The Berkeley Marina does indeed have a park, Cesar Chavez Park. (http://www.cityofberkeley.info/parks/parkspages/CesarChavez.html)

The vehicle destination is near water. The water in question is part of an inlet; described as a peninsula similar to the shape of the state of Florida.

Laci is believed to be in the inlet surrounded by rocks, some of which are smooth and could be so due to manmade changes. She is in what appears to be fresh water though it has a fishy smell. It was described using the phrase, "There is good fishing in the area." Salt water is nearby, but Laci is not in it. She is in a drainage area and there is rushing water near her, though her body cannot move because she is in a cylinder or well-like container. Though surrounded by rocks, she also has cement, possibly in the form of cinder blocks tied to her to keep her down.

(*Note:* Police found a homemade cement anchor in Peterson's boat and prosecutors showed that an anchor like that had been used in disposing of Laci Peterson's body.)

Noteworthy comments:

There was a sense of someone massaging "my" chest, though it was not clear whose chest it actually was.

(*Note:* Later, the autopsy diagnoses noted multiple rib fractures, left 5 and 6, right 9.)

The number 33 is significant but there was no specific reference.

Clock-face information:

Noreen likes to describe locations based on the positions on a clock face. Below is a graphic explanation of where she sees Laci now if Laci is at the center of the circle or clock. My comments are in italics.

- At the 11 o'clock position there is the sense of high-ness and is where the sun either rises or sets (i.e., marks east/west).

- At the 9 o'clock position is a city that is very "spread out." *(That city would be Oakland.)*

- At the 3 o'clock position there is a substantial city, possibly an industrial one. *(The city is most likely Richmond.)*

- At the 7 o'clock position is a small airport. *(The airport would be Oakland.)*

- At the 6 o'clock position is a major highway. *(That highway would be 580, which runs parallel to the marina.)*

- At the 5 o'clock position there are odors or smells like something burning. *(If Richmond were the city, then the smells would be the refineries in the area, such as Shell Oil in Marinez.)*

I never knew if the police actually used my information. They most likely wouldn't confirm it if they did use it. After working with the police for more than thirty-two years, I know that feedback on my psychic work is not always forthcoming, and I accept that much better now than I did at the beginning of my career.

Many months later, to promote Court TV's new show *Psychic Detectives*, I was a guest on *Psychic Out* with Nancy Grace. Defense attorney Mickey Sherman was also on the show.

The trial was still going on and many thought Scott would get off. When asked if I thought Scott did it, I told Nancy Grace I did feel he had and would be found guilty and then I asked, "Could they give him the death penalty?"

The jury did!

CASE NUMBER ___13701___

EPILOGUE

I've been working as a psychic detective for more than thirty years and I would like to retire soon, but I can't. I know people need me. That's why my next book will be a how-to book; my goal is to teach. I believe that all of us have the possibility of developing our psychic powers.

We are a society that encourages and rewards the logical, rational, thinking mind. And we've gone a long way with that—without our logical skills, we would never have been able to discover and develop cures for age-old illnesses; we wouldn't have the telephone and the Internet, tools that allow us to communicate with friends and loved ones thousands of miles away.

But our brain has *two* parts. We know our left brain fairly well by now—we have mapped its twists and turns, and we know how to use it to our best advantage. But the right brain—the intuitive mind—is a vast, unknown, and barely tapped territory. Even though we know that creativity and dreams and intuitive leaps spring from our "irrational" brain, our educational system and science in general tend to neglect this resource—or, afraid of it, they angrily deny its existence. Still, it's there: a dimension of intuitive, creative, and loving power that most of us have nudged aside, like a friend or child who embarrasses us and who we wish would go away or disappear.

But every so often, we hear its quiet voice in the form of a feeling we can't explain or a dream that won't let go. Sometimes, as happened to me, the intuitive mind speaks so loudly we just can't ignore it. When I teach my classes in ESP, I always ask my students to "leave their rational minds at the door." I've gotten a lot of flak about this statement from skeptics who interpret it as telling people I want them to turn off their critical faculties and blindly accept everything I tell them. Nothing could be further from the truth.

Life is balance: The rational mind and the intuitive mind, equally trained, are powerful tools. My work with law enforcement has taught me to respect a mind that hews closely to facts and refuses to be swayed by tall stories and con artists. I like to think that the law enforcement officers who have worked with me have learned to respect their own "gut feelings" just a little bit more. I love lecturing to law enforcement and hope that in the future, police and FBI investigators will be trained in intuitive techniques. In fact, it is my dream to train cold-case squad members to tune in to their own "irrational" minds. The missing people and unsolved homicides would benefit so greatly—and perhaps they won't need to call me in as often!

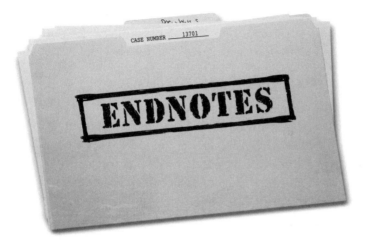

CASE NUMBER 13701

ENDNOTES

Introduction

1. Vernon J. Gerberth, *Practical Homicide Investigation: Tactics, Procedures, and Forensic Techniques*, 3d ed. (Boca Raton, Fla.: CRC Press, 1996), 423.

Chapter 4

1. In his book *Visions of Time* (Wheaton, Ill.: Theosophical Publishing House, 1979), Jones writes about his work with psychics, including Noreen Renier, in uncovering the ancient past.
2. Detective Grady's name has been changed to protect his privacy.

Chapter 5

1. Joan Krieger, "This Poltergeist Uses the Phone," *Fate* (August 1980): 87–91.

Chapter 6

1. "Over in Staunton, Lacy King was the lead investigator . . . and he's more enthusiastic about recommending psychics.

'We were not trained in the field of parapsychology or pro-filing at the time. That was a new thing.'" In "Underwater: Psychic Renier Sees Laci," *The Hook,* Issue 0217 (May 1, 2003).

2. Anne Richardson, "Ruckersville Psychic on Trail of Rapist," *Daily Progress* (December 11, 1979).

3. "Psychic's Sensitivity Is Pitted against Rapist," *Richmond Times-Dispatch* (December 16, 1979).

4. Anne Richardson, "Ruckersville Psychic on Trail of Rapist," *Daily Progress* (December 11, 1979).

5. "Psychic's Clues Help Police Catch a Brutal, Knife-Wielding Rapist." *National Enquirer* (August 12, 1980).

6. Anne Richardson, "Staunton Rape Case: Psychic's Details Mostly Accurate," *Daily Progress* (February 7, 1980).

7. "Psychic Termed Accurate," *Richmond Times-Dispatch* (February 8, 1980).

8. "Psychic Termed Accurate," *Richmond Times-Dispatch* (February 8, 1980).

Chapter 8

1. "Psychic's Clues Help Cops Catch a Brutal, Knife-Wielding Rapist," *National Enquirer* (August 12, 1980).

2. Detective Toller's name has been changed to protect his privacy.

Chapter 9

1. Tape made by the Waynesboro police, as reported in George Beetham, "A River, A Psychic, A Search Ended," *News Virginian* (photocopy, no date available).

2. "Psychic 'Tunes In' to Help Police Solve the Unsolvables," *Virginia Police Journal* 17, no. 2 (Summer 1982): 21–23.

3. Mimi Tandler, "Noreen Renier, Psychic Detective," *Frontiers of Science* (November–December 1980): 25.

4. John Blosser, "Psychic Finds Missing Man after Cops Give Up," *National Enquirer* (July 27, 1999): 1.

5. Karen Voyles, "Psychic Claims Power to Solve Mysteries," *Gainesville Sun* (June 8, 1999).

Chapter 11

1. For more on this fascinating work, see his books, especially Robert K. Ressler and Tom Schachtman, *Whoever Fights Monsters: My Twenty Years Tracking Serial Killers for the FBI* (New York: St. Martin's Press, 1993).
2. John Douglas writes about my lectures at the FBI Academy in his book, *Mind Hunter: Inside the FBI's Elite Serial Crime Unit* (New York: Pocket Books, 1997).
3. Investigator Mike McGraw, in Mimi Tandler, *Frontiers of Science* (November–December 1980): 25ff.
4. Jim Schnable, *Remote Viewers: The Secret History of America's Psychic Spies* (New York: Dell, 1997), 273.
5. Vernon J. Geberth, ed., *Practical Homicide Investigation: Tactics, Procedures, and Forensic Techniques*, 3d ed. (Boca Raton, Fla.: CRC Press, 1996).
6. "FBI Goes into Action as Psychic Predicts New Assassination," *National Enquirer* (photocopy, 1982; exact date and page not available).

Chapter 14

1. Stewart's name has been changed to protect his privacy.

Chapter 15

1. Dr. Gills's name has been changed to protect his privacy.

Chapter 17

1. Vernon J. Geberth, ed., *Practical Homicide Investigation: Tactics, Procedures, and Forensic Techniques*, 3d ed. (Boca Raton, Fla.: CRC Press, 1996), 665–670.

Chapter 18

1. John Marzulli, "Psychic Eyes Zodiac Hunt," New York *Daily News* (July 17, 1990): 4.
2. Melissa Ann Madden, "Heriberto 'Eddie' Seda." Crimelibrary.com, www.crimelibrary.com/serial_killers/weird/seda/index_html (April 24, 2004).

3. "Police Tune in the Occult for Clues to Zodiac Killer," *The Orlando Sentinel* (July 24, 1990): A-6.
4. Melissa Ann Madden, "Heriberto 'Eddie' Seda." Crimelibrary.com, www.crimelibrary.com/serial_killers/weird/seda/index_html (April 24, 2004).

Chapter 19

1. From the television show *Beyond Chance* (personal videotape).
2. *Gainesville Sun*, Gainesville, Florida (June 12, 1997).
3. Associated Press story (photocopy, no date available).

Chapter 20

1. Personal communication from Detective Ray Taylor (September 18, 1992).
2. Personal communication from Jacque MacDonald (April 2004).

Chapter 21

1. All of the names of people in this chapter, and the name of the town, have been changed to protect the privacy of the individuals and townspeople.

Chapter 22

1. *Psychic Detectives*, Court TV (March 2004, personal videotape).

Chapter 23

1. All of the names in this chapter, including the horse's name, have been changed to protect the privacy of the individuals involved.

ABOUT THE AUTHOR

Noreen Renier first lectured at the FBI Academy in Quantico, Virginia, in 1981. She is now a well-known psychic detective who has worked on more than four hundred unsolved cases with city, county, and state law-enforcement agencies in thirty-eight states and six foreign countries. She has been featured on the *Larry King Show*, *Psychic Detectives* on Court TV, *Good Morning America*, and the Biography Channel.

You can contact Noreen Renier through her website: www.noreenrenier.com.

Hampton Roads Publishing Company

. . . for the evolving human spirit

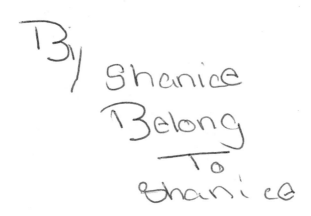

Hampton Roads Publishing Company
publishes books on a variety of subjects,
including spirituality, health, and other related topics.

For a copy of our latest trade catalog,
call toll-free, 800-766-8009,
or send your name and address to:

Hampton Roads Publishing Company, Inc.
1125 Stoney Ridge Road
Charlottesville, VA 22902
E-mail: hrpc@hrpub.com
Internet: www.hrpub.com